KEN KOEMAN

REDEMPTION
COMES HARD

Pastor Ken Koeman

Blessings Randy

Kay Koeman

My college psychology professor, Dr John T. Daling, was immensely popular with students. Earthy and straight shooting, he had a knack for challenging our naiveté. Two unsettling claims he made were:

1. The truths that are hardest to see are often the ones that are the most obvious.

2. They are also some of the greatest truths.

I am proposing to you that the title of this book is a great, and even obvious, truth. Might I also observe that it is not easily learned?

One day two young lads decided to smoke marijuana up in the third-story attic of our downtown's main retail center, Delft Square, home to over a dozen thriving businesses. This solid building had stood as the legendary centerpiece of our city's commercial core for almost a century. Somehow, as they lit up, they caused a small fire, which soon grew out of control. They fled. In minutes, the whole attic was engulfed, and soon the entire building was ablaze. In just an hour, it was a total loss. Every business in it was ruined. Year after year, the thick shell of this gutted building taunted us with, "Who of you has the chutzpa, and the cash, to fix me?" People lamented as they watched the downtown slowly deteriorate. The prospect of fixing it and finding tenants who would risk a startup business there scared most investors away. Finally, *some eight years later*, a small group of courageous investors pooled some eight million dollars, found tenants willing to risk launching a business in that location, and began rebuilding using the scarred shell, which was still intact. It took over a year of costly reconstruction. It now remains to be seen if this investment will turn a profit. The "redemption" of that building is still an open question.

Americans believe that if it's broke, we can fix it. Ours is a can-do attitude. We believe in bouncing back. Our heroes are the Louis Zamperinis and Ernest Shackletons of the world. As a result, it often takes situations so broken they defy all attempts to fix them to finally force us to come to grips with this hard truth: *the path to redemption is hard and long, and few find it.* Most of us quietly abandon the broken pieces and simply try to go on with what we can salvage out of our leftover lives.

Perhaps you remember the quarrels you had with your siblings when you were little. Sometimes these were daily storms in your early childhood, wearing your poor parents down! How often did it happen that you mended these quarrels *all on your own*? Rarely, if ever! It took all the power of your almighty parents to coerce you back into simple civility. Rarely did you find your own redemption. And, if you pause to think for just a moment, you'll notice how much this weakness carries right into adulthood. Disputes within families, institutions, and even nations defy resolution. Some go on for centuries.

You even learned the virtual impossibility of redemption on your mother's knee when she read you the nursery rhyme:

> *Humpty Dumpty sat on a wall.*
>
> *Humpty Dumpty had a great fall.*
>
> *All the king's horses and all the king's men*
>
> *Couldn't put Humpty Dumpty together again.*

There's a reason that little rhyme has endured: this great truth is embedded in it. Have you ever tried putting the broken pieces of an eggshell back together so that it looks as flawless as the day the hen first laid it? Even all the power a king can muster cannot pull that off! No, not even the president of the world's greatest superpower can heal the brokenness of the nations. There has been a great fall. It demands a superhuman redeemer.

Consider marriages that shatter. How many divorced couples do you know who refused to call it quits and actually did the humbling work of mending the old injuries they had inflicted upon each other, confessed their faults, extended forgiveness, and finally put themselves to the trouble of earning one another's trust again? Here is an understatement: *that is a road less travelled.* I know of no such couple in my almost fifty years of serving as a parish pastor.

This soon dawns on anyone who opens a Bible and starts to read Genesis. They will notice that the Old Testament is thick, and the New Testament, thin. In my *NIV Study Bible*, the Old Testament takes up 1,422 pages; the New Testament, just 510 pages. The Old Testament is almost three times longer than the New! Why? There are many weighty reasons, but surely this is one of them: God is demonstrating *what doesn't work* when it comes to redemption, and he is taking his time about it because it is just that hard to accept.

Sin and evil entered the world in just a brief, single act of what a respected catechism calls "reckless disobedience" when Adam and Eve ate the forbidden fruit. The effect was shattering. Their pristine love for God and each other instantly turned into alienation. Both of them reaped hard labor: he in the fields, she in childbirth. They lost their paradise home. Worst of all, they ended as mere dust. Their only hope of redemption was a cryptic promise that a day would come when the seed of the woman would crush the head of the serpent.

If Adam and Eve entertained any hopes that one of their children would fulfill that promise, they were quickly relieved of their naiveté. Their first child, Cain, murdered their second child—his brother, Abel. Far worse was yet to come. Evil exploded. We're only six chapters into Genesis, and the prospect of redemption looks bleak. Consider: "The Lord saw how great man's wickedness on the earth had become, and that every inclination of the thoughts of his heart was only evil all the time" (Gen. 6:5).

Note those titanic words: *great, every, only, all!* How do you redeem corruption on such a massive scale? And why did God wait so long? Might I suggest a reason: to teach us that there are *no quick fixes.* There are *no human fixes.* God demonstrated again and again *what doesn't work* to cure us of our naiveté about our capacity to fix the brokenness ourselves.

There's a mindset that says, "Get the crooks off the street. Lock them up!" God did it. He got rid of all the evil people in one great purging—the flood. Did this fix the problem? No, because those who survived, Noah and his family, carried the infection right back into their sanitized world the moment they stepped off the ark. Noah became drunk. We learn that the line between good and evil, as Alexander Solzhenitsyn observed, is not so easy to draw:

> If only it were all so simple! If only there were evil people somewhere insidiously committing evil deeds, and it were necessary only to separate them from the rest of us and destroy them. But the line dividing good and evil cuts through the heart of every human being. And who is willing to destroy a piece of his own heart? Gradually it was disclosed to me that the line separating good and evil passes not through states, nor between classes, nor between political parties either—but right through every human heart—and through all human hearts.[1]

We think sometimes that the cure lies in some form of mighty deliverance, such as a great military victory or passing landmark legislation. Again we are warned: this does not produce lasting redemption. God provided, through Moses, a massive act of deliverance for the nation of Israel from slavery in Egypt. They left the country loaded down with wealth. Within a

1 Alexander Solzhenitsyn, *The Gulag Archipelago, 1918–1956*, abridged ed. (New York: HarperCollins, 2007), p. 168.

few weeks, however, grumbling and even rebellion surfaced among their ranks, much as it did among the thirteen colonies after the Revolutionary War was won. *Liberation does not equal redemption.*

We think legislation and regulation will redeem our torn social fabric. Indeed, we need the rule of law. However, through Moses God set up a comprehensive system of laws and ceremonies designed to create a just social order and a pathway for regular spiritual purification—but it soon was usurped by the idolatry of a golden calf followed by *centuries* of repeated relapses into empty religion—or worse, total idolatry. *Neither morality nor spirituality equal redemption.*

We think a higher standard of living can set people free. It does make life easier. However, affluence easily leads to decadence. God miraculously guided his people into a land flowing with milk and honey, but their affluence eroded their once-sturdy faith, and, says the book of Judges, everyone ended up just doing their own thing, repeatedly.

We think the key to redemption is fresh leadership, as every candidate for public office claims. Again and again God provided his chosen people with fresh leadership—but every king in the Old Testament ended up with fatal flaws.

We think strong warnings (as in powerful preachers or prophetic voices) would launch redemptive change. Again, notice: God warned his people repeatedly through bold prophets, but they were routinely ignored. Many were killed.

Finally, we're told that redemption is a matter of just getting tough on crime. But notice: God finally imposed the severest discipline of all on his own people by destroying their prime city, Jerusalem, and their crown jewel, the temple, and then shipping them out of their land into seventy years of exile. Did this redeem them? Read Nehemiah and Ezra. Nehemiah ended up enraged at the spiritual slippage he found among the returned exiles. Ezra ended up in tears for the same reason. Why? Because, upon their return, it didn't take long, and they fell right back into the old ways.

And then, four hundred years of silence. Four hundred years without one hint of redemption! By the time the New Testament rolls around, God's people are living in utter darkness, enslaved to the Romans.

In the thick Old Testament, God is demonstrating to us *what doesn't work, and he takes his time about it.* Ever so slowly, it has to dawn upon us: if redemption is ever going to come, it will not be a quick fix. It will be indescribably difficult, and, we slowly admit, it will require someone superhuman. No wonder so many of the feel-good redemption movies center around a Batman, a Superman, a Wonder Woman, a Harry Potter, or a Jedi knight.

And so it was. The person who finally earned our redemption, you will remember, was human, and then some. The truth is that it took *God himself,* coming here in the person of Jesus, to finally bring about deep, solid, lasting, worldwide redemption. It demanded nothing less than a cross.

Movies have trailers—previews that are designed to whet our appetites enough to plunk down cold cash for the real thing. The ultimate story of redemption in Jesus has many trailers hidden throughout the Old Testament. One of them is the story of Joseph. It is one of the grandest redemption stories of all time, a preview of The Real One.

But you'll soon learn as you follow along with me that even this redemption, in just one family, took over two decades and involved severe suffering. More significantly, the people who were redeemed had nothing to do with it. They were redeemed in spite of themselves. It came about in a way no one would ever have guessed. It's called "Grace."

DEDICATION

To Jamison, Arianna, Isaiah, Hadley, and Andrew, my dear grandchildren on the cusp of adulthood: this book is written for you. Why? Because you will find yourself in this story—or better, this story will find you.

You will experience the brokenness of the world, and it will hurt you. Brokenness wears many faces: a fractured friendship, a frustrated career, a shattered marriage, a financial collapse, sexual misconduct. It may barge in as a tragic accident, a life-threatening disease, or yet another world war. You will face a national debt that seems insurmountable. You will face entrenched sexism, discrimination, and unequal justice.

You may experience brokenness within yourself, and it could shatter you. Your own family histories are proof enough. Just a few generations back, one of your ancestors was out for a walk in a park with his wife and children. He told her he needed to relieve himself, and he disappeared behind some bushes. He relieved himself alright: of his wife and children. He never emerged from those bushes . . . except on the other side. He abandoned them. She never saw him again. In seconds, her world turned on its head. Slowly the terrible truth dawned on her: she was on her own. How does a person recover from rejection that sudden? How is such a shattered family *redeemed*?

When some part of your world comes unglued, you will feel the weight of that question as never before. You will face situations so utterly broken they will *defy* you to believe they could ever be redeemed.

When you were little, you asked me, often, to tell you a bedtime story. So I did, wracking my brain for yet another delightful event from the days when, as you prescribed, "I was a little boy." So often they were stories of redemption.

How many times did I tell you the story of the stolen watermelons? I was around six years old at the time. Perhaps you will remember that my dad and your great grandfather, Donald Koeman, was not a wealthy man. We could not afford "store-bought" watermelon. So one year he decided to grow a large plot of them in his garden. Every day we watched as those little melons grew from the size of lemons, to footballs, and finally to plump, oblong balloons, calling out to us to be picked and savored. We kept on pestering him to harvest them, but he kept us waiting until he was sure they would be fully ripe . . . and sweet! Finally, one evening he announced that the very next day we would be eating all the watermelon our tummies could hold.

But the next morning, you'll remember, my dad's face was frozen with rage, for during the night every last one of our watermelons had been stolen. We were shattered; tears flowed. He told us that finding the robbers would be virtually impossible. It seemed that there was no possibility of redemption. You may very well have chapters like that in your life. You may very well be victimized. You might even be the villain.

But this was a redemption story in its own way. That evening my dad and your great grandfather came home from work carrying a gigantic watermelon. Even though splurging on such a luxury violated every frugal bone in his body (and *all* his bones were Dutch), he was determined that he would make good on his promise to his four sons. He sliced into it with his big butcher knife, and that evening we luxuriated in melon heaven. The juice ran down our chins just as the tears had run down our cheeks the night before. It was one of our first tastes of redemption, and, as is always the case with redemption, it was impossibly sweet.

That is why I want to tell you one final grandpa story: Joseph's. One day, in just seconds, the world of this seventeen-year-old imploded. And then it steadily got worse. Eventually he found himself utterly forgotten in a foreign prison with no prospects. And yet his story ends with a redemption so immense it restored not only his life, nor even just the harmony of his broken family, but it spread internationally, giving hope to thousands. It was one massive redemption.

But this redemption did not come easy. Redemption rarely does. It is invariably slow, tortured, expensive, and agonizing. There are very few quick fixes. I would spare you of dreaming otherwise. Don't be naive. Redemptions invariably involve some form of a cross. Someone always has to suffer first. Sometimes thousands suffer first. But that very suffering is often the catalyst that finally brings redemption.

So I dedicate this book to you. It is more than possible that you will taste the bitter brokenness in our world barging into your comfortable nests. You will learn how long redemption can take and how hard it comes. But never forget how this story ends.

And, by the way, you'll remember from your childhood the alphabet picture book titled *Animalia* by Graeme Base, the award-winning Australian writer and illustrator of children's books, which we pored over with you again and again. You might recall that Graeme hid himself (or just a small part of himself) on every page, and how much fun it was for you to search for him. There's Someone like that in this story too. It's really about him.

CONTENTS

CHAPTER 1

Catfight

Read Genesis 29:1–30:24

Joseph's story begins in a fighting family. We've got eleven kids from four different mothers all under one roof. Jacob has two wives who are full of spite toward each other. This family is so broken, it appears to be beyond redemption. You'll see dysfunctional families. But I doubt you'll ever see anything quite like this. So, you'll understand my insistence that redemption comes hard. In this family, you'll wonder if it could ever come at all.

Here's the heart of the story you just read: Joseph's father Jacob is smitten by lovely Rachel. Hard bitten Uncle Laban sees this as his chance to exploit Jacob. Oozing generosity, he says, "Just because you are a relative of mine, should you work for me for nothing? Tell me what your wages should be" (29: 15). He knew Jacob would offer almost anything in return for the hand of Rachel in marriage. Jacob offered seven years of labor. But that wasn't enough for Laban. He figured out a way to get another seven years of free labor. After the first seven years, he deceptively pawned off "weak eyed" Leah on him, justifying it with a lame appeal to local tradition, and offered Rachel a week later for seven more years of hard labor. Jacob got the raw

1

end of that deal. Twenty years later Jacob describes just how hard Laban was on him:

> I have been with you for twenty years now. . . . This was my situation: The heat consumed me in the daytime and the cold at night, and sleep fled from my eyes. It was like this for the twenty years I was in your household. I worked for you fourteen years for your two daughters and six years for your flocks, and you changed my wages ten times. (Gen. 31:39–41)

And so a family is founded on the wrong foot, set up for misery from the get-go. Jacob is duty bound to treat both sisters as his wives, but he felt nothing for Leah and everything for Rachel. God saw his coldness towards Leah. Seeing Leah's plight, God poured out great kindness upon this unloved woman and began to bless her, and only her, with children. While Rachel watched with empty arms, Leah began having babies—first one, then another, then another, and then, even a fourth: Reuben, Simeon, Levi, Judah. Each name expressed the pain of an unloved wife:

- Reuben: "The Lord has seen my misery. Surely my husband will love me now."

- Simeon: "Because the Lord heard that I am not loved."

- Levi: "Now at last my husband will become attached to me."

- Judah: "This time I will praise the Lord."

Four boys . . . and yet, no love from the man who fathered them. Leah's pain persisted, but notice: the name she gave to her fourth boy reveals that it's possible to have a heart full of praise for God even in the vacuum of human love.

You may know that Jesus descended from Judah, and it is through Jesus that we can end up living lives of praise despite the fact that, like Leah, there is obvious spiritual ugliness in us that forfeits any claim to the love of God. He sees our "weak eyes," our flawed hearts, which have no beauty in them that he should desire us. Still he desires us. It's all grace.

For Rachel, this parade of four sons for her rival and not even one for her was just too much. She exploded at Jacob, blaming him for her childlessness, insisting that if he didn't make her pregnant, it would kill her. Deeply self-absorbed, humiliated by the very woman she had always outshone, Rachel now puts on a powerful pout that sounded like a deadly ultimatum: "Give me children, or I'll die!" But Jacob shot right back at her, speaking cold truth in hot rage, pointing out the obvious with merciless logic:

- Only God can cause conception.

- Am I God? Of course not.

- You haven't conceived, and that can mean only one thing: It's God who is keeping you from having children, not me.

- Therefore, woman, you've got a problem with God, not me. If you want a child, take it up with him!

But Rachel didn't turn to God. Instead, she opted for the same godless solution Jacob's grandmother Sarah had used in her barrenness. She gave her servant girl, Bilhah, to Jacob as a surrogate mother. She was determined to have a child and do it her way. Jacob caved in, slept with Bilhah, and through her gave Rachel what she wanted. Bilhah produced a son whom Rachel claimed as her own by naming him herself. She called him Dan, a name full of spite for Leah. It means, See? God has vindicated me! Joseph grew up in a home where his mother gave his half-brother a name designed just to taunt his aunt! How can such a hate-filled home ever be redeemed?

Bilhah conceived and bore a second son. Rachel named him "Naphtali," a name fraught with self-pity and laced with the poison of triumph: "My how I've struggled against my sister, but look: I win!"

All this, in turn, was just too much for Leah. She countered by imitating Rachel's strategy and gave her maidservant Zilpah to Jacob as a competing surrogate. Once again, spineless Jacob complied, and two more boys appeared. Leah gave them names expressing vindictive delight:

- Gad: "What good fortune!"

- Asher: "How happy I am!"

The score was Leah, six; Rachel, two. And Joseph has yet to be born into this alienated family with two sisters under one roof fighting like cats, using children as pawns in their game of one-upmanship.

Leah, now long banished from Jacob's bed but still pining for more children of her own, one day spied a perfect opportunity to get Jacob to sleep with her again. Her son, Reuben, showed up in the kitchen with some mandrake roots, which, when consumed, were widely believed to induce pregnancy. Rachel saw them and immediately wanted them, no doubt, in the hope that they could cure her barrenness. So she asked Leah for some of the roots. Leah's spite spilled out at what she saw as Rachel's nerve: Wasn't it enough that you took away my husband? Will you take my son's mandrakes too? But Rachel was so desperate she offered Leah the very thing she hoped the roots would give her: the possibility of another pregnancy. So the deal was struck. Rachel got fertility roots, and Leah got a fertile man. That night hapless Jacob was compelled to sleep with plain Leah . . . as arranged by desperate Rachel, who now was consuming cooked mandrake roots as a fertility drug! What a soap opera this is!

Leah slept with Jacob that night with a prayer in her heart that this liaison would lead to a fifth child of her own. Amazingly, despite the crass deal making in the kitchen that day, God mercifully granted her prayer that night. Nine months later she birthed a healthy baby boy for Jacob. She named him Issachar in the belief that his birth was a "reward" justifying her decision to allow Jacob to father children through her servant maid, Zilpah.

This led to another liaison between Leah and Jacob, which in turn produced a sixth son of her own. Once again, longing at least for some respect, if not love, from Jacob, Leah named him Zebulon, which likely means "honor." And then she slept with Jacob yet again, this time leading to a daughter, whom she named Dinah, reputed to mean "avenged" or "vindicated." It's just possible that Leah finally felt validated with these seven (a perfect number) children around her, despite knowing that her husband had never loved her. She saw her children not just as a consolation but as a vindication. It suggests that finally, after all these years of longing for Jacob's love and never once receiving it, she ended up so hurt she couldn't help but despise him. There are few forces in the world more powerful than a woman spurned. Consider how this very likely infected her children! Later on, the animosity will run so deep her sons will drive Joseph right out of the family without a qualm of conscience.

Finally God remembers Rachel. He sees her deep sadness, despite her two half-sons. In sheer mercy, he opens her womb, and Joseph is born: Rachel's first child, Jacob's eleventh son. He was no sooner born than Rachel began pining for a second son. This is why she named him "Joseph," meaning "may he add." So Joseph grew up saddled with a name suggesting that he was not enough to satisfy his mother!

Doesn't this story have you shaking your head in disbelief? Doesn't it make you wonder, "What good can ever come out of a dysfunctional home like this one?" We have two wives, both of them mothers, who are at odds from week one. We have two surrogate moms who work right there in the tents every day. We have eleven boys and one girl from four different mothers, all living in the same compound. This is a devil's brew! This is a concoction bound to poison this family for years! It does, overshadowing the home with deadly hostility and daily tension. This is a deeply broken family, and this is the scene where God will do his redemptive work. If he can do it here, nothing is beyond his redemptive reach.

Consider this: this tragically broken family was the family through which God intended to bless the entire world, as he had promised to their great grandfather, Abraham. And he did! In fact, the names of Jacob's twelve boys adorn the twelve gates of the ultimately perfect community, the New Jerusalem (Rev. 21:12b). Every gate, adorned with a flawed name. That says something!

Here is one of the great truths from this chapter: God's power runs so deep even profoundly broken families can be redeemed. God is not limited by our limits. He is not stymied by our brokenness. He does not malfunction because of our dysfunction. He can strike a straight blow with a crooked stick. Beyond that, he can make straight what is crooked. In fact, it is his glory to do so, for his strength is made perfect in weakness. And if there is anything God wants you see with your own eyes, it is this wondrous glory. And the greatest showcase of that glory is the story of how he redeems a foul family like this.

Children who grow up in dysfunctional families are likely to enter adulthood scarred and emotionally jaded. Jacob's boys were no exception; as Leah despised Rachel, they despised Joseph. But deeper yet lies a powerfully consoling truth: there is a God in heaven who can bring his shalom even into a chaotic, polygamous family where favoritism is rampant, love is one-sided, and the children are pawns in a catfight.

CHAPTER 2

The Bald Face of Evil

Read Genesis 34

I t is sure to happen, if it hasn't already. Real wickedness will come crashing into your world, wrecking your nicely arranged affairs and plans. It could severely damage you, leaving you jaded, distrustful, and disillusioned. At times like that, you may very well wonder if there is any person you can trust. You will get hurt . . . . . .and sometimes in the most unexpected places.

It could happen in the world of your career, which you may have chosen quite humbly and obediently as a place where you could put your considerable talents to work for the sake of the heavenly Kingdom. Imagine that what you chose was an intentional Kingdom outpost, like a Christian school, mission, church, college, or charity. You went in, trusting the people who hired you and the colleagues who surrounded you. Then one day, real evil charged into this supposedly "Christian" institution. Someone mishandled money. Two colleagues had an affair. Your boss was not totally truthful with you. Office politics got the upper hand. A co-worker posted something slanderous about you on social media. For some shadowy reason, you were dismissed.

You will encounter real wickedness, if you haven't already. You may very well be victimized. Indeed, you may even see frightening forms of it within yourself, coming, as we sometimes say, "right out of nowhere." There just might be a time when you are shocked at what comes out of your own mouth. When I was around 10 ten years old, I got so mad at a neighborhood boy, I picked up a stone and slung it at him. I hit him close to his temple. I could have killed him. That moment was a revelation to me: I didn't realize I had it in me, but I most certainly did. To my immense relief, he recovered.

You should not be shocked. And you won't be if you come into adult life armed with the unwelcome truth about the hard reality of our fallen human condition. It is portrayed starkly in this chapter. The Holy Spirit, who inspired Moses to include even the most sordid details of the Joseph story, intended for us to know that real wickedness does exist, even within God's own chosen people. This chapter is meant to underscore why redemption comes so hard: look at these scoundrels!

We don't know how old Joseph was when this happened. He's not mentioned at all in this part of the story. But it is safe to say that he learned all about it, either at the time it happened or later. The clue? Simeon, one of the two primary villains, was the person Joseph chose to imprison in Egypt years later as a hostage to ensure his brothers would actually return a second time with Benjamin. One wonders if he specifically selected Simeon for this humiliation to nudge him into thinking back to this atrocity, and face the killer side in his own heart.

Study the ugliness in Joseph's family of origin. Father Jacob, upon his return to Canaan, chose to settle near Shechem, a pagan Canaanite city. There was good pasture there for his flocks, so he decided (not unlike Lot in Genesis Gen. 13: 10 – 13) to take the risk of exposing his children to the corrupting influence of the nearby pagan culture for the sake of making good money.

Trouble came soon enough. One day his daughter Dinah, apparently without a chaperone, decided to visit the women of the town. The son of the district ruler, a young man named Shechem, saw her and "violated her." Frankly, he had sex with her, and we have no idea if this was consensual. It is possible that Dinah was flattered to receive the attention of the son of the ruler of that territory, who was highly regarded in the community, making her vulnerable to his charms. Whatever it was, it was scandalous.

Jacob was the first to get wind of it. Instead of taking decisive action, he dallied, waiting for his sons to come home. Once he informed them, he was usurped from his role as patriarch to settle the matter wisely and properly. His vindictive sons, full of grief and fury, took over.

The spirit of revenge is particularly deadly because it makes us want to hit back harder than we were hit, as you well remember from your childhood fights. If your brother or sister took away your toy, you didn't merely grab the toy back; you attacked them. You clobbered them!

The Bible is forthright about the deadly power of revenge, and warns us that no one is immune from its grip. Even David, the man after God's own heart, was once so filled with revenge it took all the diplomatic skill of a smart, beautiful, quick-thinking, and gracious woman named Abigail to spare him from the disaster it would have caused. It's all in I Samuel 25. Revenge can fill us with a fury so blinding we lose all perspective. The Count of Monte Cristo, by Alexandre Dumas, is a classic tale of how all-consuming—...and self-destructive—...revenge can be. No one is immune.

Watch revenge do its deadly work here. Shechem was so smitten with Dinah that even after he violated her, he still treasured her. He spoke very tenderly to her. She ended up moving in with him (see vs. 26). He promptly asked his father, Hamor, to approach Jacob and request her hand in marriage. Hamor did the honorable thing. With Shechem, he went to Jacob with a proposal. He respectfully asked for Dinah, and invited Jacob to welcome the idea of even broader intermarriage between the two communities. He also held out the tantalizing prospect of lucrative commercial dealings between them. Then Shechem stepped forward, respectfully asked their favor, and offered to pay any dowry for the girl. He may have been a pagan, but he appears to be at least a decent pagan. He wants to make things right, or, at least, look right—, which is hardly upright.

But Jacob's sons think only revenge. With them, it's, "Don't just get mad; get even." But, though they are furious, theirs is not blind fury. They come up with a calculated scheme to get their revenge in spades. The worst element of their scheme? They use religion.

Evil is never more powerful than when religion is its driving force. ISIS is a powerful force in the world today. Its foot soldiers have no qualms about committing atrocious acts of murder. What drives them is religion, in this case a radicalized version of Islam. Indeed, it was Jewish religious fervor that crucified Jesus. Mere religion can be a dangerous thing.

Sounding very pious, the brothers of Joseph announce to Shechem that they could never give their sister to him because, unlike them, he was uncircumcised. That, after all, would be a disgrace! But, sounding equally magnanimous, they offer to strike a generous deal: if Shechem and all the males in the town would circumcise themselves, then not only could Shechem have Dinah, but they could all intermarry with each other and live as one peaceful community, happily ever after! Underneath, they were out for blood.

Shechem and his father lost no time. They went back to their city with the offer. Because Shechem was considered "the most honored of all his father's household," (vs. 19a), the men of the city welcomed the proposal, and every last one of them allowed themselves to undergo the painful surgery of circumcision. Three days later, while they were still so seriously incapacitated they could barely move, they were suddenly attacked by Simeon and Levi.

They killed every male in town, including Shechem and Hamor, and took Dinah back home. For just one sin they annihilated the entire city! The worst evildoers that you will encounter are people who commit evil in the name of a greater good; they are also the hardest to redeem, since they see their vice as completely justified.

Then Dinah's other brothers, and perhaps her half-brothers as well, joined in. They grabbed everything in and around the town: personal property, flocks, herds, women, children, and all their wealth. They looted it all. They were not only killers; they were pillagers. Their revenge made them ravenous.

Jacob protested their behavior, not because it was evil, but only because it was dangerous! He feared retaliation from neighboring Canaanite cities when the stench of what his boys had done reached their noses. He knew a counterattack would wipe him out. But his sons had no appreciation for his concern. They responded with a disrespectful, self-justifying rhetorical question meant to silence their father: *Should he have treated our sister like a prostitute?* This tells us something very significant about Joseph's brothers, which will show up later in the story: even if they felt any sense that what they had done was wrong, they certainly didn't tolerate it. This is what is always so shocking about truly evil people. They seem conscienceless.

This blindness of the brothers to their own sinfulness will show up again and again in the Joseph story. It is the great infection that will poison this family for years. Invariably it is this blindness that makes redemption come so hard, which is why Jesus confronted it so fiercely in the religious leaders of his day (Matt. 23). The journey of realizing, much less coming to grips with, the presence of serious evil in our own hearts is all uphill. We are bent toward denying, minimizing, or rationalizing the evil we do. You will encounter people who never apologize. They will never admit that it is their fault. Like Joseph's brothers, they will have their explanation at the ready, no matter how shocking their behavior. When you see this it just might leave you stunned. Don't be surprised. Confession may be good for the soul, but it is also both difficult and rare. In his insightful book, <u>People of the Lie</u>, Scott Peck wrote writes this about evil people: "The evil do not serenely bear the trial of being displeasing to themselves. In fact, they don't bear it at all. And it is out of their failure to put themselves on trial that their evil arises." (Peck, 1983).

Later on in the story we'll see how severe Joseph had to be to break through his brothers' blindness in order to lead them to a place of redemption. Their redemption will not come easily.

CHAPTER 3

Pilgrimage
Read Genesis 35

If God doesn't step into our bloody world, there can be no redemption. Though just a lad, Joseph is about to get his first glimpse of what that looks like. He likely was old enough to understand what his half-brothers did to the men of Shechem, returning with blood on their swords and corralling frightened hostages into camp. He saw the loot. He heard the bleating sheep and the braying donkeys. And then he watched God at work. God stepped into this fiasco and spoke firmly to his paralyzed father, telling him to clear out of that country. The result was Joseph's first pilgrimage.

Jacob senses danger. He fears reprisals. He knows he's outnumbered. He knows he needs to get out of there and make a run for safety . . . somewhere. After all, Jacob's typical response is flight. He ran from Esau. He ran from Laban. Now he knows he needs to be on the run again. But where?

God is never mentioned in chapter 34, where wickedness dominated the story. But chapter 35 is full of God. The name "God" appears eleven times in this chapter, and if you add in the places named after God (like Bethel, which means "house of God"), the number rises to twenty-three. In other words, redemption is entirely the work of God, and Joseph will watch it all.

God speaks. He directs Jacob to go back to square one. He orders him back to his roots, to the place that gave him his first spiritual grounding. Some twenty years earlier, Jacob had also been on the run. His brother Esau had vowed to kill him, so he fled. One night, sound asleep on bare ground, he was given a wondrous dream. Heaven came to meet him. He saw a ladder extend itself down out of heaven with the bottom legs resting right on the dirt next to him. Then he saw angels gliding, first up and then down, on the steps of that ladder, as if they were carrying his frightened soul up into the very serenity of God and then bringing it back to earth, comforted. Then God spoke to him, promising not only to protect him but to shower him with a whole cavalcade of blessings. First, God promised to prosper him so richly that he would end up owning the very spot on which he was now sleeping, and the vast country all around it. Then God promised him that his descendants would be as countless as the dust of the earth. Then a third promise: that he would someday return safely. And finally, one more promise meant to steady him during all the intervening years: God would never leave him.

When he woke up the next morning, he was frightened. He realized that he had unwittingly gone to bed on holy ground, sleeping right under God's own roof! His first response was terror. Notice that! This is a normal human response to the felt presence of God. It happened to the Israelites at the foot of Mount Sinai. It happened when Jesus miraculously produces a huge catch of fish for Peter. Jesus said it will certainly happen when people who don't know him see him return to earth on the clouds of heaven. Deep down, fallen man dreads the prospect of coming into the presence of God, no matter how much bravado we put on. The truth is that God, in fact, is *dangerous*—unless he graciously leads us into the circle of his lovingkindness, as he did for Jacob that night twenty years earlier. From the day Adam and Eve hid from God in the Garden of Eden to that final day when humans will plead to the mountains and the rocks, "Fall on us and hide us from the face of him who sits on the throne and from the wrath of the

Lamb!" (Rev. 6:16), facing God while alienated from him is utterly frightening. The Bible does nothing to ease this fear. It warns us, "It is a dreadful
thing to fall into the hands of the Living God" (Heb. 10:31).

But God has no delight in our being terrified by him, and he has paid a
very high price to lead us into the safety of knowing him as our Father. A
key element of human redemption involved Jesus experiencing our own
very real terror on the cross while he was abandoned by his Father. Our
guilt had been transferred to him so that, through Jesus, we might see that
the very face we fear is, wondrously, a face of grace, gloriously radiating the
warmth of his great love for us out of the bright face of Jesus (2 Cor 4: 6).

Now God shows that face to Jacob by sending him back to that very place
Jacob had named Bethel, a journey of about twenty miles to the south of
Shechem. And he instructs Jacob to make Bethel his true home by building
an altar there to himself, for wherever our altar is, there our heart is. We
know what we love by what we are willing to sacrifice for it!

This was no mere journey; this was a pilgrimage. This was nothing less
than an expedition designed to guide the entire family to a shrine! This
was a like a hajj for Muslims, a return to Normandy by WWII vets, or a
visit to Augusta National by golfers. This was a pilgrimage to a memorial,
a path to hallowed ground! This required thorough spiritual preparation!
Every person in the camp had to clean up their act. Foreign idols had to be
smashed. Clothes had to be changed. Bodies needed to be washed. Before
they could take one step toward Bethel, they needed to purify themselves!
This is why redemption never comes easy: any time we feel drawn to make
a clean start toward God, it invariably means making a clean break with
the loves in our lives that rival him. There's always something to leave first.
And without leaving, there can be no real cleaving. This is not only true for
marriage. It's the only way back to God.

So Joseph watched a remarkable ritual. He saw his older brothers, his mother, his mother's sister, the two surrogate mothers—every person in the camp—sort through their possessions, locate all their magical amulets and charms, their little statues representing spiritual powers (called "household gods"), and even some of their jewelry, gather it all up, and bring it to father Jacob. Imagine this huge pile of spiritual junk! Then he watched his dad enact a ritual of renunciation under an oak tree, a landmark there in Shechem. He literally witnessed his father get out a shovel or a pick, dig a cavernous hole under that oak tree, dump all this religious trash into it, and mound a thick layer of rocks and dirt over the top of it. Very likely the stash included even his mother Rachel's cherished household gods, which she had smuggled out of her father Laban's house back in Padan Aram. (It's all in Genesis 31: 34 - 35). Idolatry had infested Jacob's household. Now everything viewed as having any religious power had to be ruthlessly excised. Joseph learned a great lesson that would shape his treatment of his cruel brothers some twenty years from this moment:

- without repentance, there is no redemption;

- without repudiation, there is no restoration;

- without renunciation, there is no recovery.

He learned that it takes crucifying one's misdirected loves first before we can taste the power of a resurrection. He saw that death comes before life, and that turning toward God invariably means turning from habituated evils so entrenched in our lives that they have become domesticated. That is, after all, why they were called "household" gods!

He learned the contours of repentance as he watched all that junk buried under a pile of stones, under a tree anticipating another tree, on which all our misplaced loyalties would one day be crucified to us. Young, impressionable Joseph watched what spiritual renunciation looked like. We will never outlive our need to practice it, routinely, in one form or another. It is indispensable spiritual hygiene.

Then he experienced something equally wondrous. As his small and vulnerable family traveled through hostile territory on their way to Bethel, nobody attacked them, despite the atrocity they had committed at Shechem. He learned that "the terror of God" had fallen upon all the towns in that region, so that no one dared to even approach their little clan to exact vengeance. He saw an amazing grace as he watched the bloody hands of his brothers being grasped by an invisible divine hand and then being safely escorted out of sure and certain danger. It was one of his first glimpses into grace.

You may find yourself thinking, "This looks like God let them get by with murder! Where is His justice? They wiped out a whole city in retaliation for just one act of sexual misconduct which the perpetrator tried to make right. Is God going to just let them slip out of town without any form of punishment?" It's a fair question. Its answer involves taking a long look. Their day will come when they will feel the severe judgment of God. But right now you are looking at an example of God's long-suffering compassion. This is sheer mercy. God does not want to see them destroyed. He doesn't want any of us to perish. He protects them for the time being so that on another day, at another time, they can come to terms with the real depth of their sinfulness and be redeemed. God is immensely patient with us.

When the family arrived at Bethel, Joseph watched his father do something he had seen him do only once before: build an altar. When they had first arrived in Shechem, his dad had built an altar there and given it a name, El Elohe Israel. That altar recognized the mighty power of God, which Jacob had experienced so often over the years, and just recently in the surprising affection of Esau. However, this first altar had been built in the wrong place. Now God moved them to the right place. The first thing Jacob did upon arrival was to once again set up an altar, this time certain that he had been specifically led to the very place where he could expect to meet God as he had before. In fact, he named the altar El Bethel out of his serene conviction that he had now settled right in the very presence of God (the name means "God of the House of God"). He knew he was home. After all his wandering, he had come back to his roots, to his deep certainties, to the convictions that anchored his life. A great Shaker hymn captures the glory of finding our true spiritual home with these well-known words:

'Tis the gift to be simple, 'tis the gift to be free
'Tis the gift to come down where we ought to be,
And when we find ourselves in the place just right,
'Twill be in the valley of love and delight.
When true simplicity is gain'd,
To bow and to bend we shan't be asham'd,
To turn, turn will be our delight,
Till by turning, turning we come 'round right. (Brackett, 1848)

You too may travel widely in life, not only through different places, but in and out of any number of jobs, houses, communities, and relationships. You belong to a mobile generation, and you are global citizens. And I hope you enjoy the journey. But never forget your spiritual roots. They ground your life. The only people who are truly free to spread out their branches high and wide are the ones who stay rooted deeply in their one true spiritual home, who is the Living God. In fact, the more you are promoted and advance in your callings, the more critical this will be, since nothing is more dangerous to the soul than "moving up in life" without at the same time moving down deep into our spiritual roots.

Now that his father had journeyed to his true spiritual home, God responded by appearing to him personally. Once again, God poured out promises over Jacob, beginning by confirming his name change to "Israel," a powerful name that just might have sustained Joseph during all the struggles that lay ahead of him. "Israel" literally means "He struggles with God and prevails." Jacob had indeed struggled with God, especially the night he first arrived on the doorstep to Canaan, in a place called Mahanaim. This was one time Jacob could not flee; there was no place to run. Behind him was Laban; ahead of him was Esau. Both were fearsome adversaries. He had no choice but to face what faced him. There he met a man who wrestled with him all night long. As daybreak arrived, Jacob had locked up the man in a grip so tight he couldn't break free. He had him "pinned," as wrestlers would say. The man, seeing daybreak coming, begged Jacob to release him. Jacob sensed that the man was more than just another human being; he believed he had been wrestling with God. So he very forcefully refused to release the man from his grip unless the man first blessed him. The man did—by changing his name to Israel. That name was spiritual bedrock for Jacob, because it defined him with a very rare quality: he was a man who had wrestled with God . . . and had overcome! In other words, his struggle with God had not led to the despair and cynicism that has crippled so many people who have battled with God over why he has allowed so much suffering into their personal lives, family, or the world itself. Nor did it mean that his struggle against God had forced God to give in to his demands. It meant that his struggle with God had opened his eyes to see that God is always at work for good, even in the most shattering experiences of our lives. That is what it means to wrestle with God . . . and overcome. It means to have learned a paradox: in the very battle with God we finally discover that God is and always will be, for us. He seems opposed to us; he's actually allied with us. Joseph may indeed have made a special note of it! A few years later, he would need every bit of the promise that name carried!

So now, once again, God astounds Jacob with a recital of blessings on a scale far beyond his own safety:

- An entire nation will come from you.

- Kings will be among your heirs.

- This very country, which I promised to Abraham and Isaac, will all come under your ownership in due time. Your descendants will possess it.

Redemption is cosmic. It is far more than having our sins forgiven so that we go to heaven when we die! Redemption means the renewal of all things under the kingship of Jesus Christ, transforming all of life and leading to a new heaven and a new earth where God himself comes to live with us forever. The immensity of this vision had to stagger Jacob's mind.

And then, as Jacob (and Joseph?) watched, God "went up from him," suggesting a solemn, visible ascension, not unlike that of Jesus.

Then Joseph (and I can imagine the entire family) watched his father do something he may have never witnessed before. His father set up a stone pillar, a tall, visible landmark that was sure to attract the attention of anyone who was traveling by. He watched his father anoint the pillar by pouring first a drink offering over it (perhaps wine) and then a second covering of oil, designating it as an earthly structure endowed with heavenly significance. Then he heard his father give the pillar and the ground on which it stood a name. In the Bible, when God or people named something, it was a revelation of its true identity, its essential meaning. When Jacob stepped down from anointing the top of this pillar, he announced to everyone in his family: This place is "Bethel." He wanted to be sure than no one in his family ever doubted again, no matter what lay ahead, that God himself had stepped into their lives in this very spot and issued promises to them that they could count on for the rest of their lives. This place was a holy place. It was their spiritual home from that day forward.

Joseph experienced three other significant events as they continued their journey. Surely, the most significant was the death of his mother Rachel, who died in childbirth on the way to Bethlehem. Her labor was intense . . . and deadly. She knew she was dying, so just before she passed away, with one of her final breaths she insisted that the baby should be named "Ben-Oni," which means "son of my trouble." This powerfully suggests to us that all along she had never been a joyful woman, despite her stunning beauty. Jacob wouldn't allow the name to stand. He renamed the baby "Benjamin," which means "son of my right hand," a name of high honor and rich favor. It suggests that after God visited him at Bethel, Jacob had moved from fear to favor, and so he wanted his final son's name to be a testament to his new hopefulness.

The second significant event was a scandal right in the family. Joseph's oldest brother, Reuben, Leah's firstborn son, had sex with his father's concubine, Rachel's servant Bilhah, the mother of his two half-brothers Dan and Naphtali. This act was not only shameful, it was arrogant. Reuben, the firstborn, was acting as if he was entitled to something that was not his to claim. His dad heard about it but did nothing. How could he? He himself had taken something that was not his to claim either, years earlier, when he deceived his father and stole Esau's birthright. The very sin he committed against his own brother was now perpetrated against him by his own son! You do well to remember this as a grim reminder that there are certain sins and weaknesses that travel in families and can boomerang back upon us.

Finally, we're told, Joseph's childhood was also marked by the death of his grandfather, Isaac. He witnessed a remarkable sight: a reunion of two brothers who lived apart for most of their lives. He watched as they both came and laid their father into the good earth of Canaan. He saw that alienation does not have the last word. And that reassuring truth is one he would need to hold onto in the years ahead.

I hope you notice one thing from this chapter: God is a rescuer. God saves people. This family was in deep trouble at the end of chapter 34. But, at the end of chapter 35, despite plenty of blood on their hands, they are still alive, and even hopeful. This great revelation was given to Joseph as a young lad. We do not know how deeply it registered with him. We do know that years later he would see it all happen again, and this time God would not only rescue him, but rescue his whole family through him. God is a rescuer! And that is why we believe that even the most broken places can be redeemed.

CHAPTER 4

Joseph's First Act: Courageous Whistleblowing

Read Genesis 37: 1 - —2

"...He brought their father a bad report about them." (Genesis Gen. 37: 2b)

The first reported act of Joseph is what referees do: he blew the whistle. He was seventeen years old . . . . ..and surprisingly courageous. Without whistleblowing over real wrong, there simply is no way redemption will ever happen. If real wrong is not exposed, redemption cannot happen. Redemption demands truth, first.

Joseph was doing his job: taking care of his father's sheep. He was the youngest member of a five-man squad, made up of four older half-brothers, Bilhah's two sons (Dan and Naphtali), and Zilpah's two sons (Gad and Asher). The more he watched their conduct, the more troubled he became. We're not told what they were up to, but we already know from earlier chapters in Genesis that shepherds got into serious fights over water rights (Gen. 26: 20), would go so far as to plug up the wells other shepherds depended upon (Gen. 26: 18), or and were known to rough up shepherd-esses (Exod. 2: 17). Whatever wrong Joseph reported, it was likely serious enough to endanger Jacob's whole operation. And so he blew the whistle. He summoned up the courage to report what was really going on, even though he was outnumbered four to one. It would end up costing him dearly. Centuries later, Jesus Christ blew the whistle on hypocritical religious leaders. It cost him his life. But real redemption can never happen without first coming to terms with bringing the truth to light.

We hate exposure., Whistle blowers are rarely looked upon with favor by those they expose. They shine the light of day upon what others, usually higher ups, are determined to keep hidden. It is not at all unusual for whistleblowers to be demoted, or simply fired. This happened to Eileen Foster when she exposed the corruption in her mortgage company, Countrywide Financial. A similar fate befell Richard M. Bowen III when he began to expose serious fraud at Citi Group, and triggered the subprime mortgage crisis of 2007. You would be wise to read their stories on Wikipedia, and watch the "60 Minutes" programs with Steve Kroft that chronicles their pain. You will see for yourself that invariably the few intrepid souls who dare to tell the truth hit a stone wall of denial and end up suffering immensely, paying dearly for their honesty.

Some people quickly interpret this as tattling. It would be a serious mistake to dismiss it so easily. Instead, this is the first evidence that deep down, Joseph was a young man of absolute integrity. We also call it "uprightness." Here's why: it's consistent with the rest of the story. There is a very remarkable fact about Joseph: not once is he ever recorded as having done anything wrong. Look as hard as you may, you will not find any record of his ever committing a sin. This is so shocking as to make us want to look again just to be sure we're not imagining things! Abraham, Isaac, Jacob, Moses, David, Solomon—all their sins hit the headlines in the Bible. But not even a hint of wrongdoing is ever recorded about Joseph. So why would we see this as tattling? It is more honorable than that.

Moreover, consider what Joseph has already learned, and how deeply his heart has been shaped during his younger years as a child close to his father. He watched as his dad and Grandpa Laban had harsh words, but he witnessed how God protected his father from his grandpa's rage. He saw his father walk with a limp and learned how he had wrestled mightily with God and ended up securing a great blessing from God. He watched as his dad fearfully approached brother Esau, and he saw dread turn into relief as the two brothers embraced. He watched the murderous behavior of his half-brothers at Shechem and saw how deeply it troubled his father. Then, at Bethel, he learned the story of the dream of the ladder and the protection, prosperity, and safe return God had promised his father. He had seen the very real presence of God, first hand, in his father's life. Everything he knew he had learned from his father, just like Jesus. And because of the special bond he had with his father, this family history shaped a keen awareness of the presence of God upon his heart. Later in the story it this is obvious: *Joseph was acutely aware of the immediacy of God.* It protected him in times of temptation. It sustained him when he suffered injustice. And it kept him humble when he exercised his gift of interpreting dreams. At seventeen, Joseph was tuned in to the immediate presence of a very alive God who saw and heard it all.

It is almost bound to happen that you will uncover corruption, not only in yourself, but in others. You will discover slipshod quality control, racism, skimming profits, and padded expense reports. You will see widespread sexual misconduct. You will be powerfully tempted to look the other way . . . to keep your job! Know this: the brokenness you witness will never be redeemed unless the truth first comes out.

This is a preview of what Joseph will do when he was second in command in Egypt and his brothers showed show up. This same determination to get at the truth and bring it out to the full light of day will show up again. Marvelously, that is what will finally bring redemption. The truth would will finally see daylight, and the truth, as it always does, would set his family free.

So Joseph blows the whistle. In the short term, that one act of bringing secrets to light and costs him dearly. He will lose everything and end up banished to a distant land as a slave, far from the presence of his father. But in the long term, the very long term, that courageous deed also sets in motion the events that ultimately end up winning the greatest prize of all—the complete redemption of this broken family.

Why does redemption come so hard? It is because the almost impossible step is to face our own depravity. That's why we bristle when people we respect, and who we know love us, shoot straight with us. It stings, and we fight back. But, if we are, in fact, at fault, there can be no redemption without facing it head on, admitting it, and seeking mercy. In our story, that moment is over twenty years away for these brothers. It just takes that long, sometimes, to finally come to terms with the truth about our own hearts. Some never do, sentencing themselves to an unreal daily existence deformed by self-made and fiercely defended illusions.

CHAPTER 5

The Clothing of Redeemers

Read Genesis 37: 3–4

You know this part of the story very well. As kids, you colored pictures of this "coat of many colors." You're adults now; time for a closer look.

Surely you have noticed the effect clothing has: it can endow you with dignity, beauty, even authority. When you graduated from high school, what happened? You were robed in a graduation gown. Just putting on that gown transformed you from a student into a graduate, announcing the beginning of adulthood. Such is the impact of clothing. A prom dress can transform the girl next door into a glamorous young lady. A tux can turn the kid who mows lawns for extra cash into a prince.

There's more that clothing can do. It can even call you into a vocation! Think of the time you first wore a baseball, cross-country, or track uniform. Just putting on those threads (that's all they are, after all: dyed cotton, nylon, or polyester threads!) filled you with pride and moved you to aspire to all the uniform represented. The clothing compelled you, pulled at you. It called to you to become an athlete! When a young person is first issued the dress blues of a United States Marine uniform, once again his or her identity is transformed. That uniform commands them to step into becoming one of the few, the proud, the Marines! What one wears calls out to the wearer: be how you are dressed!

So you can well imagine just what this coat of many colors did for seventeen-year-old Joseph: it transfigured him! It catapulted him to most favored status in the family. It sealed his rank as the most beloved son of father Jacob. Even though his body wore that coat only a few weeks before it was ripped off and smeared with the blood of a goat, his soul wore it the rest of his life. Why was this significant? I invite you to consider this reason: to be the redeemer he was one day going to become, he first needed to know who he was before he would ever be ready to do what he would be called to do. He needed to learn that he had been chosen to be the first among his brothers for a holy purpose. You can already see that God is pointing us to Jesus, the One who is presented to us as the firstborn of many brothers (Rom. 8:29) whose authority is already evident at the tender age of just 12 years old.

Why did Jacob select Joseph for this coat? Was this simply a case of favoritism? Many have thought so, and for plausible reasons. We know that Jacob loved Joseph's mother more than any of the mothers of his other children. Twice in this section of Genesis 37, we're told plainly that Jacob loved Joseph more than any of his other sons (vv. 3–4). Jacob's other sons were very quick to notice this. They watched as Joseph was repeatedly favored. It grated on them, so much so that they "couldn't speak a kind word to him" (vs. 4b).

This streak ran in the family. Great-grandfather Abraham favored Isaac over Ishmael. Grandfather Isaac favored Esau over Jacob, and Grandmother Rebecca favored Jacob over Esau. This "favoritism" had its reasons. After all, Isaac was the child God promised, whereas Ishmael was the child of a slave woman. Rebecca favored Jacob because of a promise made at his and twin Esau's birth, namely that he would rule over Esau. Still, in every case it caused friction in the family. It would again, now in the third generation.

And yet there is more to this than what appears. Jacob was signaling to Joseph as well as to each of his brothers that he had made a choice. He had decided to choose Joseph as his true and rightful heir and had bequeathed to him both the authority and the blessings of the first born. It's as if Jacob had rewritten the will and chosen Joseph as the future head of the family. Here are the clues:

1. The Bible gives the reason for Joseph's selection as the most beloved son: the time in Jacob's life when he was born. We're told plainly that Jacob poured out greater love upon Joseph because he had been born to him in his old age (v. 3). Was this just a sign of Jacob's own vain pride in his enduring virility as an aging man?

    Or might this hearken back to another story, the birth of his own father, Isaac, to two people who were very old? Abraham was one hundred; barren Sarah, ninety! This suggests that just as Abraham knew his miracle son was the one through whom God would keep his promise to bless the whole world, so too Jacob believed that Joseph was also born to bless the whole world. If so, might this be yet one more link to that other miracle baby: Jesus, earth's ultimate redeemer?

2. But there is a second compelling reason for seeing this as much more than mere favoritism: Joseph was the only one worthy of the honor. Look at what we have already been told: the firstborn son, Reuben, had forfeited his rights as the firstborn by only recently defiling his father's bed (Gen. 33:22). Later on, we're told explicitly in 1 Chronicles 5:1 that his incestuous act of defiling his father's marriage bed led to this result: "his rights, as the first born, were given to the sons of Joseph, son of Israel." So, with Reuben disqualified, Jacob was free to designate any of his sons to receive the rights of the firstborn.

3. Just before telling us about Reuben, Moses also made sure to expose the wickedness of the other sons in the massacre of the Shechemites. One reason we are told that story is to help us see that Jacob's options for someone worthy of the rights of the firstborn had narrowed down to just two of his sons, Joseph and Benjamin, both of whom were far too young to have engaged in that dastardly deed.

4. Moreover, right after this chapter, Moses inserts yet another sordid story, this one about Judah, his fourth son. It portrays Judah as a man without a conscience, who is brought up short by his own daughter-in-law. And yet it seems to have left him unchanged. Surely, Judah was not qualified at this point to be given this place of honor and responsibility. And so all four sons of Leah end up being disqualified: Reuben because of his incest, Simeon and Levi because of their murderous deceit, and Judah because of his callous conscience. All the other sons, except Joseph and Benjamin, were born to slave women. Jacob knew God's history with his family. He remembered that God refused to allow a son born from a slave woman, Hagar, to be given the rights of the firstborn. (Indeed, Paul, in Gal. 4: 21–31 insists that all true believers must learn to see themselves as children, not of a slave woman, but of the free woman.) So none of them were qualified either. This left only one candidate for this honor: the firstborn son of his other legitimate wife: Joseph, son of Rachel.

Consequently, a careful reading of the context around this "coronation" of Joseph tells the whole story: there is no one else worthy in this family except the whistleblower who has the courage to speak up when he sees wrong, no matter what it will cost him. Who was left to receive the defining uniform of the richly embroidered robe that future royal family members wore (see 2 Sam. 13:18)? A solid case can be made that Jacob was entirely justified in setting Joseph up as prince among his brothers (Gen. 49:26), designating him as such by adorning him with this royal robe. He had nobody else. There was no other son worthy of the honor. And once again, does this not remind us of our older brother, Jesus, who alone is worthy to be recognized as the firstborn among many brothers and sisters? No wonder Handel's "Worthy Is the Lamb" explodes with such power each time it is sung in Messiah.

This robe was undoubtedly expensive, but it was also very costly for Joseph to be seen wearing it. When the other brothers saw Joseph adorned in that princely robe, it stoked their hatred. Notice this, because it points to something you too will surely face if you choose to clothe yourselves with Christ (Col. 3:12). You will be hated. Whatever role you are called to take in extending the redemptive work of Christ in this world will awaken resentment, even fury, in those who feel exposed by your integrity. But remember this: we know that Jesus was hated as well, and one of the reasons he infuriated his enemies was the simple fact that his goodness exposed their evil hearts. So they tried their best to find something, anything, wrong with him. Their sharp eyes scrutinized his conduct. They tried to trap him into saying something that might incriminate him. They failed, and so they hated him all the more. He warned us that we also will be hated, and without cause: "If the world hates you, keep in mind that it hated me first. If you belonged to the world, it would love you as its own. As it is, you do not belong to the world, but I have chosen you out of the world. That is why the world hates you" (John 15:18–19).

But how does this coat speak to you today? Well, think about it this way: when you were little, you saw pictures of this splendid coat in your Bible story books. You may very well have colored pictures of it in Sunday School. I suspect your teacher let you choose the colors, and I suspect you picked bright reds, greens, blues, oranges, yellows, and purples. And then you showed your parents. You were proud of your coloring, and as you presented it to them, you waited to hear what they would say. They may very well have smiled approvingly, praised you right out loud, and perhaps even stuck it to the refrigerator door or on the wall in your bedroom. Right at that moment, it was as if they dressed you up in your own "coat of many colors." Being praised by a parent is like being dressed up in a splendid new outfit. You felt yourself shine!

At the time it is very likely that you did not realize just how important that praise was to you, and how much you hungered for it, even craved it. But here is a great truth: if it had been withheld from you, and if you had grown up in a home where you were never appreciated and never heard one word of commendation, you would have entered adulthood severely crippled, desperate for someone to convince you that you somehow had some value somewhere. You would have emerged starved for love. And that would have driven you into all kinds of behaviors (some of them life-long!) designed to get somebody, anybody, to notice you, value you, and affirm you. You would have been launched on a desperate journey of trying to prove yourself to the world. Your love hunger could have lured you into a destructive marriage. It could have turned you into a hard-driving athlete, like Harold Abrahams in *Chariots of Fire*, compulsively absorbed in his pursuit to prove his dignity as a Jew in his anti-Semitic world. And you would have had a lot of company. The world is full of driven people desperate to hear just one word of affirmation. We all crave to be validated. It is deep within us. We hunger for someone to say a "Yes" to our existence, and when it comes, it's like salve on a sore soul. It's a kind of glory. It's like a "coat of many colors."

The coat that Jacob presented to Joseph was, in truth, glorious. It was magnificent. Scholars have tried to describe the full intent of the Hebrew terms used to describe that coat by saying that it was a "richly embroidered" coat. The two Hebrew terms for this coat suggest that this was a flowing tunic that reached all the way to his ankles and wrists. This was not a working man's normal wear. This was regal. Use your imagination. Try to picture it. Whatever its appearance may have been, one thing is certain: it radiated dignity. What was that like for Joseph when Jacob slipped it onto him, draping it over his shoulders? He had to be stunned, watching his father's beaming face, feeling his arms and torso wrapped in the textures of that warm, soft, all-embracing adornment. At that moment, Joseph felt everything the word "favor" contains: preciousness, beloved-ness, importance, significance, value, affirmation, and worth. And one more thing: delight. At that moment, as Joseph realized how deeply his father delighted in him, he had to be filled with a unique kind of delight, for there is nothing that fills a child's heart with greater delight than to know that their parents take delight in them. Strange, isn't it? Delighting in someone else's delight in you? But so it is. That is the real "dress up."

Think of this delight over being favored as a kind of clothing, or being dressed up, and you'll understand the deep meaning this richly embroidered coat had for Joseph. And you'll begin to understand the language in the Bible about clothing and why it was so important in God's redemption of the world.

For example, think about this: you could say that Jesus also was given a "coat of many colors." He was dressed up in a splendor that outshone anything that anybody around him could possibly have worn. It happened on a mountaintop, and it was witnessed by three of his disciples. Suddenly, the clothing that Jesus was wearing was transformed right before their eyes. His robe, perhaps made of ordinary linen or muslin, suddenly began to glow brighter and brighter until it radiated such brilliance that Peter, James, and John could barely look upon it. His clothing blazed with light so luminous that pure whiteness radiated out of him like the sun at high noon. Matthew says that "his clothes became as white as the light" (17:2). Mark says that "his clothes became dazzling white, whiter than anyone in the world could bleach them" (9:3). Luke describes his clothes this way: "his clothes became as bright as a flash of lightning" (9:29). The Gospel writers are using metaphors of luminosity to tell us the glory of Jesus's clothing right at this very moment. And what did all that brilliant clothing mean? It meant favor! Why, at this moment, did God dress up his son like this? Because he was on the very cusp of undertaking our redemption, which would not come easy.

What lay ahead for Jesus after his transfiguration was the ordeal of his passion, culminating in his crucifixion. The moment he was transfigured, both Moses and Elijah appeared and spoke very directly to him about "his departure (literally, his 'exodus'), which he was about to bring to fulfillment at Jerusalem" (Luke 9:31). What sustained him during that indescribable ordeal of injustice and abandonment? The deep reality of his Father's favor poured out upon him, signified and sealed to him by that brilliant transformation of his ordinary clothes. That defined him so that he would know who he was in order to enter into what he had to bear, the hellish reality of becoming, for three hours of darkness, the unbeloved Son for our sakes.

And now, not knowing what Joseph was about to endure, Jacob was saying the same thing about Joseph when he dressed up his most beloved son in that radiant coat of many colors: this is my son, whom I love; with him I am well pleased. Listen to him as your leader. It was a message of favor that imparted high-octane power to Joseph—power he would need for the immense suffering that lay ahead. There is no redemption without suffering. Moses and Elijah each played in key role in God's redemptive work. Both suffered intensely. But they knew who they were and that they were set apart for their mission from their birth.

What does this say to us? The New Testament reveals that this same brilliant clothing, representing the favor of the Father, is something all believers are dressed up in as well. Here's how it's presented in Galatians 3:26–27: "You are all sons of God through faith in Christ Jesus, for all of you who were baptized into Christ have clothed yourselves with Christ."

This says that when the Holy Spirit gave you a new heart, which we call the baptism of the Holy Spirit, and transformed you from the inside out, you were actually "dressed up" in all the righteousness of Jesus. You were adorned with a robe of inner holiness—his holiness. It was "credited" to you. It was infused into your very spirit, transforming the very core of your being. All of this was promised to you from the very start of your lives, when you were presented for baptism as a little babies by your parents. Even then, what you wore was so important to them as a symbol of this sacred gift to which you were an heir, that they even dressed you up in something pure white. It is possible they still have your baptismal gown. They clothed you in that bright gown with a prayer on their lips: that someday, by the baptism of the Holy Spirit, you would put your faith in Jesus Christ, and experience at that moment the greatest gift possible for any human being to receive: being so dressed up in his glorious righteousness that you would "shine like stars in the universe as you hold out the word of life…" (Phil. 2:15–16).

What lay ahead for Joseph was a twenty-year ordeal of immense suffering preparing him for his redemptive role, not just in his family, but in the whole Middle East. What sustained him during all that temptation, injustice, and loneliness? It was not just the dreams. It was the far deeper reality of his father's favor upon him, signified and sealed to him by that wondrous coat. You could call it a sacramental garment.

Over the years, your parents bought lots of clothing for you, and nothing brightened up your day like a brand-new item in your wardrobe—except this kind of "clothing." When your parents beamed over you in pride, which is a picture of the favor of God himself upon you, the "dressing up" dignity with which that praise adorned you rivaled the sharpest outfit you ever wore. It made you just glow. We know. We saw that radiant smile on your faces so often as you basked in your parents' praises for you. We saw that deep delight in you. We saw that glory on you!

But all that human favor that was heaped upon you was merely preliminary to the real favor that has the power to adorn and define the very core of your identity! Just like Joseph and Jesus, the real adornment that fills us with glory and sustains us in our mission to be agents of renewal in this broken world, ushering in the kingdom here on earth, is the favor of a Father, the living God Himself! He is for you. Whatever it is that comes up against you is no match to who you are in Christ.

Favor is a big word in the Bible. When you were young, your teachers made you learn Luke 2 by heart. So, you found yourself, probably in a Christmas program, reciting these very words from the heavenly host as they praised God upon the birth of Jesus: "Glory to God in the highest, and on earth peace to men on whom his favor rests." (Luke 2:14)

That favor has presented itself to you, in Christ. If you receive him and allow yourself to be dressed up in him, you will shine! You will also be able to face the dark places that very likely will come your way. For Joseph, what lay ahead was a cistern, slavery, temptation, injustice, and two years in a dark dungeon. *But he had worn the coat!* That is what carried him through the hell he was about to endure in preparation for the great redemption of this broken family that would not come easily.

CHAPTER 6

The Dreams

Read Genesis 37: 5—11

Redemptive work is invariably excruciating. Without a compelling dream that turns your face into flint, you'll quit before you get even halfway through. Dreams are to redeemers what jet fuel is to airplanes.

Joseph was given a double dose. His first dream is local: a wheat field. His second dream is cosmic: the spacious expanse of sun, moon, and stars above us. In both dreams there's movement: toward Joseph. The movement is respectful submission. The sheaves of wheat all glide over the field and tip their golden heads down flat before Joseph's sheaf. The sun, moon, and stars all sweep down toward the horizon of the night sky and assemble below Joseph's star high overhead. The message from God is unmistakable: Joseph is going to be elevated to a place of such prominence that not only will his family honor him; so will thousands more. All redemption is local. Think of how Jesus restored Peter after the denial (John 21). But its reach is cosmic. Through Peter, the rock, thousands received redemption.

Joseph reported those dreams to his brothers. The Bible says twice that he "told" them to his brothers. You just might wonder: how did he tell them? Was he bragging? Was he retaliatory in the face of their sneering spite over his robe? Was he haughty, like kids can be, reporting his dreams with an in-your-face spirit of "So, there! Take that!"? Was he just being a brat about it, telling them off in the tone of an impudent little punk? If so, it would seem plausible given the way they resented him, the little snitch, parading around the compound in his uppity uniform! Many people read pride and arrogance into Joseph's behavior. But let's be cautious here. It is possible that Joseph was unwise, or even naive, to report these dreams. But there is another way of looking at this. It is very possible that Joseph's reporting these dreams was an act of obedience to God and concern for his family. To quote James Montgomery Boice, he may have "sensed a God-given responsibility to make a divine revelation such as this known" (Genesis: An Expositional Commentary, p. 24). After all, these dreams involved all of them, and besides, there was not just one dream but two, the first being backed up by an even weightier second one.

You'll notice the Bible doesn't tell us how he told them. It simply says that he "told" them. And then it goes right on to tell us how they took it from him. That is what we need to know because it shapes the rest of the story. It made them seethe with rage. Notice the temperature gauge on their animosity spiking as chapter 37 moves along:

- "They hated him and could not speak a kind word to him" (v. 4)

- "They hated him all the more" (v. 5)

- "And they hated him all the more" (v. 8)

This is what the Holy Spirit wants you to notice. He wants you to see that dreams may inspire, but they can also generate resistance! He wants you to see that a legitimate dream can actually make life worse for you! A day will come when wise men will be warned in a dream to not return to King Herod. They take another road home. Herod gets furious. Babies die. Dreams guide and protect redeemers, but they also kindle hatred.

When Joseph reported the dreams, his father "kept the matter in mind." In the days of inconsolable grief that lay ahead for Jacob, this may have been the one thin thread that kept his hopes from collapsing entirely. But the hatred of his brothers is now at a boiling point. The handwriting is on the wall: Joseph's days are numbered.

But for Joseph, these dreams are sobering. They are weighty. They are divine oracles. Knowing as he does that dreams come directly from headquarters, heaven itself, they carry clout. They are, you might say, a divine summons. He is being shown that he will be assigned all the weight of pre-eminence, which is no small cross to bear.

Plus, he would need them just to survive the crucible ahead. You've heard this story often enough to know the descent into hell that's awaiting him. His brothers would nearly kill him, callously tossing him into an empty cistern and ignoring his cries. They would casually sell him off into slavery. A seductive woman would lie about him, and he would be tossed into the slammer. For over two full years he would sit in the blackness of a dungeon, totally forgotten by an official who promised to be an advocate for him. Any person (much less a young adult!) going through an ordeal like that could easily collapse under it . . . without a God-given dream. Joseph's dreams were his lifelines. They carried him. They never died. They were the ballast that kept his small craft afloat in the storm that lay ahead.

As we go through this story, always remember what Jesus told the couple on the road to Emmaus. He began with Moses (that would be Genesis!) and "explained to them what was said in all the Scriptures concerning himself" (Luke 24:27b). You know that Jesus also was the only beloved Son of his Father. His birth, interestingly, was accompanied by five dreams, all designed to protect him at the very outset of his mission on earth, just as Joseph's dreams were meant to carry him through the ordeals that lay ahead. (If you count, you'll notice an interesting footnote: there is also a total of five dreams in the Joseph story.) His glory was announced, not by a coat of many colors, but by a thunderous voice right out of the sky (John 12: 28–30) and confirmed through the miracles, wonders, and signs God did through him (Acts 2: 22). Jesus was very clear about the role that he would play as a redeemer: he would become the firstborn among many brothers (Rom. 8: 29) so that he might bring "many sons to glory" (Heb. 2: 10). But Jesus's vision of God's will for him also led him right into the jaws of death. It led to the suffering of a redeemer. It would be the same for Joseph. This is a theme that runs all through the Scriptures: it is through suffering that God brings redemption.

The theme of this book is that redemption comes hard. Even the preparation of the redeemer is a hard process. Both Joseph and Jesus faced immense hardship on their way to the place where they would do their redemptive work. It was a harrowing, painful journey Joseph was led on before he became second in command in Egypt, there to rule on behalf of Pharaoh. It was an even more harrowing and painful journey Jesus was led on before he ascended into heaven, there to rule on behalf of his Father. The life of a redeemer is a cross from start to finish.

Yet both knew that they had been chosen for this role. They were shown a dream or a vision right at the very beginning. Joseph was given the dreams in this chapter; Jesus was given the vision of the dove descending upon him at his baptism, and the voice of his Father singling him out as the son whom he loved. (See the connection to Joseph as the son Jacob loved?) That vision and voice at his baptism was so compelling it launched him into his journey, which immediately put him in a place of great temptation, just like Joseph's dreams would. Yet that vision and voice were so defining, he not only survived the Enemy's three onslaughts in the wilderness, he went on to launch his great mission of redemption. And it was immense. When he preached his first sermon in his hometown of Nazareth, he could boldly claim:

The Spirit of the Lord is on me,

Because he has anointed me
To preach good news to the poor.
He has sent me to proclaim freedom for the prisoners
And recovery of sight for the blind,
To release the oppressed
To proclaim the year of the Lord's favor.
. . . and he began by saying to them, "Today this scripture is fulfilled in your hearing." (Luke 4:18–21)

From day one, both Joseph and Jesus were given the clear message: you have been set apart for a holy mission.

God still gives people dreams and visions today. Sometimes they come when we are sleeping. More often, they come when our eyes are wide open. They are promised in the book of Joel and echoed in the announcement of Peter on the day of Pentecost:

In the last days, God says,
I will pour out my Spirit on all people.
Your sons and daughters will prophesy,
Your young men will see visions
Your old men will dream dreams. (Acts 2: 17)

It is possible, but not necessarily certain, that you also might be given a specific dream or a night-time vision for your life. But it is also possible that God might guide you in other ways. There is no doubt that you are here for a reason. We have been summoned to be part of God's redemptive work in this world, completing what is still lacking in Christ's sufferings for his church (see Col. 1:24)! Besides, there is no doubt that God is fully able to reveal to you just what your part in that mission is.

Sometimes he speaks to you through the guiding principles Jesus announced when he said that his followers are to be a light in the world and the salt of the earth. Beyond that, he may leave it up to your own discernment as to how you can best do so in your generation. Sometimes he is more specific.

He gives you a powerful inner compulsion, or a defining experience, that compels you in a particular direction. He may use a forceful person who urges you to embrace a particular challenge. He may burden you over a compelling need in our world that cries out to the depths of your heart. Be on the lookout for it. If it comes, embrace it. Never let it go. It will carry you all your life. And don't be afraid to tell people, especially your family.

CHAPTER 7

When Evil Hits Home

Read Genesis 37:12–36

On any given day, you will hear about evil. Murders, mass killings, sexual misconduct, terrorism, injustice, political corruption, whatever: it will be the media's breaking news just for you. Their mantra is, "If it bleeds, it leads." You may pay attention, or you may not. Then, you'll go have lunch . . . or whatever. It will barely register with you.

Then one day it will come crashing right into your own calm, predictable, safe little world. Violence will land right on top of you. It will be marked by four elements: it will come from someone close to you whom you trusted, it will be a complete surprise, it will be violent, and you will experience it as utterly undeserved. Evil will hit home with you. And when it does, this part of the Joseph story will resonate with you. It will fit you. Very likely, your first response will be: there is no way this can be redeemed. In fact, I don't even want it to be redeemed. I want justice!

As I already told you back in chapter 2, the Bible doesn't gloss over the ugly side of God's people. What we saw the brothers do to the people of Shechem was appalling, but it didn't hurt Joseph. Now that same brutality of these sons of Leah and the slave women will victimize him. They will almost kill him.

The day seems to begin so normally. Father Jacob sends Joseph on a mission to see if all is well with them. Obedient son that he is, his response is instant, wholehearted compliance: "Very well." (Once again, Joseph reminds us of Jesus, who, over twenty times, spoke of himself as having been *sent* here to earth, often mentioning that the One who sent him was his Father.)

Joseph leaves, makes the fifty-mile mile trek to Shechem, begins searching, but can't find them anywhere. He doesn't give up, scouting out one pastureland after another. An alert local watches him wandering around and asks him what he's looking for. When Joseph tells him he's looking for his brothers, it just so happens that the man is in the know. He's overheard them suggest to each other that they move on to Dothan, fifteen miles to the north. Joseph heads up to Dothan. He is determined to complete the mission on which his Father has sent him. He spies them off in the distance. Filled with joy, he hurries to them.

And then it happens: all hell breaks out over Joseph. The brothers saw him from a distance as well; he was clearly recognizable because he was wearing his richly ornamented robe. Before he even had a chance to arrive and greet them, they had decided exactly what they were going to do. (This may remind you of a parable Jesus told about himself. He portrayed himself as the son of the owner of a vineyard, dispatched to confront the workers in the vineyard because of their mistreatment of his inspectors. There we read these words, almost a perfect echo of what the brothers say to each other in this story: "This is the heir. Come, let's kill him and take his inheritance." [Matt. 21: 38]) Their hatred was so deep that the sheer sight of him, alone and far from his protective father, fired up their imaginations with a perfect scheme to eliminate him. They thought it all up in just minutes. When evil sees its chance, it's amazing how quickly it can devise its strategy. That dry country was filled with cisterns, deep holes in the ground designed to catch and hold rainwater runoff, and there was a handy one right nearby. Instantly they had it all figured out: grab him, strip off that despicable coat, kill him, throw his body down into the cistern where it would likely never be found, bloody up his coat with goat blood, bring it home, tell dad that they stumbled upon the coat, and let him draw his own conclusion.

This is what the evil that will hit you might very well look like. It will be raw, cold, merciless, vicious, without a single qualm, brutal, heartless. Let this challenge the dreamy notions you may entertain regarding the goodness of humanity. This is what the people around you are capable of doing to you. Truth be told, without the restraining grace of God upon your heart, this is what you are capable of doing to them. This is why British Prime Minister Margaret Thatcher once said, "The veneer of civilization is very thin." There is a brutality that lurks in the souls of all of us, and if it were not for the restraining hand of the rule of law—much less the strict training in proper behavior you were privileged to receive, much less a wondrous grace from God upon all of us that collars our lawlessness within his own constraints—who knows what kind of brute any one of us could become?

One of the most formative experiences of my childhood took place when I was about ten years old. I was playing with the neighborhood boys when something happened that made me very angry with one of them. His name was Jim. I do not remember what triggered this, but I do remember that suddenly I became so angry at him that I picked up a stone and slung it at him with all my might. It hit him right in the head, just above his left eye, near his temple. It could have killed him. He screamed in pain and ran home, holding his bleeding head. I saw the blood. Slowly, too slowly, I became afraid of what I had done. Minutes later, his mother pushed him into the family car, quickly backed out of their driveway, and tore down the road . . . very fast. I trembled all the more. A couple of hours later, she returned with him. His head was heavily bandaged, and she took him directly into the house. I told my mother what had happened. She immediately insisted that I go to his house and apologize. When I knocked on the door, his mother, her face stern, opened it. I asked if I could enter. She said, "Yes, you may." Then she told me, her face grave, that her son's head had six stitches. I felt the chill of a cold alarm. I do not remember how he hurt me; I only know that I hurt him worse.

Later I learned, to my horror, that this put me in the company of one of the Old Testament's most notorious villains, a man named Lamech, who boasted to his two wives about his power to excel in getting even, dealing out death to a young man who merely injured him. You can read all about this vile man in Genesis 4: 23–24. I could only blurt out a stumbling apology. I had always thought of myself as a good kid, a nice kid—until that day when I was given a priceless gift. My eyes were opened to a frightening reality. I was forced to face a spirit in me that, when provoked, could instantly erupt into thoughtless, unrestrained, self-justified brutality. For the first time in my life, I was afraid, not *for* myself, but *of* myself. Inside of me lurked a killer! That was no small revelation.

If it hadn't been for Reuben stepping in and appealing to their consciences, begging them to not shed the blood of a brother, Joseph would surely have been slaughtered. But Reuben, being the firstborn, commanded just enough respect to restrain their thirst for blood. He urged that they dispose of him another way without actually killing him. He proposed that they dump him into the cistern alive and abandon him there to die of thirst and starvation. At least, he argued, they would then not be guilty of outright murder! (It's amazing how creative we can be when it comes to finding respectable ways of being vicious!) Well, six of one and a half-dozen of another, it didn't much matter to these exterminators as long as they never needed to lay eyes on this pain in the neck again. They just wanted to be rid of him. So as soon as Joseph stepped into camp, they grabbed him, stripped him, and tossed him into the cistern. And then they calmly sat down and had lunch together, as if nothing of any consequence had just happened. That is the depth of callous perversity from which they would need to be redeemed. They were totally unmoved by the pleas of Joseph, begging for his life from the bottom of the cistern right nearby.

Over twenty years later in the story, when Joseph, as the ruler of Egypt, turns the tables on them and has them incarcerated, we are allowed to listen in on their conversation from their "cistern," an Egyptian prison cell. It gives us a vivid picture of just what happened here during lunch:

> They said to one another, "Surely we are being punished because of our brother. We saw how distressed he was when he pleaded with us for his life, but we would not listen; that's why this distress has come upon us." Reuben replied, "Didn't I tell you not to sin against the boy? But you wouldn't listen! Now we must give an accounting for his blood." (42: 21–22)

Reuben could castigate them because, at the time, he had had his own secret plan to rescue Joseph. Once they moved on, leaving Joseph behind to die, he hoped he could slip away and then, unnoticed, circle back, pull Joseph up from the cistern, and swiftly escort him back to the safety of home. Moses does not reveal the motive of Reuben. It's possible that Reuben knew how much his father loved Joseph and how the death of Joseph would break his father's heart. It's possible that, unlike the other sons, he had actually come to care about Joseph. But there's no evidence for this so far in the story. Instead, there's another possible motive that would have been entirely self-serving. Reuben had lost the favor of his father by shamelessly committing incest with one of his father's concubines, Bilhah. The most likely motive behind Reuben's sudden intervention to save Joseph's life was that, by rescuing Joseph, he could somehow, by his own efforts, atone for what he had done and get back into his father's good graces again. If so, then the truth is that there was no one in this scene, no one, who was truly looking out for Joseph. There was no one who cared about him for his own sake. Here too, in this moment of complete abandonment, Joseph's helplessness is a picture of what David later on, and then Jesus most of all, suffered. David described it is Psalm 69: 19–20:

> You know how I am scorned, disgraced and shamed;
> All my enemies are before you.
> Scorn has broken my heart and has left me helpless;
> I looked for sympathy, but there was none,
> For comforters, but I found none.

(G. F. Handel included this in "The Messiah" as a haunting recitative, No. 29. Sung by a tenor soloist, it is deeply moving, helping us feel the depth of this kind of suffering—of Joseph, David, Jesus, and perhaps, one day, even you.)

Suffering itself is painful enough, but to suffer alone, without one person caring for you—that is a taste of hell. But this too is part of the great redemption story: Joseph as a prototype, and then Jesus as the true redeemer, endured the ultimate hell to spare us from the hells into which our own perverse hearts can so easily lead us.

And so Reuben slipped away, planning to return once the brothers moved on and pull off his rescue plan. It never happened. Instead, we are looking at a situation in which it seems that evil has triumphed. Reuben is gone, Joseph is trapped, and the brothers are enjoying lunch! But there is Someone else there. He is always there. And he is looking out for Joseph. So now, when all seems locked in the grip of evil, God quietly but powerfully orchestrates his own rescue of Joseph—though to Joseph it surely would not look one bit like a rescue. While the boys were munching on their sandwiches and Joseph plaintive cries were spilling over the lip of the cistern, God mercifully sent, in disguise, his own unlikely rescuers: a caravan of Ishmaelites, of all people!! These men were distant and estranged relatives of the brothers. They were descended from their grandfather Isaac's half-brother, Ishmael, who long ago had been driven away from the family. It "just so happened" that their caravan was passing by this very spot as they traveled on their way to trade their goods in Egypt. God chose them, the unlikeliest of all people, to actually be his agents in Joseph's rescue.

As they pass near the camp, Judah noticed them and immediately spotted a fast way to make a buck. He suggested they at least make some money for themselves by pulling Joseph out of the cistern and selling him off to these merchants. He even made his greedy offer sound downright charitable by saying, "After all, he is our brother, our own flesh and blood." So they struck a deal and sold their brother (their brother!) for a mere twenty shekels of silver, which, these days, is about $170. His brothers sold him for next to nothing, much like Jesus would be sold, centuries later, by his betrayer.

When evil hits you, it is very likely you will experience it as a betrayal. Someone you thought cared about you will turn on you. It will feel like being stabbed in the back. It will shock you. You will feel violated, perplexed, and likely enraged.

The deal was struck, and suddenly Joseph is turned over into the hands of heartless strangers. He is forced down an unknown road to a distant country as nothing more than a commodity meant for sale . . . and a big profit. Who can imagine the agony that kid endured on that long, dusty road through Gaza and down to Egypt? What had been a goodwill mission had suddenly been flipped over into something Joseph had never expected. He was totally blindsided. There was nothing ahead of him but uncertainty. In his heart he must have felt exactly like the dark ending of Psalm 88:

> From my youth I have been afflicted and close to death;
> I have suffered your terrors and am in despair.
> Your wrath has swept over me, your terrors have destroyed me.
> All day long they surround me like a flood; they have completely engulfed me.
> You have taken my companions and loved ones from me;
> The darkness is my closest friend. (vv. 15–18)

Might I observe that you also might, and very likely will, find yourself experiencing this kind of darkness at some point in your life—perhaps even at several points. You will feel that your world has collapsed around you. You will feel that no one cares. Your heart will be wounded at the injustice of how you are being treated. The future will fill you with apprehension. You will feel utterly alone. You will feel that you are falling, falling, falling into an abyss from which there is no escape. You might even wonder if life is worth living any more. You may even contemplate suicide. And perhaps the worst part of it all is the powerlessness. You see no escape.

And so it was that Joseph found himself being hauled off to a slave auction in Egypt! Still, deposited deep in his soul were two treasures nobody could strip away. They were part of him. They came with him:

- Nobody could take away the favor his father had given him.

- Nobody could take away the prospect his dreams had promised him.

Perhaps, looking back later on, he could even glimpse all the ways that God had actually protected him that day when his fortunes were so reversed. For, after all,

- Reuben had intervened to spare his life.

- The cistern just happened to be dry.

- The Ishmaelites arrived just in the nick of time.

- And Judah's scheme to make money off of him actually allowed him to live another day.

Perhaps he saw, despite it all, that he was under divine protection. It would not be too great a stretch of the imagination to say that powerful but invisible angels were dispatched to that very same spot, where Joseph was outnumbered and overpowered, surrounding him and setting limits to just how far the Destroyer could go. Doesn't the Bible promise this? Consider Psalm 91:9–13:

> If you make the Most High your dwelling, even the Lord, who is my refuge—
> Then no harm will befall you, no disaster will come near your tent.
> For he will command his angels concerning you to guard you in all your ways;
> They will lift you up in their hands, so that you will not strike your foot against a stone.
> You will tread upon the lion and the cobra; you will trample the great lion and the serpent.

Consider this: just a few centuries after this story, at that very same location, one solitary man would end up being surrounded by an entire army sent to capture him. By night, this army of horses, chariots and soldiers had stealthily set up a cordon around the entire area, making escape impossible. It was one man against thousands. Or was it? You can read the story for yourself in 2 Kings 6: 8–23. The place was Dothan. The man was Elisha. But he had his spiritual eyes wide open. In a situation we would call desperate, he remained surprisingly serene. Why? Because he saw another army, an angelic host surrounding the army surrounding him. They too had chariots and horses—of fire! What looked lopsided was lopsided—but the other way around!

A day may come when you will find yourself in a situation where you feel as outnumbered and overpowered as Joseph . . . or Elisha. It will be your Dothan day. But even there, more going on than meets the eye. This is why Paul could describe his Dothan moments like this:

> We are hard pressed on every side, but not crushed;
> perplexed, but not in despair;
> persecuted, but not abandoned;
> struck down, but not destroyed. (2 Cor. 4: 9)

Joseph looks like just a bewildered kid, being carted off by strangers to be sold at a slave auction in a foreign land. But there is always a "but." In the upside-down kingdom of heaven, things are rarely the way they seem.

CHAPTER 8

Thriving In Exile

Genesis 39: 1 — 6b; 20 — 23

The time will come. You will experience exile. Your first taste of it was when your parents imposed a "time out" on you for bad behavior, or, for some mysterious reason, your circle of friends shut you out. Exile comes when…

- You leave home for the first time and experience a homesickness you never imagined.

- You lose a job you thought was secure and find yourself adrift in the world of the unemployed.

- You don't fit into the culture where you live or work.

- You can't find a church where you feel you fit, or, far worse, you feel out of sync in a congregation where you've been a member for years.

Exile is an acute form of torment for the soul, marked by a haunting conviction that you don't belong where you are. When John Steinbeck wrote his book *Travels with Charlie*, he observed that many of the people he and his dog Charlie met along the way (they spent a year travelling all over

America) wished they were someone else, doing something else, living somewhere else. The sense of exile runs deep within us. The Bible puts it right near the very beginning, in Genesis 3. Adam and Eve felt deeply at home in paradise. Then they rebelled against the God who was their true home in paradise, and suddenly they went into hiding. That was their first taste of exile. Then they were expelled from the garden. The sense of exile hit them full force, and humanity has been pining for its true home ever since. Christians can never (and should never) feel completely at home in this broken world, even though every square inch of it belongs to Jesus, and he is redeeming it through us. Our exile will only end when he returns, lives among us, and transforms it into our permanent home.

Joseph would never feel at home in Egypt, even though he would end up living the rest of his life there, which amounted to just over ninety years. When he died in Egypt he ordered his heirs to make sure to take his bones back to Canaan with them when they finally left their long exile there. Some 430 years later, he was finally carried to his true home (Exod. 13:19).

This sense of exile is now the new normal for Joseph. One day he's at home in Hebron, living in the favor of his father. Every face is family. Every routine is familiar. Less than a week later, this seventeen-year-old kid finds himself on exhibit at a slave auction, with a price on his head and people inspecting his physique as if he were a mule. A stranger buys him. The next day he finds himself doing menial labor, mucking out animal stalls or slaving away at field work. He is a stranger in a foreign land: strange language, strange customs, strange dress, and strange people.

Surprisingly, Joseph thrived in his exile! Whatever he undertook flourished. Whatever he touched, as the saying goes, turned to gold. People noticed. The boss noticed. And one of the great laws of economics went into effect: the reward for work well done is . . . more work! Joseph found himself being promoted . . . frequently.

And then we're given the reason. To make sure we don't miss it, Moses tells us *seven* times. In stark contrast to chapter 37, where there is not so much as even one reference to God, chapter 39 is dominated by an insistence that God is the whole story here. Notice:

> v. 2: The Lord was with Joseph
> v. 3: The Lord was with him . . .
> . . .the Lord gave him success in everything he did
> v. 5: The Lord blessed the household of the Egyptian because of Joseph . . . the blessing of the Lord was on everything
> v. 21: The Lord was with him . . .
> v. 23: The Lord was with Joseph and gave him success in whatever he did.

It's as if the whole point of chapter 37, even with its episode of dicey temptation in the middle, is to let us know, in no uncertain terms, that God's presence is all we need to thrive even in a place where you very much don't want to be. The culture around you frequently deals with exile by changing location; finding a better job, climate, or country. Or the culture will tell you to buck up and make the best of it.

Just listen to them talk to you:

> *"If you can dream it, you can do it." (Walt Disney)*

> *"The mind is the limit. As long as the mind can envision the fact that you can do something, you can do it, as long as you really believe it 100%." (Arnold Schwarzenegger)*

> *"My dad drilled it in my head, you know, if you want it bad enough and you're willing to make the sacrifices, you can do it. But you first have to believe in yourself." (Jennie Finch, softball pitcher who helped lead Team USA to the gold medal at the 2004 Summer Olympics)*

"Be magnificent. Life's short. Get out there. You can do it. Everyone can do it. Everyone." (Andy Serkis, who won an Oscar for his role as Gollum in Lord of the Rings)

"I write about the American Dream: if you set your mind to do something, you can do it." (Jackie Collins, wrote thirty-two novels, all of which appeared on the New York Times bestseller list)

"If it's going to be, it's up to me." (Lenny Krayzelburg, four-time gold medalist in Olympic swimming)

No small number of ministers have preached this message of the American "Can Do" dream, including Robert Schuller, whose entire empire, based on this "gospel" of positive thinking, collapsed, finally dying in 2010 when his Crystal Cathedral Ministries declared bankruptcy. His magnificent thirty-four-acre campus was sold to the Catholic Diocese of Orange for $57.5 million in 2011. That's what his "can do" dream came to!

But chapter 39 has nothing of this "gospel of believing in yourself" in it. The secret to Joseph's success here had nothing to do with Joseph. There's not a word in it about his drive, his ambition, or his efficiency. Nothing! The real actor here is "the LORD." This is God's story. The first sentence in Rick Warren's bestselling book, *The Purpose-Driven Life*, is profoundly true: "It's not about you." And that fact is 180 degrees opposite of the "You can do it!" creed governing the oceanic culture all around you in which you will swim your whole life.

Watch **God**. He selects the person who buys him as a slave. He just "happens" to be one of Egypt's top officials. His name is Potiphar, and he is the captain of the guard, a high post in Pharaoh's administration. So, from the get-go, it is God who positions his man Joseph right next to someone who knows how to manage major responsibility and has a good eye for people who are effective. Today, we would call them "high capacity" people.

Head hunters prize them; executives are always on the lookout for them. Potiphar knew one when he saw one.

So, when Potiphar noticed that whatever Joseph was assigned to do ended up being done with excellence, plus resulted in profits, he began to promote him up the ladder . . . rapidly. It's really quite wondrous. If he began living off in the lowly servants' quarters, he was quickly moved right into Potiphar's manor. When Potiphar noticed Joseph's success in the manor, he promoted him again, this time making him his own personal assistant as well as appointing him chief of staff over all domestic operations at the manor. That went so well that eventually Joseph was put in charge of "everything Potiphar owned," which suggests that Joseph ran the whole show.

Once he began his work as CEO of Potiphar, Inc., the entire operation just took off. Profits came pouring in. People got along. Potiphar ended up in a place owners of major enterprises can only dream of: he had no worries. He was in "boss heaven!" He didn't have to even bother with productivity reports or personnel issues. If anybody in the company had a complaint, he could confidently and easily handle it by saying, "Talk to Joseph. He'll work it out for you." It got to the point, says Moses, that after a while the only concern Potiphar had was, "What's for dinner?"! Why? God's favor, period. No doubt, Joseph was conscientious and industrious. We know that. But nowhere does Moses attribute Joseph's climb up even one rung of the ladder to his enterprising spirit. It was all God, all the time, in all the places of Potiphar's operations.

Later on in the chapter, it's the same song, second verse. Once again, Joseph suffers a painful injustice and is exiled all over again. Neither his position nor his performance protected him. Overnight, he finds himself in another pit, this time a prison, because Potiphar believed his wife's lie, claiming that Joseph had attempted to rape her. Suddenly he is in Egypt's worst prison, the place where the king put his personal enemies. Imagine the emotions that had to be swirling around in Joseph's heart as he was subjected, a second time, to undeserved cruelty.

- He had to be struggling with rage at the terrible injustice of it all.

- He had to be feeling dread at the dim prospects of ever being released.

- He had to be feeling the cold chill of fear over what kind of torture he might have to face.

The truth is, he was descending, for a second time, into a kind of hell. Psalm 105:18 describes the cruelty: "They bruised his feet with shackles, His neck was put in irons."

And yet, wondrously, when Joseph was marched into that dungeon, the Lord marched right in ahead of him. He caused the warden to notice Joseph and be impressed. Joseph noticed special kindnesses coming his way: perhaps better food, or better quarters, or an extra blanket for cold nights. God kept right on moving in the heart of the warden, making him notice that Joseph was no ordinary prisoner. He saw that Joseph had a way about him, with an air of authority, expertise, and leadership. There was something regal in his bearing. Joseph didn't have to try to impress the warden. All he had to do was simply be the person God had made him to be, and the warden couldn't help but be impressed.

It is by no means a simple or easy thing to impress a warden. These men have seen it all. Prisons have plenty of con men. Wardens are not easily fooled. Joseph was simply himself. And so it came to be that the warden did the very same thing Potiphar had done: in time, he put Joseph in charge of the whole prison! Imagine this: he managed the guards, controlled the inmates, and oversaw all the operations. This time it was the warden who was in "boss heaven," so free of concern he "paid no attention to anything under Joseph's care" (v. 23). It is mighty high praise for a manager when your up-line has so much confidence in you he or she doesn't even bother to read your reports!

What is this telling you, especially when you are a victim of discrimination, abuse, or raw injustice? It happens. What does this say to you in a place where you very much do not want to be and, in some cases, don't deserve to be?

You will notice how others deal with this. Some will put up a noisy protest. Some just quit. Some just go along to get along. Some resign themselves to it and just put in their time until retirement. You will meet people who have become cynical, who are merely surviving, whose aspirations have long since gone flat. The truth is that in yourself, you are no match for the entrenched, institutionalized corruption that will come your way.

But what if this story is actually more than an isolated incidence of divine favor? What if this story is, in fact, the *norm* for the children of God? What if this is a story that is a template you can count on for your story?

You don't have to even wonder. For the rest of Scripture never ceases to chant a larger truth: *our story is never divorced from God's story.* Our story is part of his grander story. It fits into it as a critical element of what he is doing in this world. As a result, if we go through fire or flood, it is still part of a much grander drama. This is bedrock, biblical truth. This is truth you can build your life on. In fact, it is very likely that what Moses wants the nation of Israel to learn from the Joseph story, is that this is a picture of their own exile in Egypt. As a nation, they would be brutalized, but despite long odds, they would be delivered because God had chosen them, out of all the peoples of the earth, as the nation where his presence would dwell. As they traveled through the desert, not a day passed without that presence, as a pillar of cloud by day, a pillar of fire by night, and as the bread of the presence in the tabernacle. And as Moses faced their uncertain future during their wilderness wanderings, he was convinced that the only hope he had of ever bringing them to their final destination in the promised land was The Presence. He could not lead, and the people could not advance, without it: "Then Moses said to Him, 'If your Presence does not go with us, do not send us up from here. How will anyone know that you are pleased with me and with your people unless you go with us? What else will distinguish me and your people from all the other people on the face of the earth?'" (Exod. 33:15–16)

That presence found its ultimate expression in Jesus, Immanuel, God with us. Today, that presence is the Holy Spirit, God in us. Every time we celebrate the Lord's Supper, we taste, smell and take it right into our bodies. That presence transforms all our exiles into a place we can call home.

When kids are very little, some sing that favorite Sunday School song, The wise man built his house upon the rock. It is cute to watch them belt it out, with their pudgy little hands busily doing the motions, from pounding their hammers to clapping out that loud smash at the end when the foolish man's house broke up into smithereens. Yes, it was a cute little song, and it may seem to those reading this that they have long ago outgrown it. Not so fast. If you sang it as a little child, the reality is that you were singing about a vital reality you will need as you emerge into adulthood. You will most surely experience the rain, the flood, and the blasting wind. You will get hit hard, and that is one of the reasons I am so passionate about writing this book. Most of us will experience something like Joseph experienced. What is revealed in this chapter about God, if we believe it, will be the only ballast we need when we get our taste of exile.

The American "Can Do" myth is sand; what you see in this chapter is rock. Consider that both the wise man and the foolish man built houses. Both houses were impressive, and both appeared unshakeable. Both houses stood firm as long as there were no storms. But the day of exile, the day of the storm, the day when the world collapses around you, the day when "the rain came down and the floods came up" and the wind blows and "beats" upon your house will most surely come. You have probably had a minor storm or two already. That day will expose what is otherwise invisible: your spiritual foundation. It will reveal what lies beneath. If you build your life and career around your own can-do resolve, that day will shatter you. Just look around at the wreckage and see for yourself. Consider people like Robin Williams, a highly gifted and superbly honed actor. That man was ambitious! He believed in himself. He built a very impressive "house" out of his career, but when the storm finally came, it revealed the invisible sand underneath. When his own inner demons surfaced, and the life-long depression he had fought for years hit him full force, it was too much for even his "can do" spirit. He buckled and took his own life. The day came when his dead body was discovered in his bedroom, where he had hung himself. And he is not alone; these days the suicide rate is rising at a steady pace (roughly 41,000 Americans in 2013), and among its victims over the years are some very impressive names, like Kurt Cobain, Junior Seau, Ernest Hemingway, and Aaron Hernandez. You grandchildren may not even realize that you have two distant cousins among them. This strikes close to home. Few families are spared the pain of that terrible line which concludes the entire Sermon on the Mount: "and it fell with a great crash" (Matt. 7:27b).

With some reluctance I am going to tell you a story from my own life. As you know, for over twenty-six years I served as the pastor of a particular congregation. In January of 2006, the elders of the church, among whom were dear friends of mine, out of love for me informed me that it was in my best interest and that of the congregation for me to conclude my ministry there. We acquiesced to this decision because we believe that God rules his church and our lives through the elders. This was our greatest storm ever: we felt exiled.

We chose to simply rest in God and count on him to carry us. Wondrous events began to occur, two that we will never forget.

Within just a month of this shock, we received an inquiry from another church inviting us to an interview. They were looking for an interim pastor. They chose us, and God blessed us there so richly the congregation voted to call us as their permanent pastor. We stayed there four wonderful years, and at the end, the farewell they gave us was one of the most celebrative events we've ever known.

The second occurred the month after we bid our final farewell to our church. To give our spirits time to heal, we took a month off and spent it in caring for you grandchildren while your parents went on a mission trip to Africa. During those few weeks a most unusual event happened, something which has never happened to us, before or since. A couple from your church invited us over to your home for a backyard barbeque. They had a swimming pool for the kids to enjoy. So we went and had a great time. Then they told us to come again, soon. Amazingly, over a three-week period, this happened seven times! Each time we were shown such kind and lavish hospitality, relaxing by the pool, enjoying cool drinks, and savoring delicacies off the grill, it was like a salve being worked into our wounded spirits. At the end of our final visit, I told our gracious host that he was about to hear some Bible trivia. I told him that as far as I was concerned, his real name was Barzillai, the Gileadite. His blank stare proved me right: he didn't have the foggiest idea who that was. So I invited him to read the story for himself in 2 Samuel 17:27–29. It's an account of one of the lowest moments in the life of King David, when he found himself exiled by his own son, Absalom. Utterly exhausted, he and his army had just fled for their lives, crossing the Jordan River by night, escaping into the land of Gilead, and arriving at the town of Mahanaim, the same place angels had greeted Joseph's father Jacob when he escaped from Laban. There he was met by this man, along with his two friends, Shobi and Makir. They were like angels to David and his dog-tired army as they presented them with a feast fit for a king. In fact, the entire menu is reported in the account! It completely refreshed David and his men. And, I told our host, that is exactly what he had unknowingly done for us. We left his home refreshed for our new ministry. And we had nothing to do with all this goodness that was poured into our laps. It was all of God, just as, in this storm in Joseph's life, the favor poured out upon him was all of God. That is the rock at work, gripping a house firmly while "the rains came down and the floods came up."

This story of Joseph flourishing in exile may prove a life saver to you. One of the reasons this story, and many others like it, is in the Bible is stated in Romans 15:4: "For everything that was written in the past was written to teach us, so that through endurance and the encouragement of the Scriptures we might have hope."

"Everything" includes this story and its countercultural truth. It is meant to teach a rock-solid truth: regardless of where you find yourself in your life of exile as a pilgrim here upon the earth, be it a place of your choosing or one forced upon you, the presence of the living God is in fact right in that very place. In the words of Andrew Murray, you can say to yourself, "I am here, by God's appointment, in his care, for his purpose, and until his time." If you allow that reality to settle into your spirit, you will be given the power to endure, and more. You will be given the power to thrive, even should your place, for the time being, seem like a prison.

CHAPTER 9

The Test

Read Genesis 39:6b–20a

---

 ecently, in our little town, the news broke wide open. It was in the
papers because it involved a very public person. It was whispered in the
coffee shops. People with grave looks on their faces asked each other, "Did
you hear about . . . ?" It was yet another alleged act of sexual perversion. In
a small town like ours, such scandals have all the privacy of an earthquake.
Worse, redemption looks impossible. People wonder how such a person
can ever recover their good name after such a shameful exposure

This person represents legions. Thousands of men, and some women as
well, with good names and promising careers have seen their reputations
shattered and their futures blow up in their faces because of sexual misconduct. Even as I write this in late 2017, allegations of sexual misconduct
dominate the news. Well-known Charlie Rose is the latest casualty.

We've known of this danger for centuries, which is why the wisdom of
Proverbs issues such ominous warnings for sexual strays:

> Now then, my sons, listen to me: pay attention to what I say.
> Do not let your heart turn to her ways, or stray into her paths.
> Many are the victims she has brought down;

Her house is a highway to the grave,
Leading down to the chambers of death. (Prov. 7: 24–27)

Though every generation has been tainted by sexual deviancy, you are growing up in a culture where societal norms for sexual behavior have been relaxed in a much more permissive direction. In your generation it is increasingly common for teens to become sexually active. In 2011–2013, among unmarried fifteen to nineteen-year-olds, 44 percent of females and 49 percent of males have had sexual intercourse. (See www.guttmacher. org/fact-sheet/american-teens-sexual-and-reproductive-health.)   The Guttmacher Institute reports that this level has been steady since 2002. Cohabitation rates have seen a rapid rise as well. Since 1960 the number of cohabiting couples in the United States has increased fifteen-fold to over six million. The emotional costs of cohabitation are now a matter of statistical record, laid out in a frightening book titled, *The Ring Makes All the Difference*, by Glenn T. Stanton. It is into this sexually permissive culture that you have been injected. My concern as your grandfather is not just to protect you from its corrosive influence but to challenge you to stand up against it. This part of the Joseph story, can, I believe, give you a head start on that lonely journey.

Be forewarned: sexual perversion is an indiscriminate predator. No one is exempt from its appeal, regardless of their position in society. It almost took down a president, Bill Clinton, when a lowly White House intern, Monica Lewinski, caught his eye and drew him into an "inappropriate relationship." At the same time, here in our little town of Lynden, any number of ordinary people have had to come into my office and admit to an affair, from members of law enforcement to respected financiers. Most were married, and for most of them, it marked the end of their marriage. Adultery shatters the bond of trust in a marriage so completely, Jesus even allowed for divorce in such cases. (He did not mandate it, since it is actually possible, through the power of deep repentance and the hard work of rebuilding trust, for couples to recover; but this is one redemption that comes extremely hard.) So study this part of the story with me. At the very least, I hope it will sober you. But I would hope for more. I would hope it would convince you that sexual purity is a noble ambition, and it is entirely attainable. That means going back to the story behind Joseph's imprisonment.

Joseph is thriving in the house of Potiphar. He's been promoted to CEO of Potiphar, Inc. He is running an empire on a small scale. He enjoys the trust of the owner and the respect of the workers. The slave has become a sovereign and the reject, a ruler, all because of the steady favor of God. Joseph is living a charmed life!

Then, from an unexpected quarter, he is sexually ambushed. I doubt that he ever saw the final attack coming, centered as he was on "attending to his duties" (37:11). Of all people, the very wife of the man who totally trusted him gets eyes for him. She notices how handsome his face is and how perfectly sculpted his young body is. To her, he is the perfect Adonis!

It is no small burden to be handsome or beautiful. I have often felt compassion for photogenic folks. It's not only because their beauty can breed vanity. It's because their good looks can easily move people around them to be drawn to them only for their appearance, rather than their character, and as a result, they are not always sure whom they can trust.

So Joseph's beauty puts him in jeopardy. As Mrs. Potiphar feasts her eyes on his stunning good looks and magnificent body, her fantasies inflame her imagination. She begins to coddle a dream of having such a magnificent hulk come to bed with her. Then, one day, her passions get the best of her. Suddenly she jettisons whatever cautions or fears she may have had, throws herself at him, and boldly lures him with this sweet enticement: Come to bed with me!

This is how some temptations come: on an ordinary day, conscientiously going about our ordinary business, it attacks us out of nowhere, blindsiding us, pulling at us with a force that seems irresistible. Why is this? It is because lurking behind temptations is a tempter, a malicious evil spirit. He prowls, looking for the opportune moment to strike. He is both smart and patient. Like a cagey lion, he bides his time until he finds us in an unguarded moment. Then, he strikes. After Satan tempted Jesus three times, and was rebuffed every time, he simply waited: "When the devil had finished all this tempting, he left him until an opportune time" (Matt. 4:13). Timing is everything.

When the tempter strikes, there is usually little time to think. Why is there such a thing as "emergency preparedness?" It's because, as every disaster response team knows, when the hurricane strikes is not the time to practice drills! So here: if Joseph's defenses had not been prepared in advance with solid convictions and sound judgment, his story would surely have become that of the simpleton in Proverbs 7:

> At the window of my house I looked out through the lattice. I saw among the simple, I noticed among the young men, a youth who lacked judgment. . . . Then out came a woman to meet him, dressed like a prostitute and with crafty intent. . . . She took hold of him and kissed him and with a brazen face she said, "Come, let's drink deep of love till morning; let's enjoy ourselves with love!" With persuasive words she led him astray; she seduced him with her smooth talk. All at once he followed her, like an ox going to the slaughter, like a deer stepping into a noose till an arrow pierces his liver, like a bird darting into a snare, little knowing it will cost him his life. (vv. 6–7, 10, 13, 18, 21–23)

Those are the high stakes here. Joseph is facing a temptation that could cost him his life, shattering everything he has achieved, undoing everything God has done for him.

But Joseph is not "simple." A simpleton is a person who cannot (or will not) see ahead and consider carefully the consequences of his actions. A simpleton acts first and (perhaps!) thinks later.

But Joseph doesn't! Why? If you remind yourself of all the goodness and blessing that has been poured into his life, you'll begin to grasp just how well defended he was. Remember everything you've been told about him so far:

- his father, looking upon him with favor,

- his robe, adorning him with dignity,

- his dreams, bequeathing him a destiny,

- and now the kindness of God, pouring out a cascade of blessing upon his work as a slave in the house of Potiphar

You can see for yourself the hedge of protection God has built around him. His one defense, and the first one he needed to stay safe in the face of this attack, was the settled conviction that God's hand had been laid upon him, that God's favor "hemmed him in—behind and before" to use the language of safety found in Psalm 139: 5. Therefore, he knew he was not one to be trifled with! He was inoculated again this intense exposure to real evil by nothing less than his high status as the favored of God.

Consider this: on the one hand he was being offered a momentary sexual favor from Mrs. Potiphar, while on the other hand he savored, every day, the immense favor of God, father Jacob, and Potiphar himself. Why would he give up the gold of that grand favor for the straw of this momentary favor? That would be pure folly. But those were the stakes! He would have defrauded himself of his grandest assets! Indeed, this is the same defense our Lord was given in his baptism before he came under attack by Satan in the wilderness, when his father said to him, "This is my beloved Son, with whom I am well pleased." Ponder this with me: it is all the accumulated favor of God, which he has poured upon you through your parents, your teachers, your coaches, your grandparents, and especially through his Son

Jesus that is your most powerful wall of protection against any temptation to compromise your sexual purity. You are too valued for something so cheap. Ask anybody from Solomon to Tiger Woods what it cost them when they fell for this little favor. They gained a penny's worth of pleasure at the cost of a dollar's worth of dignity. It's a Faustian bargain.

But evil does not die a quick death. Mrs. Potiphar was not easily put off. One "No!" is rarely sufficient to stop our Enemy, as we learn from the temptation of Jesus. Satan came at him three times. And so we read that "day after day" Mrs. Potiphar kept up her seductive overtures. She was convinced she could wear Joseph down into finally capitulating. What she did not realize, however, was a great truth about overcoming temptation: her persistence was actually hardening his resistance. When we lay down our first "No!" it changes us! It launches in us a momentum toward deeper and deeper resolve for holiness, a mighty dynamic of "going from strength to strength" (Ps. 84:7). The more we say "No," the more we are empowered to keep on saying "No!" An old song puts it this way: "Each victory will help you some other to win." Moral muscles, like physical ones, get stronger with exercise, especially, as all athletes know, against increasing resistance! Those of you who have run cross country know this well: it's the hills that build stamina!

Joseph's resistance was hardening! But look closely at how Mrs. Potiphar refuses to let up: "she spoke to Joseph, day after day" (v. 10). Take a moment to imagine all the subtle ways she tries to entice him. Think of all the ruses she might have used:

- Who will know? No one! I promise: I'll never tell.

- This is just a little fling—what could possibly be wrong with that if both of us consent to it?

- C'mon. Your life is hard here. You deserve a little fun in life, don't you?

- How could this possibly hurt you or me?

Day after day after day she kept coming at him, determined to wear him down.

How did Joseph ever manage to withstand such an unrelenting attack? We're told, and this is his second line of defense: reasoning. Joseph cared enough to expose to her the true dimensions of the "little fling" she was pining for. He attempted to open her eyes to the seriousness of an affair.

He began by bringing another person into the picture. It was as if he was saying, "This is not just a tryst for two; there's another person involved here, and he happens to be your husband!" Here's how he put it: "With me in charge, my master does not concern himself with anything in the house; everything he owns he has entrusted to my care" (v. 8). Joseph wanted to shatter her illusion that this would be a private event.

Then he continued by warning her about the impact such an affair would have on the entire staff. He said to her, "No one is greater in this house than I am" (v. 9a). He's not bragging; instead, he is confronting her with the fact that the handsome hulk she had eyes for just happens to be a person who was chief of staff. He wanted her to see that she was not just tempting a person but assaulting a position of such trust that if he ever violated the standards of behavior required of a person holding that office, it would damage all those under him. In the heat of illicit sexual passion, who gives the slightest thought to how many other people will be harmed?

But Joseph had more to say in his attempt to get her to see her folly. His third warning attempted to shame her by comparing her disloyalty to Potiphar with Potiphar's loyalty to her: My master has withheld nothing from me except you, because you are his wife. In effect, he's telling her: "Look at the loyalty in your husband! When you consider just how generous he is (he's let me have the run of the house) and realize how eager he has been to lavish me with every possible kind of gift, haven't you noticed that even in the context of all that appreciation and generosity, he has set one limit and only one: you? That is how loyal he is to you. And now you want to step over the very line he drew because of his loyalty to you?"

This is worth pondering. The real danger in sexual sin is not merely the risk of venereal disease or even personal shame. The real risk is that it violates the boundaries in life which protect the trust between people, trust that is vital to being able to flourish in life. Those boundaries enable us all to know our place, keep us in that place, and then thrive in that place. Perhaps you watched me transplant young, bare-root peach trees I bought at a local nursery. I didn't just plant them; I staked them, tying their trunks tautly to two sturdy posts, one on each side, so that they would be held firmly in their place when the winds blew. Without being bound in place by those posts, the gusts of wind from the northeast that can barrel through our town at terrific speeds could have easily pushed them over, since they had barely any roots. And that would have ruined their greatest joy: producing their impossibly sweet fruit! So I confined them. I restricted them. You might say I imprisoned them in just one spot in the garden. I tied them down, which is exactly what marriages does for us, and which so many in your generation fear about marriage. True enough, marriage does "tie us down," but even my peach trees, if they could talk, would tell you a peach tree cannot flourish unless it is confined to one place. Commitment is like those two sturdy posts safeguarding a tender young tree; it anchors us so we can flourish.

Finally, Joseph brings in God. This woman did not share his religion, but that didn't mean she had no awareness of a divine being. Like all human beings, Egyptians were religious people. Romans 1:20 assures us that Mrs. Potiphar was well aware of the existence of God when it says, "For since the creation of the world God's invisible qualities—his eternal power and divine nature—have been clearly seen, being understood from what has been made, so that men are without excuse." We are inescapably religious. How often don't your peers text "OMG!" when something wows them? So Joseph tried to put the fear of the God Mrs. Potiphar knew was right there into her by confronting her with the unsettling truth that an affair with her would in fact be "a wicked thing" and "a sin against God" (v. 9). What she minimized, Joseph maximized. Joseph's final attempt to reach into this woman's heart, consumed as it was by lust, was to challenge her notion that this would be only a little tryst by confronting her with a powerful rhetorical question meant to awaken her to its true size.

Joseph used the word "wicked" to describe this affair she was pining for. This is not a word we commonly use anymore in its true meaning, yet the Bible uses it almost six hundred times. It's a word with teeth in it. In the Bible, its core meaning is distortion. Bribery, for example, is considered wicked precisely because it distorts proper payment for goods and services so seriously that their actual value is lost. So what is "wicked" sex? It is intercourse that twists sex into mere physical pleasure rather than the whole-souled experience of rich love it is meant to express. Such sex is so far from its original intent that people who have an affair don't even know what they're missing. They have no idea of what real sexual intimacy could actually be like, and so they rob themselves of its true beauty. Consequently, wicked people are constantly shortchanging themselves. They're settling for a caricature of pleasure when an infinite joy could be theirs.

However, this carefully crafted warning from Joseph, expressed with respect and tact, failed to stop Mrs. Potiphar. You might wonder why such a reasonable argument didn't change her mind. I hope you do wonder, because there is truth here I don't want you to miss: our lives may be shaped by what we think, but they are driven by what we want. James K. A. Smith summarized it well in the title of one of his recent books: *You Are What You Love*. The old wisdom of the ancient Jewish scriptures put it this way: "Above all else, guard your heart, for everything you do flows from it"

(Prov. 4: 23). Joseph addressed her head, as he should have, and he spoke a whole lot of good sense into it. But she wanted him with her heart. And the heart is so powerful, it will jettison even the most sensible ideas in the head to get what it wants. Sin, at its core, is un-thinking. It is sense-less. It doesn't deliberate! It just wants what it wants and won't stop until it gets it. Desire trumps truth.

Joseph knows this very well as he watches Mrs. Potiphar sidle up to him again and again. This launches his third defense: he decides to keep his distance from her. If his first defense was the dignity of his person, and the second, the data of the facts, his third line of defense was simply distance: "He refused to . . . even be with her" (v. 10b) Why? Because there are some temptations that are so powerful our only defense is to keep our distance. In Proverbs, there are weighty words about just how critical this counter-measure is:

> Now then, my son, listen to me;
> do not turn aside from what I say.
> Keep to a path far from her,
> do not go near the door of her house,
> lest you give your best strength to others
> And your years to one who is cruel. (Prov. 5: 7–10)

That's *distance* talk. These words are there to dispel any proud notions you might harbor that you can flirt with this sin and not get burned. In the long run, what is really required to win this battle is something you may never have guessed. It takes a kind of humility! It demands the side of humility that enables you to face up to the reality of your own vulnerability. You are simply not as strong as you may think you are. Listen to an old catechism (The Heidelberg Catechism): "By ourselves we are too weak to hold our own even for a moment. And our sworn enemies—the devil, the world, and our own flesh—never stop attacking us" (Q&A 127).

Joseph, knowing his own vulnerabilities as a man, decided to do the one thing he could do in this situation: all day long, he kept on managing his feet. The moment he saw her in the distance, he instructed his feet, "Walk the other way!" Don't ever think that you are so strong you will not need to give your own feet (and eyes) the same lecture! For example, you may well need to tell your feet to get your body into the house or the dorm room on time, since the old line is just too true to ignore: Not much good happens after midnight.

This is why, in the Bible, the way of the wise is also the way of the humble. Humility is a twin to wisdom. Humility protects us from the dangerous pride that makes us think that we are an exception to all those other weaklings who capitulate to sin. Humility enables us to take the true measure of the perversity lurking in our own hearts and face up to just how weak we really are.

But Mrs. Potiphar never stopped looking for her opportunity to ensnare Joseph, despite all his defenses. One day she saw it. Joseph just happened to be in the house, doing his job, with no one else around at the moment. This is very significant because it alerts us to the protective power of community in the face of temptation. You will notice how often Satan struck his victims when they were alone:

- It was because David was not in the company of his army but rather strolling the roof of his palace late in the evening by himself that he was ambushed into adultery at the sight of Bathsheba.

- Cain suggested to Abel that they go out to the field, and it was out there, away from family, that the first murder happened.

- And, as you well remember, Judas Iscariot executed his betrayal of Jesus after he left the community of disciples in the upper room.

It's revealing to consider how much we are protected by being in community. Not only do we learn right from wrong in community. Not only do we see role models in the community. Not only do we hear warnings from the community. Actually, our last line of defense is (more often than we care to admit) the rather self-serving question we ask ourselves when we are being pulled into some sin: if I do this evil thing, what will my parents think of me? How would I face my old teachers and coaches? What will my friends think of me? I can't let them down!" It may be a rather prideful defense, but who can doubt its power?

And so it was that in those brief moments, when Joseph was not protected by the community of the workers around him in the compound, that Mrs. Potiphar made her move. She grabbed him by his cloak and brazenly tried to entice him to come to bed with her. And at this lonely moment, Joseph had only one defense left: running. Rather than fighting over his cloak, he just let her have it because, in that moment, losing his cloak meant nothing compared to losing his purity. He didn't care if this meant running out of the house in his underwear . . . or worse. A moment of embarrassment is nothing compared to a life of disgrace. Watch him run! If ever there were a champion runner, you're looking at him right here.

Once again, here is a moment in the story worth hitting the pause button on and freeze-framing it long enough to allow it to speak to us. There are actually two sides to the coin of character. The positive side is cultivating virtue through practicing good habits. So, you practice such habits as "first things first," like doing homework right after school. You practice saving your babysitting money rather than blowing it on your newest whim. You steel yourself to keep your promises even when it's really inconvenient. You get to bed on time. You do your best to honor authority, even though you just don't like some of the people over you. All of this could be described as "making a good run at virtue."

But there's a negative side to cultivating virtue, and you are seeing it right here in the story as you watch Joseph, virtually naked, flying out of Potiphar's house, racing down the road, looking for some kind of refuge, perhaps in a barn somewhere. Look at that young man on the run and learn that here is a terrific lesson in cultivating character, especially sexual purity: it could be called "growing up by running away." You'll find plain talk promoting this in the New Testament:

> Flee from sexual immorality. All other sins a person commits are outside the body, but whoever sins sexually, sins against their own body. (1 Cor. 6:18)
>
> Therefore, my dear friends, flee from idolatry. (1 Cor. 10:14)
>
> Flee the evil desires of youth and pursue righteousness, faith, love and peace, along with those who call on the Lord out of a pure heart. (2 Tim. 2:22)
>
> For the love of money is a root of all kinds of evil. Some people, eager for money, have wandered from the faith and pierced themselves with many griefs. But you, man of God, flee from all this, and pursue righteousness, godliness, faith, love, endurance and gentleness. (1 Timothy 6:10–11)

Flight! This is the way of the wise.

- They have the guts to walk right out of a bull session when the conversation turns raunchy.

- They steer their cart clear of the aisle in the grocery store filled with fattening foods and empty calories.

- They delete games on their computers that they know have the power to steal their time.

- They button their lip when they're tempted to retaliate at an insult, and often walk away in silence.

Strangely, this is the other side of growing character. It's a lifestyle marked with one determined flight after another!

But was his virtue rewarded? Did his obedience lead to blessing? Did God honor him for his integrity? It surely doesn't look like it. Smoldering with rage over the humiliation of being rejected, Mrs. Potiphar bides her time until her husband comes home. Then she presents him with Joseph's cloak, spilling her carefully fabricated story and charging Joseph with attempted rape. She called it "making sport of me." She claimed she had even screamed for help, but her screams had only caused him to run for his life. Who was there to question it? Nobody had been around at the time, so there were no witnesses. Once again, emotion trumped reason. Potiphar's rage blinded him to even consider that his wife's story just didn't add up given all he had seen of Joseph's integrity for so long.

The sobering truth is that in the short term Joseph's rectitude resulted in nothing less than ruination! Within hours, Joseph finds himself arrested by his boss and tossed into the slammer. Once again, Joseph is subjected to the sharp pain of a sudden injustice, just as he was when his brothers had tossed him into the cistern. Who of us can even imagine his agony? His act of true loyalty to Potiphar by refusing to violate his own wife is suddenly met with an act of deep injustice by the very man he tried so hard to protect.

Doing right may lead to great suffering. There is, indeed, such a thing as being "persecuted for righteousness sake," and our Lord warned us that such suffering is far from occasional; it is normal. It is, in fact, an honor, and when the early Christians found themselves being persecuted, they counted themselves most fortunate to have even been considered worthy enough to suffer for the name of Jesus (Acts 5: 41). Paul reinforced this in Philippians 1: 27: "For it has been granted to you on behalf of Christ not only to believe in him, but also to suffer for him." Strangely, the suffering of a Christian for doing what is right is viewed as worthy of high commendation. Peter put it this way: "If you suffer for doing good and you endure it, this is commendable before God" (1 Pet. 2: 20). It is far better to suffer a taste of hell on the way to heaven than to savor a taste of heaven on the way to hell. What carries us when we suffer injustice for doing good is not just the assurance that justice will ultimately prevail, it's also the comfort of experiencing virtue as its own reward. Even as Joseph found himself thrown into prison, he could hold his head high, savoring the sweetness of a clear conscience, the delight of a duty kept, the dignity of a sacred trust honored.

Integrity can make your life miserable. Once again Joseph is about to experience a radical reversal of fortune. In just one day, he will be bounced from the pinnacle to the pit, from being the top manager of a major enterprise to being a castaway in a dungeon. And once again, it will all revolve around a cloak! The first time his life was "ruined" was triggered by the richly embroidered coat from his father's hands. This time it was a manager's cloak, given to him by the fatherly heart of his owner. But now that cloak was being held by a woman he had spurned, and, as the English writer William Congreve said so unforgettably, "Hell hath no fury as a woman spurned" (a common paraphrase of words spoken by Zara in act 3, scene 8 of *The Mourning Bride*).

And so this episode in Joseph's topsy-turvy life ends with fresh agony as he finds himself suddenly under lockdown in one of Egypt's worst prisons. His future looks bleak indeed. But even here the wisdom of Corrie Ten Boom makes us think twice: "There is no pit so deep, but He is not deeper still." Could this dungeon be the launching pad for the great redemption God is planning? God's middle name is, after all, "Surprise."

CHAPTER 10

The Darkness Deepens

Read Genesis 40—41:1a

—————————

Abide with me

Fast falls the eventide

The darkness deepens,

Lord, with me abide

When other helpers fail

And comforts flee

Help of the helpless

O, abide with me.

—Henry Francis Lyte, 1847

If you thought that Joseph has suffered much in his young life, then let me put it this way to you: you ain't seen nothin' yet. This next chapter in his life is far worse than anything he's endured so far. Up to this point, we've heard the repeated refrain: "The Lord was with Joseph." But now those words will be missing. Like Jesus, Joseph is about to experience a sense of abandonment by God. Joseph is about to "descend into hell." It is described this way: "The chief cupbearer, however, did not remember Joseph; he forgot him. When two full years had passed . . . " (Gen. 41:1a).

Don't skip over this season in his life, this 730-day stretch in his journey, because you may very well experience it yourself if you haven't already. It's a time when (it seems) God has gone silent. You knock on heaven's door, but you hear no footsteps approaching, no sound of the latch opening, no door swinging wide, no voice greeting you.

Heaven can go silent. Days become gloomy; nights, oppressive. You watch the world around you humming along but feel bypassed. No one seems to care. And then, aggravating this ache is the cruel reality that it was a blatant injustice that put you in your dark place. You are in a dungeon you don't deserve. Even worse, you have no one to appeal your case. No one returns your phone calls. No one answers your emails. No one visits. Nothing.

This is where we will find Joseph at the end of his imprisonment. But this is not just simple despair; this is despair with a cruel bite to it. There's ordinary suffering, the kind that happens when trouble comes crashing into our lives. But then there's a far more acute form of suffering. It happens when a ray of light comes into our dark world, and for the first time in many days we actually take the risk of daring to hope again. For the moment we slowly dare to allow a fragile expectation to rise in our beaten-down hearts—slowly, because it is devastating to allow a wounded hope to rise once more, only to see it shattered yet again.

The Shawshank Redemption (1994) is a movie with close parallels to Joseph's story. It centers on a young banker named Andy Dufresne, who has been innocently imprisoned. One day Andy enters the cafeteria, after having just spent two weeks in "the hole," the tiny cell used for solitary confinement. Looking perfectly relaxed, he joins his buddies at breakfast. They ask him what his time in "the hole" had been like. He calmly states that it was the "easiest time he ever did." They're astounded. The hole is an inmate's worst nightmare. So his remarkable claim led to this conversation between him and his friend, Red, sitting across the table from him:

Andy: "I had Mr. Mozart to keep me company . . . [points and taps his head]; it was in here." Then he gestures to his heart and adds, ". . . and in here. That's the beauty of music. They can't get that from you. Haven't you ever felt that way about music?"

> Red: "Well . . . I played a mean harmonica as a younger man. Lost interest in it, though. Didn't make too much sense in here."
> Andy: "No, here's where it makes the most sense. You need it so you don't forget."
> Red: "Forget?"
> Andy: "That there are places in the world that aren't made out of stone. That there's, there's somethin' inside that they can't get to; that they can't touch. It's yours."
> Red: "What are you talkin' about?"
> Andy: "Hope."
> Red: "Hope? Let me tell you something, my friend. Hope is a dangerous thing. Hope can drive a man insane. It's got no use on the inside. You'd better get used to that idea."

Red had been turned down repeatedly for parole; he knew just how dangerous hope can be. Getting your hopes up, only to see them crushed again and again is a pain so acute most people do exactly what Red warned about. They get used to the idea that hope has no place in their world. Truth be told, hope does not spring eternal in all human breasts. Among those of us with a trail of smashed ambitions, the smart ones are extremely careful about ever getting any of their hopes up again; the jaded ones dismiss hope completely.

Joseph will be brought dangerously close to this precipice. It began when two of Pharaoh's top officials were escorted into the prison one day. Both had offended Pharaoh. One morning they showed up with long faces. Each of them had seen vivid dreams the night before but had no idea what they meant. They believed, as did most Egyptians, that dreams predicted their future. But now, unable to decipher them, they were frightened.

Little did these men know that the God of heaven, whom they did not know, was working out his own perfect plan at this moment. God had sent these very dreams to show them a side of Joseph they had never seen: a God-given capacity to interpret dreams. So when Joseph noticed their long faces that morning and asked what was troubling them, he found himself being led right into the surprising workings of God.

In answer to his question, they told him their quandary. Instantly Joseph, who all along had experienced the hand of God orchestrating his life, testified to them, "Do not interpretations belong to God?" (v. 8b). It was a powerful question inviting them to move beyond the shadowlands of their dreams to the bright light of the God Who Is Right Here. Then, exuding holy boldness, he invited them to divulge their dreams.

Moved by his confidence (and with no other options), the butler went first. He described a dream that seemed to have unfolded with time-lapse photography. He saw himself by a single grapevine with three branches. Suddenly, buds appeared. The next instant, they were in full bloom. The next instant they produced clusters of grapes. Holding Pharaoh's own cup in his hand, he quickly squeezed fresh grape juice from the clusters into the cup and placed the cup in Pharaoh's hands. Then, suddenly, the fast-paced dream ended.

Joseph immediately saw the meaning and laid it out. The three branches represented three days. The action in the dream was a preview of the action Pharaoh himself would take: just as the butler had taken the cup of Pharaoh and squeezed grape juice into it, within three days Pharaoh himself would release him, give him back his cup, and authorize him to fill it up and place it back into Pharaohs hand, just as he had always done. It was a promise of nothing less than a resurrection from prison within just three days, and it all revolved around a cup.

There's more here than meets the eye. There will be another resurrection later on in chapter 45. It will be the resurrection of the dead brotherhood between Joseph and his siblings, and it too will revolve around a cup. And then, centuries later, there would be yet another resurrection in just three days, the resurrection of Jesus, a resurrection that would ultimately lead to the fulfillment of a very similar promise he made to them the night before he died: "I tell you, I will not drink from this fruit of the vine from now on until that day when I drink it new with you in my Father's kingdom" (Matt. 26:29). The butler held a cup; Joseph owned a cup; Jesus drank a cup. In all three cases, resurrection followed.

Joseph saw more than just the meaning of the dream. He also saw an opportunity. He saw how that dream, once fulfilled, could lead to his own resurrection from prison. He knew his interpretation was from God, and so he knew beyond doubt that in just three days the butler would stand in the very presence of Pharaoh, the one and only person to whom he could appeal his case. Joseph seized the moment and asked the butler to return the favor: "When all goes well with you, remember me and show me kindness; mention me to Pharaoh and get me out of this prison" (v. 14). He quickly briefed the butler on his case: "I was forcibly carried off from the land of the Hebrews, and even here I have done nothing to deserve being put in a dungeon" (v. 15). In simple terms he laid out the injustices he had suffered, trusting that somewhere in the heart of that butler there just might be an impulse to return the favor. Surely this man, once restored to his position and filled with joy, would remember him! But Joseph may not have known that his hopes were being hung on a very thin thread. After all, Egyptians despised Hebrews. They refused to even eat with them (Gen. 43:32). His request was met with an ominous silence.

Instead the baker, seeing the butler had been given not only an interpretation but a very hopeful one, jumped in and asked for his dream to also be interpreted. But his dream had a dark side: birds eating bread meant for Pharaoh! Joseph caught it instantly and was compelled to inform the butler that in just three days he would be executed by hanging, and birds would gorge themselves on his corpse.

It turned out to be exactly as Joseph had predicted. Pharaoh was celebrating his birthday, and he used the occasion to restore the butler . . . and execute the baker.

Then come the darkest words in the story: "The chief cupbearer, however, did not remember Joseph; he forgot him" (v. 23). It may have been deliberate (Gen. 41:9). The fact is that once the butler began to savor the perks of his restoration, he simply forgot all about that young man back there in the dungeon.

But what was this like for Joseph? His hopes had to be sky high three days later when a palace official knocked on the prison door and both the baker and the butler were summoned and released. Why, he may have thought, it was only a matter of a few hours and some official from the palace would return, knock on that same door, and ask for him! F. B. Meyer, in his book Joseph: Beloved-Hated-Exalted (1910) invites you to imagine the next few weeks:

> Perhaps later in the day, there would have been another knock at the door. Joseph would have jumped up and run to the door, certain that a palace official was standing there, calling for him to appear before Pharaoh. But no, it was someone else, on some other business.
> The next day, another knock. Again, Joseph jumped up and ran to the door, only to be disappointed again.

A few days later, another knock. This time Joseph didn't run. He walked. Again, disappointment.

A few days later, another knock. This time Joseph didn't even get up. He just looked over at the door and let someone else answer it. Sure enough, it was not for him.

A week later, another knock. This time Joseph didn't even bother to look at the door.

Slowly Joseph was forced to face a very hard truth: the cupbearer had completely ignored his simple request. Deeper yet, he was facing an even harder truth: putting your hopes in other human beings is, ever so often, a path to certain disappointment. Slowly that reality sunk deep into his very soul, leading him to one conclusion, which was critical to keeping him fully alive and free from bitterness: there is only one truly safe place in which to deposit one's treasured hopes, and that is in the very character of God himself and nowhere else. The fact that two years passed after the butler forgot all about him suggests to me yet a third vital truth: it takes a lot of time for any of us to master this posture of the heart and learn to stay there with unshakeable confidence. It is one thing to say, "In God we trust." Thousands do, but even as they do, they also are busy making sure they have their ducks in a row and their bases covered. But there comes a time when there are no more ducks and no more bases. There is nothing! It is then that God, in his severe mercy, leads us to a far deeper and far better place where we finally are compelled to say, "In God alone we trust."

Why would God put us through such an ordeal to lead us to that place? Why would he strip away every human support, every viable option, and every "last resort" to finally bring us to a level of such unalloyed dependence upon himself alone? Why would he work to simplify our faith to such an elemental level? It is because in that place there is waiting for us a delight few people ever experience. In that place there is the possibility of a joy that is simply unimaginable, an explosion of pure euphoria at the amazing workings of God that is simply astounding. It is a privileged vista afforded to a very few. For at that moment, when we have been "reduced" to trusting in God alone, and God finally steps in and makes his move, it is enough to take our breath away! When some good finally comes our way that is pure God-at-work, it is awesome, stunning, and so rapturous it far transcends any other human delight. We finally see God fully in all of his power and mercy! I am certain that God longs for us to see that glorious vision. But it does take a kind of hell to lead us to that heaven. This is no secret. This is common knowledge among seasoned saints. There are many songs about it. Here's an excerpt from an "oldie" by Annie Flint (1866–1932) titled "He Giveth More Grace":

> *When we have exhausted our store of endurance,*
> *When our strength has failed ere the day is half done,*
> *When we reach the end of our hoarded resources*
> *Our Father's full giving is only begun.*
> *His love has no limits, His grace has no measure,*
> *His power no boundary known unto men;*
> *For out of His infinite riches in Jesus*
> *He giveth, and giveth, and giveth again.*

Everybody wants to enjoy the gravy train of "giveth, and giveth and giveth again." Sorry. This rare bounty is reserved only for those who have finally reached "the end of our hoarded resources." The journey to that "end" can take a very long time. In Joseph's case, it took over 730 days. Only then did the knock that counted finally come. When it did, Joseph would find himself catapulted, in just one day, into the highest position in the land of Egypt, second only to Pharaoh himself. You can be sure that when it happened, there would be not one whiff of self-congratulation in the heart of Joseph, not one shred of pride. There would be nothing of that American spirit that says, "I worked my way up the ladder, and I earned this." The truth is, God took two full years to empty Joseph of any reliance on other people or even himself. And as a result, when this moment came, it was (might I now finally use that overworked word?) awesome!

88

A day will surely come, if it hasn't already, when you will struggle with that age-old question, "Why do bad things happen to good people?" This is why I urge you to think deeply about this season in Joseph's life and its outcome. For no chapter in Joseph's life aligns itself more closely to the final suffering of our Lord than this one. On the cross our Lord experienced a similar abandonment, except far worse: he was forsaken by his very own Father. Philippians 2:7 describes it as "making himself nothing." His was a journey into . . . nothing. This is the hardest part of suffering: it creates a vacuum, an empty place, a nothingness where there was once (what seemed to us) such fullness, vitality, promise, life! And yet, as at the dawn of creation itself, out of that nothingness can come an explosion of life so full of energy it far outshines any degree of brightness and joy we once savored in the treasure we lost.

I know. It is hard to fathom, for our losses wound us deeply, and leave us utterly bereft. We cannot imagine such a possibility. We cannot imagine such a "resurrection." And yet that is precisely where the suffering of Joseph and Jesus (and, might I add, Job) led: to a level of life beyond anything they had known before. For Joseph, it created a fullness that spread new life over the entire western Mediterranean—and for Jesus, over the entire world. In a recent newsletter, reflecting on the tragic accidental death of student Tara Oskam, Calvin College president Michael LeRoy pointed to this promise by quoting these words from Peter Wehner:

> *For those of the Christian faith, God is a God of wounds, where the road to redemption passes directly through suffering. There is some solace in knowing that while at times life is not easy for us, it was also hard for the God of the New Testament. And from suffering, compassion can emerge, meaning to suffer with another—that disposition, in turn, often leads to acts of mercy. I have seen enough of life to know that grief will leave its mark. But I have also seen enough of life to know that so, too, will love. (Michael LeRoy, "This Square Inch," April 2017)*

The suffering of Joseph led to an outpouring of mercy, compassion, and love, not just for the Egyptians, but for his own family. It birthed redemption itself.

Should a day come when the darkness descends on you, I want to ask something hard of you: to do all in your power to see it, in due time, as a gift—unwelcome as that gift may be. It could become a doorway into releasing nothing less than the redemptive power of God in and through your life, provided you steel your soul to quietly keep your trust in God alone . . . there in your dungeon.

CHAPTER 11

The Divine Majesty

Read Genesis 41:1—49

It began as just another ordinary day in the prison. Two full years had dragged by, and not one possibility of release had come Joseph's way. The butler had long ago decided to forget about that Hebrew kid with the uncanny ability to interpret mysterious dreams and for two years had lived quite serenely with his little secret. Meanwhile everything in Joseph's world seemed to contradict the long-cherished, thirteen-year-old dream he had received. Instead of blessing his family as their benefactor, he was managing jailbirds! Worse, he himself was one of them.

And so it was that on this very ordinary day, Joseph was simply doing his job. Likely, he was wearing standard prison-issue clothes. His world was grim; his future was bleak. And yet, in all that desolation, he was not alone, and he knew it. All along he had witnessed a ray of light: the invisible hand of the living God. Joseph was living by a light that could not be extinguished in a world that afforded him not one ray of hope!

So it was just another ordinary day, but it was not a dark one. The light still shone, the hope still lived, and the dream could never die, because its taproot was a divine revelation. When God gives you a dream, it may dim, but it cannot die.

And now, finally, on this ordinary day, the movement of God to fulfill that dream was about to charge into his world. God was about to make his move, displaying his glorious divine majesty in the unlikeliest of places, transforming Joseph from a prisoner into a prince, from managing a small jail to running a huge country, from being second in command to a warden to being second in command to a Pharaoh! Most of all, God was about to position his key player in the redemption plan he had in store for the broken family of Jacob.

And so it was that this time the knock at the prison door meant something. It was a messenger from the palace asking for Joseph! He was being summoned . . . by the Pharaoh himself! Joseph didn't waste a second. Quickly, he cleaned up and shaved his beard. He was given a presentable set of clothes to wear. And, perhaps within the hour, he stood before a Pharaoh.

But this Pharaoh was troubled, which can only mean that the court officials around him were nervous! When the boss is upset, the staff walks on eggshells. Overnight, there had been an unsettling development: the dictator had dreamed a double dream, and not one of his magicians or wizards were able to unravel its meaning. It's no wonder they were distressed, for as you may well remember, a later dictator named Nebuchadnezzar threatened to kill every one of his magicians if they could not come up with the content and meaning of his dream. Why would this be? In the ancient world dreams were believed to contain "actionable intelligence," reliable information vital to the future—in some cases of an entire country. This was their CIA.

Immediately Pharaoh told Joseph his quandary: he had had a dream, no one could explain its meaning, and he had been informed Joseph could decipher dreams. Joseph (God-conscious Joseph, God-alert Joseph,

God-marinated Joseph) responded instantly. He boldly testified to the Pharaoh that there was a God in heaven, and that he, not Joseph, could be counted on to give Pharaoh exactly what he needed to know. Notice the courage of a person who has come to see and practice the very real presence of the living God in every single situation. It is remarkable! Joseph immediately brings the reality of the living God into the crisis and doesn't stop doing so. He'll do it three more times (v. 25, v. 28 and v. 32), and it will be this dimension in Joseph, this obvious endowment with the very spirit of God himself, that will impact Pharaoh even more than the interpretations Joseph will reveal. Later on he'll turn to his officials and, based on this short first impression of Joseph, will claim that standing before them all is a person "in whom is the spirit of God" (v. 38b). This is what elevates Joseph, and this, above all else, is the one quality you will need to flourish all the days of your life. More crucial than education, honed skills, character, a great network, or natural talents, this is the key to lasting, authentic stature.

This also shows you something about people who might seem to be irreligious: they can be very quick to discern the presence of spiritual power (or, "gravitas") in people. For example, Pilate quickly sensed a spiritual authority in Jesus so august he became afraid of him. King Saul sensed this in David and feared him. The Sanhedrin sensed it in Peter and John (Acts 4:13) and felt quite impotent in their presence. When God reveals his divine majesty to us and then enables us to see it, that vision has a profoundly transforming impact upon the impression we make on others. It gives our bearing a regal quality and our words weight and authority. It fills us with no-nonsense boldness, and pagans, even those in high positions, soon sense that we cannot be bought off or pushed around. Joseph was a complete stranger to Pharaoh, and yet, in just moments, Pharaoh has recognized the light of the living God shining in him and become deeply impressed.

So, I repeat, it is this quality, even more than any educational degrees you may earn, athletic achievements you may accomplish, or skills you may develop, that will shape your life and influence. This quality is richer than sterling character; it is more critical than learned competencies. This is the one quality that keeps you grounded. It defines who you are.

Pharaoh does not respond to Joseph's claim. He neither argues with him nor agrees with him. He is so anxious to find out the meaning of his dreams that he plows right ahead into the details. And they are weird enough to rock any monarch's throne!

In his first dream, he is taken to Egypt's river of life, the Nile itself. While standing on the bank, he notices seven cows walk up out of the river. They look terrific. They're the very picture of health: fat and sleek! They began grazing among the reeds, and it's easy to imagine Pharaoh, at this point in his dream, savoring this symbol of wealth. That is exactly what any leader wants: a thriving economy! Then, out of the same river came walking another set of, yes, seven more cows. But this time, ominously, they looked dreadful, even menacing. They were nothing but skin and bones, and so ugly no farmer would want them. And then the worst part: these grotesque creatures descended upon the seven beautiful cows and proceeded to consume every last one of them. And yet even stranger, their meal of Grade A beef did nothing for them: they looked just as skinny and horrid as when they first stepped out of the Nile.

This was frightening enough, said Pharaoh, to wake him right out of his sleep. Suddenly he found himself back in his bedroom. It had been just a dream. So he went back to sleep, only to be assaulted with a second dream, even stranger.

This time he saw a single stalk of grain. At its tip were seven heads of grain, which is quite phenomenal since most grains, like wheat, produce just one head per stalk. Each of them were blue-ribbon quality: bulging, full of kernels, and free of any blemish—a farmer's dream! But then he saw the strangest sight. On that same stalk of grain another set of seven heads sprouted, and their kernels were exactly the opposite. They were wrinkled and shriveled with no body to them at all. They looked as if they had been withered down to just a hull, which was known to happen to grain in Egypt when the hot desert wind from the east blew for days through their fields. And then, once again, an unnerving sight! The withered heads of grain suddenly rose up, latched onto the healthy heads, and consumed every last one of them. Once again he woke up, and this time he knew for a fact that these were not dreams to be ignored.

And that is why he had summoned every one of his wise men and magicians to report immediately to the palace. Standing among them was his ever-present butler. Pharaoh described his dreams, and his butler watched in growing horror as they all looked completely baffled, at a total loss to figure out just what the dreams might mean. Finally his conscience convicted him so deeply he stepped forward and confessed that he had tolerated a "shortcoming" in his life. He then told Pharaoh that for the last two years he had known about a remarkable young man whom he had met in prison. He told Pharaoh the whole story, how he and the baker had both been given mysterious dreams, and how, to this young man, their meaning had been as plain as day. Moreover, he admitted, the interpretations had turned out to be completely true, even though he was a Hebrew. So Joseph was immediately summoned.

What is remarkable now is that Joseph did not need to ask for time to figure out the meaning of the dreams; he knew instantly! Even as Pharaoh was describing each dream, the spirit of God was unfolding its meaning. When Pharaoh finished his description, Joseph knew the exact meaning of every significant detail in the dreams: the sevens, the healthy cows and full heads of grain, the gaunt cows and withered heads of grain, the power of the second set to destroy the first set, and the significance of two dreams instead of one. In front of Egypt's top officials there in the country's Oval Office, this young thirty-year-old spelled it all out, making sure to emphasize that these meanings came directly from God, not him:

1. Both dreams described the same event.

2. The first described it in terms of what it meant for animals, and the second for plants. In other words, it covered all of agriculture, the basis of Egypt's entire economy.

3. The sevens were years.

4. Fat cows and full heads meant great bounty.

5. Skinny cows and scorched heads meant great famine.

6. The fact that the seven skinny cows and scorched heads ate up the seven fat cows and full heads had a most ominous and urgent meaning: the seven years of famine would completely obliterate all the gains the land would enjoy during the seven good years. They would ruin the country!

7. The fact that there were two dreams meant that God had firmly decided that these events would indeed happen. God was doubling down on the royal court to ensure that no one second guessed either the interpretations or their ramifications.

And then Joseph took a very bold step. Being the trained and trustworthy manager that God had fashioned him to be during his two "internships," he courageously summoned up the chutzpah to become a self-appointed royal adviser! Before Pharaoh had even a moment to consult his officials for their expert guidance in the light of this frightening prediction, Joseph capitalized on the shock of the moment as well as the expertise he had just demonstrated, daringly asserted himself, and immediately urged Pharaoh into a specific course of action. This was truly audacious, and, if the presence of God's divine authority had not been so evident in him, it could very well have moved any number of Pharaoh's officials to dismiss him as an impudent and presumptive young man who needed to be reprimanded. Even Pharaoh himself could have viewed Joseph's daring to give advice as the unwelcome intrusion of a brazen young man into matters that were none of his business and sent him packing right back to prison with the words, "Young man, you don't need to advise us on a course of action. We can figure that one out for ourselves."

But Joseph was on a God-inspired roll! He had seen clearly in the dreams what God was going to do, and now he had no doubt whatsoever what God was leading Pharaoh to do. He knew, and such deep conviction that you are standing in the very center of the truth has the power to fill you with a boldness that will astonish people and demand that they take you seriously! You'll find other instances of this very same boldness later on in the story of redemption. You'll see it in a young David informing Saul that he could handle Goliath and, moreover, could do it very well without any of Saul's armor. You'll see it in a twelve-year-old Jesus questioning the teachers in the temple. It is nothing less than a divine "unction" or anointing, and God gives it to all of us who have put our faith in Jesus, received his Spirit, and immersed ourselves in his truth. Such boldness surfaces naturally in people who have been trained in God's truth and witnessed his hand in their lives. That's the power of knowing his divine majesty: it gives us boldness, even before kings!

So Joseph charged right ahead and spelled out a seven point plan of action:

1. He needed to appoint just one person to guide the country through the next fourteen years in such a way that the nation would survive what was coming.

2. That person needed to be wise and discerning, because this would be a massive operation. There would be no time to train someone. It demanded an expert manager from day one.

3. That person needed to be given significant authority over the entire country to make sure that what now needed doing got done without any resistance. In fact, he would need a level of power second only to Pharaoh.

4. The country-wide scope of this enterprise demanded a whole suite of solid middle managers.

5. The policy would be simple: one-fifth of all the food grown each of the first seven years, the years of surplus crops, was to be stored. Joseph was savvy enough from his years running Potiphar's operation to know that one-seventh would not be enough given the realities of spoilage, sabotage, or theft, to say nothing of the very likely possibility that neighboring countries might need to purchase food from Egypt.

6. The purpose of the plan was as critical as it was simple: it was a matter of national survival.

7. And all of this needed be done under the authority of Pharaoh and with his seal of approval.

What is most amazing about this scene in Pharaoh's court is the winsome bearing of Joseph, and, behind him the divine majesty which had trained him, now radiating out of him. Look at him! Look how confident he is! Notice his fearlessness in the presence of a potentate! See his poise! Notice how well he uses words. See his respectful deference to Pharaoh balanced with his daring to prescribe a policy! What is most astounding and rare is this: he has gone through a foul smelling, putrid sewer of servitude, injustice and then incarceration over the course of thirteen years during the prime of his life and come out the other end a leader!

How do you explain a phenomenon like that? There is only one explanation: because of the grace of God upon his life, Joseph ended up actually being trained by his adversity. He benefitted from it! He had been given the gift to see it as a kind of fitness regimen, a workout designed for his own good, where his soul grew muscle and his spirit grew endurance. It was a thirteen year spiritual formation project, it's result exactly what is promised in Hebrews 12: 11:

> No discipline seems pleasant at the time, but painful. Later on, however, it produces a harvest of righteousness and peace for those who have been trained by it.

In the mystery of God's providence there are certain hearts who are given the capacity to receive discipline as a gift, an opportunity to grow deep in patience, humility, and steadfast trust. These are the people who emerge ready to face "It is what it is" with utter realism on the one hand, and gritty hope on the other. On the one hand, they have outgrown all naiveté. On the other hand, they refuse to acquiesce to "It is what it is." They are not dreamy idealists, nor easily rattled visionaries; they are people of seasoned judgment and uncommon confidence! Such people are sought out because they are the ones that can be trusted to lead governments, corporations and the great institutions of society. A county executive once told me, "All I do, all day long, is just solve one problem after another;" but she said it with such quiet, calm confidence. She knew that God had placed her in that position and would surely use her to bring more and more of his shalom into that part of his kingdom.

There is another aspect to this part of the story I want you to see: you are looking at the critical moment in the life of Joseph, standing there in the court of Pharaoh. Such a decisive moment may come into your life.

Overnight, you may suddenly find yourself face to face with one of the most critical decisions or greatest opportunities you will ever face. Such moments are pivotal, since they usually occur only once or twice over the course of a lifetime and the future course of your life will turn on just what you do at that very moment. This is why we call them "defining moments." All the character you will have accumulated up to that moment will suddenly come into play. You will be exposed for who you truly are. This was Joseph's moment. He seized that moment, daring to tell a monarch, without even being asked his opinion, exactly what he should do.

Such moments will surely come to you. There will be little time to think. The crisis before you and the character within you will converge, shaping how you choose to behave at that moment. It will be like that moment on January 15, 2009 when Captain "Sully" Sullenberger's passenger jet with 155 souls onboard suddenly encountered flocks of geese upon takeoff from LaGuardia Airport in New York City. The geese were swallowed right into the turbines of both engines on the plane, which rendered them useless. The plane was completely crippled in an instant, but NOT THE CAPTAIN. At that moment, with only 35 seconds to plot his course of action, Captain "Sully" revealed the character that had been formed in him over the 59 year span of his life. In half a minute, he knew exactly what he needed to do. He decided to bring his plane to as smooth a landing as possible on the safest surface available to him, which happened to be the Hudson River. He did it with expertise, caution, courage and confidence and brought that plane to rest on the surface of the water in such a way that it stayed perfectly level, without any serious damage, giving him just enough time to safely evacuate all 155 souls on board before the plane slowly disappeared beneath the waves. Not one person died, and for days the whole world stood in awe at "The Miracle on the Hudson."

An event on that scale was unfolding right at this moment in Egypt's palace, and God had orchestrated the whole thing. Even as Joseph was laying out his prescription for a plan of action God was convincing Pharaoh of the correctness of Joseph's interpretation and the wisdom of his plan of action. He looked to his officials for their vote of confirmation. Head nodded all around. It was unanimous: "the plan seemed good to Pharaoh and to all his officials" (vs. 37). So Pharaoh clinched the matter by asking a rhetorical question with an obvious answer: "Can we find anyone like this man, one in whom is the spirit of God?" (vs. 38b)

Without hesitation, Pharoah issued his orders:

- Joseph was to be immediately put in charge of the palace. You just can't miss the parallelism here as this is now the third verse of the same song!

- "Potiphar put him in charge of his household." (39: 5)

- "The warden put Joseph in charge of all those held in the prison." (39: 22)

- "You shall be in charge of my palace." (41: 40)

- Every person in the empire was commanded to submit to Joseph.

- The only position closed to Joseph was the throne itself.

And so it came to be. Joseph was placed into office immediately, and Pharaoh immediately organized an inaugural display of glory for Joseph to ensure everyone knew it.

- First, a public announcement: "I hereby put you in charge of the whole land of Egypt" (vs. 41).

- Then, the bestowal of the official seal of the new position: "Then Pharaoh took his signet ring from his finger and put it on Joseph's finger" (vs. 42). The ring represented the power of Pharaoh himself, and the fact that Pharaoh took it off his own finger and put it on Joseph's finger is nothing less than a transfer of power at the highest level. Plus it was a signet ring: it was engraved with a royal logo or emblem which was used to imprint a seal upon official documents, giving them absolute authority. There is a strong similarity here to the baptism of our Lord. At that moment, the Father put, not a ring, but a dove upon our Lord. That dove represented the Holy Spirit, imparted to Jesus by the power and authority of the Father. And, even more wondrously, this is what happened at Pentecost as the Father, at the request of the Son, poured out his spirit upon US! Who wears the signet ring of authority today? All those who have received the Spirit!

- Then, once again, the robes. This time Joseph was given not one but a whole wardrobe of richly embroidered robes. How could he not have connected the dots and remembered the robe of favor his Father had given him? Surely, at this moment he must have known that this was the very fulfillment of what his Father had seen in him so long ago.

- Then, a golden chain around the neck. Nothing illustrates the transformation of Joseph's position in life more dramatically that this golden chain. For it was not that long ago when that same neck wore another chain...of iron (Psalm 105: 17, 18)!

"And he sent a man before them—Joseph, sold as a slave. They bruised his feet with shackles, his neck was put in irons."

- Then, Pharaoh arranged for a public display of his brand new official, so he arranged for a presentation similar to a ticker tape parade down Broadway. He prescribed a chariot ride down the main street of the city for Joseph. Thirteen years earlier, as Joseph was carted off to Egypt, he may very well have found himself dragged behind an Ishmaelite camel. Now the one who was dragged down is being raised up. The reject is now the revered! Don't let this detail slip past you; it's a preview of what would later on happen to Jesus certifying that he is our one true redeemer. He put it this way to the religious leaders of his day who despised him:

"Have you never read in the Scriptures: "'The stone the builders rejected has become the cornerstone; the Lord has done this, and it is marvelous in our eyes'?" (Matthew 21: 42)

- Then, a new name. He called him Zaphenath-Paneah. Interestingly, not once is Joseph ever openly referred to by that name in the rest of the story. And yet, it may have served a vital purpose: it's not hard to imagine that later on, when his brothers first showed up, they were instructed that they had to bring their request for food to "Zaphenath-Paneah," thus safeguarding Joseph's real identity.

- Finally, one more blessing: a wife, who herself came from a highly regarded family. Her father was a priest, and Egyptians revered their priests. This too may have been one more way in which Pharaoh sought to publicly elevate his new, prized talent in the eyes of the entire country.

This is how Pharaoh ensured that no one in his empire would ever question the authority he had given to Joseph. His position was solidly established, publicly acclaimed, and firmly settled in every heart. His supremacy was beyond question. There would be no toleration of any disrespect. What happened to Joseph was nothing less than a resurrection from being virtually dead, and now Pharaoh was using every lever at his disposal to announce to the world that this young man was now seated in a place of power at his very right hand. And all of this is a preview of how God himself would not only raise his own Son from the grave and seat him at his right hand but also reveal this fact publicly. Jesus appeared, alive, to hundreds of people after his resurrection. The disciples boldly proclaimed it and never backed down from their testimony, even at the cost of their lives.

Now take a deep breath and let this sink in: in just a couple of hours Joseph's circumstances are suddenly revolutionized. His dark world was instantly flooded with brilliance. Everything turned around on a dime! He woke up in a prison and went to sleep in a palace! He woke up an unknown and went to sleep known throughout the city. Is this not just stunning? Can you even imagine that such a transformation could actually happen? It would be as if the President of the United States summoned a prisoner from Rikers Island in New York City and within just two or three hours made him Chief of Staff in the White House! This kind of thing just doesn't happen. It never happens, except in the kingdom of heaven.

You will remember, I trust, that this is par for the course with God. Did he not select a young unknown virgin to be the mother of Jesus, and did he not reveal his birth to lowly shepherds? Didn't Paul tell us that "God chose the foolish things of the world to shame the wise; God chose the weak things of the world to shame the strong. He chose the lowly things of this world and the despised things—and the things that are not to nullify the things that are, so that no one may boast before him" (1 Cor. 1:27–29). What you are witnessing here is what our God not only is able to do but what he loves to do! He delights in showing his divine majesty by taking nobodies and making them somebodies. He loves to lift people up and set the prisoner free!

This is what he did on Easter! One day Jesus was lying dead in a borrowed tomb, his body bearing the marks of a cruel crucifixion, having submitted himself to becoming a slave for our sake. His "fortunes" were so low none his disciples attended his burial. He lay there, still as a stone, and it seemed as if this was to be the end of his brief life. He had become a nobody in the eyes of the world. Then God made his move, and overnight he went from death to life, from weakness to power, from shame to glory, from the abused to the Almighty! He was set free, just as Joseph was at this momentous time! In his Pentecost sermon Peter put it this way: "It was impossible for death to keep its hold on him" (Acts 2:24b). This is the single greatest display of the divine majesty, and here in Genesis we are being shown a preview! This is your God! Psalm 113 is full of worship and wonder as it highlights this particular beauty in our God:

> The Lord is exalted over all the nations,
> his glory above the heavens.
> Who is like the Lord our God,
> the One who sits enthroned on high,
> who stoops down to look
> on the heavens and the earth?
> He raises the poor from the dust
> and lifts the needy from the ash heap;
> he seats them with princes,
> with the princes of his people.
> He settles the childless woman in her home
> as a happy mother of children. (Ps. 113:4–9)

And so it came to pass that Joseph stepped into his place of power and immediately set to work managing the entire economy of the country for the good of every man, woman, and child in the land. The first step he took was to tour the realm. Then he began the stockpiling as the seven good years commenced. He levied his 20 percent tax in kind on all the grain, gathering it up and socking it away in huge storage facilities. God confirmed his dreams by producing bumper crops seven years in a row. So much grain came in it was compared to the sand of the sea, and the sheer abundance soon became so unmanageable Joseph simply stopped keeping records. Pharaoh may have arranged for a public presentation of Joseph, but God did a public, seven-year-long confirmation of Joseph. By the time it was all over, Joseph's position of power was solidly established throughout the land. And that power was critical to the great task that lay before him: the redemption of his family.

Why? Because, it takes power to be a redeemer. When you were young, you would often get into fights with your siblings. And then we watched as someone with awesome power (one of your parents) would step in and exercise that power to redeem the situation. They would sentence you with a "time out." They would raise their voice and give you a stiff lecture. They would announce that you had forfeited some special privilege because of your behavior. And their words and decisions had clout because of the position they held in the family: they held the POWER. It takes power to be a redeemer.

The same is true on a much larger stage. Disputes between corporations and labor unions often bog down into stalemates as workers strike and owners refuses to budge. Mediation fails. What does it take to redeem a situation like that? In most cases, it requires someone with absolute power. It may require a back to work ruling by a judge. Often the only option left is binding arbitration: a person or team is appointed to hear both sides and then empowered to declare a settlement which both parties agree, in advance, to honor. It takes power to be a redeemer.

This is one of the reasons why the power of Jesus Christ is repeatedly portrayed to us in the gospels. You grew up learning all the stories of his amazing power. In one display after another, he healed the sick, cured lepers, stilled storms, fed multitudes from a single lunch, and even raised the dead. Have you ever wondered why the Gospel writers spent so much time recording all these displays of the power of Jesus? It is because all these accounts lead up to one final display of that power which dwarfs all of them.

When Jesus suffered on the cross, he certainly did not look powerful at all. He looked every bit the weakling, humiliated by the power of the Roman empire. But you must look past the surface. You probably remember how, just before he died, Jesus spoke about drinking a cup. What is so difficult about drinking a cup? Nothing, unless the cup contains a poison so lethal one drop could kill you instantly. In our Lord's case, the prospect of drinking the cup assigned to him was so horrifying, he actually asked his Father, if it were possible, to allow him to take a pass on it. He prayed, "My Father, if it is possible, may this cup be taken from me. Yet not as I will, but as you will" (Matt. 26:39). The agony behind that prayer made him break out into a perspiration so profuse the drops of sweat actually rolled off his face. What was in that cup to produce such agony?

I think you will understand why the contents of that cup were so impossibly difficult to drink if you think back to the times you were really angry at someone who had done something to you that was downright dastardly. It didn't just hurt; it made you furious. It filled you with rage. What they did to you was so awful, so unfair, and so cruel, it left you boiling. You may have even begun plotting your revenge. If you can recall such a painful memory, it will give you a small taste of what was in that cup. Then think of the great atrocities you have witnessed, from mass killings of innocent people to horrific sexual misconduct. Do they not arouse your rage? This cup contained nothing less than the full measure of God's perfect wrath against not only your and my sins, which are many and serious, but the sin of the entire human race. One example of the cup is found in Revelation 14: "If anyone worships the beast, he too will drink of the wine of God's fury, which has been poured full strength into the cup of his wrath" (vv. 9a, 10).

To redeem us, Jesus needed to possess the power to drain the contents of the cup so completely that every last bit of God's holy wrath against sin was finally satisfied. That required a power far greater than the power to make a blind man see or a lame man walk. It takes immense quantities of supernatural power. It takes a power that far exceeds any power known to man, even atomic power. It takes divine power. It takes all the power of God himself. The Heidelberg Catechism puts it this way:

Q.: Why must he [Jesus] also be true God?
A.: So that,

by the power of his divinity,
he might bear the weight of God's anger in his humanity
and earn for us
and restore to us
righteousness and life. (Lord's Day VI, Q & A 17)

In other words, for Jesus to be our redeemer he had to be able to satiate the justified divine wrath by taking it all into himself. That required nothing less than the power of a divine being. Simply put, it required the power of divine love to satisfy the power of divine wrath.

This is what lies at the heart of how Jesus redeemed us, and this part of the Joseph story is a preview of that greatest of all redemptions. This is why Moses emphasizes here both the ascent of Joseph into power and the extent of that power. This is why he paints such a glorious picture of all the elements of that power, from the regal robes to the royal signet ring, from the golden necklace to that shining chariot. And this is why he shows us just how "successfully" Joseph wielded that power, so that after seven years of bounty, the storehouses of Egypt were bulging with abundance. Behind it all was the divine majesty adorning Joseph with authority so absolute and unquestioned it would finally serve its real purpose: to bring his strong-willed, hard-hearted, mule-headed brothers to a place of such brokenness they would begin to move down the path they avoided for over twenty years—the path of repentance that leads to salvation, heals a shattered family, restores God's covenant community, and moves them on to become a blessing to the nations.

But it took the divine majesty breaking in and, with breathtaking speed and an astounding reversal of fortune, endowing their redeemer with awesome power to begin this impossibly difficult project. For, as we will see, the redemption of this family will not come easy.

CHAPTER 12

A Qualified Redeemer

Read Genesis 41: 50–57

Joseph is now poised to become a redeemer on a massive scale. Not only Egypt but all the neighboring countries are facing a crisis. It's all wrapped up in just one word: severe. The famine finally hits, and it is mean. Though it affects thousands of people, it is aimed specifically at Joseph's brothers. This famine is God's hammer slamming down on their hard hearts. It will, in time, do its deep work; it will shatter them. It is God's disguised mercy, because it's a severe mercy. You'll remember that it was a famine, a severe mercy, that brought the prodigal son back to his father (Luke 16:14).

Famines have many faces: often, they are severe adversities we bring upon ourselves because of our own evil behavior. The sexual abuser loses his reputation. Think Harvey Weinstein. The greedy Ponzi schemer loses his wealth. Think Bernie Madoff. The crooked politician loses the White House. Think Richard Nixon. And sometimes famines, mercifully, transform their victims. Think Charles Colson.

Jacob and Sons, Inc. is hit hard. The grasslands turn brown and dusty. Plants droop. Sheep get thin. Wells go dry. Finally the flocks, their very livelihood, begin dying off. Then a good news/bad news quandary: there is food in Egypt! But the sons don't want to go. They dilly-dally, looking at each other with clouded faces, hesitating. You can imagine why. Egypt is the last place they would want to visit. What if they ran into Joseph? What if they came face to face with the brother they had evicted so long ago? So begins a valiant struggle to make the best of it, getting by on rations and hoping for rain.

When we resist coming to terms with our own misconduct we reduce ourselves to living on rations and hoping for rain. We find ourselves living an impoverished life but are too stubborn to deal with its root causes. But God has no intention of bringing rain until his famine has done its purifying work.

Finally Father Jacob gives them a forceful shove! He says to them, "Why do you just keep looking at each other? I have heard that there is grain in Egypt. Go down there and buy some for us so that we will not die" (42:1–2).

Will they finally do it? Not one of them could ever forget the final sight of him being dragged off to Egypt by those Midianites some twenty years earlier. Now they are being coerced into travelling that very same road they forced him to take. The pressure is on. It is either go to Egypt . . . or die! Only when their father tells them that the whole family is staring death itself right in the face do they finally budge.

The one thing they dread is, in fact, going to happen. They will find themselves being led by an invisible hand right into the very presence of Joseph. He will instantly spot them, though they will not recognize him at all. (You can understand why they wouldn't. He'll be called an Egyptian name. He'll speak the Egyptian language. He'll be dressed like an Egyptian. Besides, twenty years will have changed his features from the time he was seventeen.) They just won't see him for who he is behind that natural disguise! Besides, they certainly would not expect to encounter him in a high government position. But right there, without their even knowing it, the great redemptive encounter will begin as they all bow down before him precisely as those old dreams had predicted.

They were not ready to meet Joseph. The real question, however, is: was Joseph ready for them? It doesn't look like it. It looks like he has never forgotten the dastardly way they treated him, because it appears that when they finally come under his power, all his stored-up rage just explodes at them. Look at his first response! He speaks "harshly" to them. He accuses them of being spies. And then he summarily throws them in jail. It looks like his anger, his righteous and justified anger, smoldering in his heart all these many years, finally bursts out on them. He blasts them!

Or does he? Is that what is happening here? Is this vindictiveness? Is this a spirit that says, "You put me through Hell, and now I am going to give you a taste of your own medicine!" Is this revenge? On the surface, it sure looks like it. After all, isn't this how we might treat someone who has made our life unbearable for some thirteen years? Wouldn't we just savor the opportunity to finally unload all our rage on them and make them pay in every way we could possibly think of? Would we not more likely react like Edmund Dantes' in Alexandre Dumas' classic, *The Count of Monte Cristo*? Edmund had been betrayed by his closest friend, Fernand Mondego. As a result he was wrongfully imprisoned for many years. But he escaped, acquired a fortune, and set about getting revenge on those responsible for his terrible suffering. This was no ordinary revenge. He was convinced that it would be far too easy on his enemies if he just quickly killed them off. No! He wanted to torture them. Now that he had them in his power, he wanted first to make their lives as miserable as he possibly could. He said, "Death is too good for them. They must suffer as I suffered. They must see their world, all they hold dear, ripped from them as it was ripped from me" (Reynolds, 2002). He wanted to put them through Hell first, and then finish them off.

Is that what we see when the brothers first come under Joseph's power? A closer look tells a different story: Joseph's harsh treatment of his brothers is all an act, a charade Joseph compels himself to put on because it is the only way for them to be forced to finally face up to their old sin. If you could look into Joseph's heart at the moment his brothers first showed up, you would have seen nothing but affectionate love for them. You can watch it leaking out in the scenes that follow as again and again we are told about the tears of Joseph:

> 42: 24: "He turned away and began to weep."
> 43: 30: "Deeply moved at the sight of his brother, Joseph hurried out and looked for a place to weep. He went into his private room and wept there."
> 45: 2: "And he wept so loudly that the Egyptians heard him, and Pharaoh's household heard about it."
> 45: 14–15: "Then he threw his arms around his brother Benjamin and wept, and Benjamin embraced him, weeping. And he kissed all his brothers and wept over them."

Vindictive people do not break into tears like that. They stare at the misery of their enemies with cold pleasure. Not one single tear flows as they watch their enemies grovel. Not so Joseph. He wears a hard countenance and speaks with harsh words, but his heart is moved with longing for their redemption, just like the heart of our Lord yearned as he wept over the city of Jerusalem for all the ways they had murdered the prophets that were sent to them. But for the time being, his tender affection needed to put on a different face—the face of a tough prosecutor whose love compels him to confront their deeply entrenched evil in the hope of leading them to the brokenness that is the doorway to redemption.

To convince us that Joseph's severe treatment of his brothers sprang from love and not revenge, Moses makes sure we know what had been happening to Joseph all along during his time in Egypt, and especially during the last seven years, the years of plenty. He tells us that during those years, as

Joseph ruled Egypt and gathered in the bounty of one bumper crop after another, he was being blessed in another wondrous way as well. He was given a family of his own. Joseph not only was given a wife from a highly respected family, but he also became a father. His wife Asenath, the daughter of Potiphera, the priest of On, gave him two sons, and the names he gave to his sons show us his heart. In the Bible, names describe the character or destiny of a person. The names Joseph gave his sons reveal to us that if he had ever had a spirit of vindictiveness (which we don't know), it had been washed away by God's sweet presence over the last twenty years, and especially by his rich goodness to him in the last seven years. Look at the names he gave those boys!

The first son he called "Manasseh," which means, "It is because God has made me forget all my trouble and all my father's household" (41:51). At first this sounds ominous, as if Joseph had deliberately decided to erase the painful memory of his family from his mind once and for all. But this doesn't mean "forget" in the sense of suppressing a painful memory. Joseph would never forget his troubles nor his family of origin, especially his father. Joseph never wrote off his family in that sense. So what does this "forgetting" actually mean? Might I suggest it means that whenever Joseph recalled his troubles or his father's household, he deliberately moved the pain of the memory *off to the side*. He refused to let it stand between himself and his brothers. He refused to stew in it. He didn't rehearse it and allow himself to get hot all over again. It was over! He had "let it go."

A redeemer must be a person who, though having every right to his anger because it is a righteous anger (not all our angers are!), is able to *relocate* that anger by putting it off to the side so decisively that it does not control his behavior toward the person who has offended him. He has to be able to move past—or better, around—his anger to see the person who has so deeply hurt him with eyes that still see value in that person! A redeemer has to have set his rage aside enough to be able to look past the sin of the person who hurt him so deeply that he or she is able to see there a person who still, in spite of their abysmal behavior, remains a person to be valued. I know. That was a hard sentence, and when you were children this did not happen when you had your fights. You were so mad at each other, you couldn't see anything good in each other!! Your rage created just one spirit in you and that was a determination to hit back, and hit back a lot harder than you were hit, because, suddenly, your brother or sister had become a monster to you!

But you are children no longer. And there may very well come times in your adult life where you will have an opportunity to make a redemptive move to heal a broken relationship, perhaps with your spouse, a neighbor, or a co-worker. If your childhood response is still alive in you, and if it shapes how you respond to being injured, then I must say to you that you are still childish. Far too many adults still are. They are punchers. They hit back. And they glory in it. If this is still your response to insult or injury, let me say this to you quite plainly: *"Grow up!"* It is time (past time, since you are now emerging into young adulthood) to put such childish things behind you and do something that is not natural to any of us but is critical for you to learn in order to be used of God to be one of those blessed peacemakers Jesus honored: you will never redeem the broken relationships in your life if you insist on hitting back. The key change is this: you will, sometime, finally, have to learn *how to make a move against your own anger.* This is what Joseph did, and the name he gave to his first son testifies to it: Manasseh! What a name!

There can be no doubt that he was initially steamed at his brothers for what they did to him. Who wouldn't be? There was plenty in his life in Egypt to fire that anger up even hotter. He had every right to be infuriated all the more when Mrs. Potiphar treacherously lied about him, and then when Mr. Potiphar threw him into the slammer without a proper investigation. He had every right to feel deeply aggrieved at his brothers all the more when that selfish butler deliberately let him just sit there for two long years! Moving against his own anger at his brothers was no cakewalk for Joseph because it kept on being stoked by fresh sufferings in his exile.

Some of us never do succeed in moving against our own anger, so much so, that our anger can even begin to define us. In some cases, if we let it go *we wouldn't know who we are*. This was the great threat Joseph faced. He had been repeatedly mistreated, and his sufferings had been acute. So, how did it ever happen that he reached a place where he could name his first son with a title telling us that he had been able to set all that anger aside?

The most obvious answer is this: the repeated kindnesses of God in his life. All along the favor of heaven had washed over him. Then it had gushed out like a torrent when, overnight, he was elevated to manager of the entire country. Then he was given a wife to love, and, I can only imagine, one who loved him. And then, a child! If he had carried rage in his heart, all of this surely would have softened it. How fitting it would be for him, in return, to cultivate kindness towards those who had been so unkind to him. This is one of the sweetest fruits from being loved by God, in Christ our Lord: "We love because he first loved us" (I John 4:19). That is how we find the power to move against our own justified angers.

There may have been something else as well. Perhaps during his years of suffering he had come to view his brothers with a different set of eyes: to see that they were not only villains, but, in a certain sense, *victims*. They were villains alright; but, they were also the poisoned fruit of the dysfunctional family tree in which they had grown up. Perhaps he saw more clearly how the blatant favoritism of his father, robbing them of the love they needed, had harmed them to the point it crippled their capacity to love anyone at all. *Some people are more beat up than brought up.* Perhaps that perspective softened his heart. In other words, even though they were to blame for their cruelty to him, perhaps he saw that they were not *entirely* to blame. They were to blame, of course; what they had done was pure evil. But perhaps he saw more and more that the brothers themselves had also been damaged. This is almost a truism among counselors today: hurt people, hurt people.

Then, perhaps, there was something even more. Perhaps the fact that they were *still his brothers*, that the relationship binding them to each other was much older than the offense which had driven them apart, was also a heart softening consideration. One key to being able to move against our anger is remembering the history we may have with that person who has hurt us which is usually much older than the offense. We grew up with them! They are family! They worshipped side by side with us for years. We worked at the same company for decades, cheered the same teams. We went camping, hunting and fishing together for years. We still share not just the same genes but the same story, the same legacy, and, in the case of the family of Jacob, the same promises! What we have in common with them is still, in spite of real injury, far more substantial (come to think of it) than the crime that drove us apart. This too may have been a factor in softening whatever anger Joseph may have felt.

Manasseh! What a name!

Then there came a second son! When Joseph cradled him in his arms, he was so moved by the joy of holding him he said something like this: "I have suffered so much! But now, holding this little boy in the very land where I have endured so much pain—what a rare kind of delight is this! I feel so rich right now, but what is so unique about my wealth is that I am savoring it in the unlikeliest of all places: the very place where I have suffered so much! Is it actually possible to taste such joy in such exile? Is it really possible to find any light at all in such a dark place as this? Is it possible to know this kind of delight in the very place where I still feel deep sadness over being far from my father? Yes, it is, because the God who is with me specializes in this very thing! He makes the very deserts themselves bloom, and the very rocks themselves pour forth fountains of water. So I'll call him Ephraim, 'because God has made me fruitful right in the land of my suffering'" (41:52b).

This surprising discovery, so often revealed in the Bible, still sounds strange to us. Our culture says that you only find real living by figuring out a way to get away from it all. You don't "stay" where you are right now, that place of such frustration, pressure, and ordinariness! No, you have got to get out of there!! You tell yourself, "Life where I am right now is rotten, but if only I could get out of this lousy job (marriage, city, school, corporation, etc.), life could be so much better." We think escape. Well, Joseph couldn't escape. Instead, he learned to abide. He learned to be where he was. He learned that it is actually possible to find everything you long for by just staying put. He learned that staying where you are at and letting adversity do its deep work in your heart, produces character that can be cultivated in no other way.

This little baby's name, calls out to you to ask different questions: can heaven be found in hellish places? This name, Ephraim, says, "Yes." Indeed, the entire thrust of the Holy Scriptures is a resounding, "Yes!" Here is a biblical jewel that seems foolish to men but is in fact one of the great insights of the Christian faith: we have a God who can look at a world where darkness covers the face of the deep places, say the words "Let there be light," and suddenly right there, that very world, that selfsame abyss of blackness, can be instantly flooded with light. It's all there, right at the very start of the Bible. This is not a big secret! And yet it remains, to this day, one of the most difficult of all the mysteries to embrace.

Joseph, trained in God's school of adversity and kindness, was ready to take on his greatest task: being a redeemer, with a heart full of light, shining in a dark world.

The darkness first surfaced in Egypt. When the seven years of abundance came to an end, precisely as Joseph had said, the seven years of famine began, right on schedule. Year number eight in Egypt was a disaster. So was year nine. Every Egyptian knew, looking at their barren fields, that Joseph's prediction was confirmed.

It was not long before all the people began to cry out to Pharaoh to help them. Pharaoh was ready. He knew exactly what to tell them: "Go to Joseph and do what he tells you" (41: 55b). They did. The people listened as Joseph and his commissioners directed them to the nearest storehouse. In city after city a steady stream of people from all the outlying villages poured into each of the store cities Joseph had established. There, Joseph and his commissioners experienced one of the most delightful moments in the career of any government official. They unlocked the doors to their vast storage facilities and showed the people the mountains of grain just waiting for them: tons, ready to meet their needs for years. What a sight! And then began the delightful operation of selling it to all the citizens and gathering in the profits for Pharaoh. No doubt the price was fair, and the people were fully able to pay, given the fact that they were just coming off the seven bountiful years. So everyone was happy: the citizens, the officials, Joseph, and especially Pharaoh. Moreover, there was no fear of any shortages. The supply seemed endless. Those were happy days, right in the heart of the famine. Isn't that a wondrous scene?

But it had even larger dimensions. People from other nations heard the news that there was plenty of food in Egypt, and soon enough the whole world (41:57) began to beat a path to Egypt. They came from Ethiopia, Libya, Syria, and Arabia, on pilgrimage to the benevolent banker. Not one of them was disappointed. They came anxious and left assured. They came with empty sacks and left with bulging sacks. Egypt became the shining city on a hill, the banquet for a starving world.

Centuries later, people from these same nations, spiritually hungry, would find their hearts filled with the Holy Spirit . . . at Pentecost. And right in the middle of it all stood Joseph, a prototype of Jesus, who, on Pentecost, poured out the fullness of his Spirit!

Surely you must see that there is so much more here than meets the eye. If you look at this scene of benevolence and bounty, you surely will recognize Jesus in Joseph. Look at Jesus. No one caught on at first that He was the ultimate "Joseph." But then he fed a crowd of five thousand men (along with women and children) an amazingly abundant meal that originated with just five loaves of bread and two fish. Everybody ate their fill, and there were twelve basketfuls of leftovers (Matt. 14: 13–21). People started to take notice! Then he did it again, this time feeding four thousand men (along with women and children) using seven loaves and a few small fish. There were seven basketfuls of leftovers (Matt. 15:29–39). Then people really started talking. This was miraculous!

Then he began to offer a radically new kind of nourishment—a spiritual food for the soul, more pure and potent than anything you can buy, even in the best organic food store. He told a love-starved woman by a well, who had already worn out five husbands and was about to ruin the sixth, that if she drank the water he gave her, it would actually turn into a spring of love inside of her and she'd never be desperate for a man's love again. Strange! Later on he told a vast crowd that if they truly wanted to live, they needed to eat his body and drink his blood. That was so bizarre they thought he was crazy, and most of them stopped following him. Yet today millions of us, his followers, do just that, some of us every week, as we partake of the Lord's Supper in our churches. We experience the very life of Jesus being infused into us, nourishing us at the very core of our beings with eternal life. Joseph could only keep people from starving, but the food Jesus gives us does so much more: it generates a vitality in us so powerful it is called eternal life. It is the very life of God being fed into us, and when it nourishes us something beautiful happens inside of us: we are rescued from our self-absorption, and knowing we are deeply loved, we begin to find the power to love God and others.

So don't skip over those clear and simple instructions Pharaoh gave to his frightened people crying out to him for relief as the famine began to strangle them: "Go to Joseph, and do what he tells you" (41:55b). For this much is certain: you will experience more than one famine during the journey of your life. You will travel through some very dry places. It could be that your marriage will grow cold, or one of your children will break your heart. It could be that dear friends will fail you just when you need them, or you find yourself suddenly dismissed from your job, which you thought was so safe. It could be that you'll contract a fatal disease at a surprisingly young age and find yourself facing death itself. It could be that a thick fog of depression descends upon you and threatens to smother your spirit. This is virtually as certain as the sunrise tomorrow: life is difficult. In his bestselling book, *The Road Less Traveled,* Scott Peck began with these words: "Life is difficult. This is a great truth, one of the greatest truths. It is a great truth because once we truly see this truth, we transcend it. Once we truly know that life is difficult—once we truly understand and accept it—then life is no longer difficult. Because once it is accepted, the fact that life is difficult no longer matters." (Peck, p. 15)

Peck goes on to recommend a regimen of personal disciplines as the recipe for coping with the difficulties of life. They are wise and fitting. But where does one find the strength to practice those regimens so vital to human flourishing? That is THE question. At this point in the Joseph story we are provided with the answer: "Go to Joseph and do what he tells you." Today Jesus is the true Joseph. And this is what he told us to do when life gets really difficult: "Come to me, all you who are weary and burdened, and I will give you rest. Take my yoke upon you and learn from me, for I am gentle and humble in heart and you will find rest for your souls. For my yoke is easy and my burden is light" (Matt. 11:28–30). Teacher Jesus would have us learn this: "Live like me. Live a surrendered life. My life does not belong to me; it belongs to my Father. He has put his Spirit in me. It is the Spirit Himself who is the guide and the power of my life. He is my wisdom. He is my energy. He is both my pathway and the power to walk on it. I live, because He lives in me. Join me. Slip your head into the yoke next to me (we oxen pull in pairs), and let my great power come alongside of your dwindling strength. You'll find it is a lot easier than what you are trying to do, managing life on your own. Life is far too difficult for you to make that work. Surrender."

People listened to Pharaoh. The whole world did go to Joseph. They did what he told them to do, and they survived. But now the true Joseph is here, and he has the key to storehouses bulging with the real food, spiritual food for the whole world. When life gets difficult, as it most certainly will, go to Jesus and do what he tells you. And you will do more than survive. You will thrive, because the food he gives you is his very self, living in you. For this is what he said about that powerful food:

> I am the living bread that came down from heaven. If anyone eats of this bread, he will live forever. . . . Whoever eats my flesh and drinks my blood has eternal life, and I will raise him up at the last day. For my flesh is real food and my blood is real drink. Whoever eats my flesh and drinks my blood remains in me, and I in him. Just as the living Father sent me and I live because of the Father, so the one who feeds on me will live because of me. This is the bread that came down from heaven. . . . Whoever feeds on this bread will live forever" (John 6:51, 54–58a, 58c).

And so it was that Joseph redeemed thousands from certain death. This is history, but it is also prophecy. The greatest redemption was yet to come . . . it wouldn't be easy. . . and it would revolve around a lavish banquet of food.

CHAPTER 13

Forgive? Not so Quick

Read Genesis 42: 3 — 38

This chapter in Genesis just might trouble you. Joseph's brothers are facing desperate times. Their only hope is to find food in Egypt. They are prepared to pay for it. After a long, hot journey, they finally show up in Joseph's presence. They bow low before him. And how does Joseph respond? Harshly! You may wonder, "Is this any way for a redeemer to behave?" Actually, yes, it is.

As we learned in the last chapter, this is not pent-up rage boiling over. Surely, you can see, by now, that his heart has to be overflowing with grace and kindness. All along Joseph has been very alert to what God was has been up to. He was tuned in, as he demonstrated when he mentioned the hand of God so often the day he first appeared in the presence of Pharaoh. Surely by now it has dawned on him why he was evicted from his family and sold off as a slave to Egypt: he was sent here to save thousands, including his own family.

We can be fairly certain that he knew, as he watched people from the countries all around pour into Egypt for food, and heard their dire reports of just how devastating the famine was in their homelands, that it was only a matter of time before his own brothers would have to make their way to Egypt as well. They had to be suffering, and you can be quite sure that he was expecting that any day now they too would be standing in line with all the others, clutching their pouches of money, desperate for food. I can imagine him keeping a close eye on the foreigners crowding into his distribution center. And then, one day, there they were, ten of them! He was ready. He made his move.

But not with mercy! Not with forgiveness! Not with a warm embrace! Not with those wonderful words he would later say to comfort them, "Don't be afraid. Am I in the place of God? You intended to harm me, but God intended it for good to accomplish what is now being done, the saving of many lives. So don't be afraid. I will provide for you and your children" (Gen. 50: 19 – –21). Why not? Where's the forgiveness, Joseph? Not one word of kindness, after all the kindness that has been shown to you? What gives here?

Oh, it's there all right. Joseph is full of forgiveness. He is rich in mercy. He is a forgiveness millionaire! But he had to restrain himself from extending that forgiveness to them because *they were not ready to receive it*. They were not ready for redemption. They were nowhere near the place where their hearts were ready for that side of grace's face. He had to first show them the other side of grace's face—the side that helps us see our need for grace! His task was now the same task the angel Gabriel told the old priest Zechariah his future son, John (the Baptist), would be called to do: to "make ready a people prepared..." (Luke 1: 17c). Joseph's first job was the tough task of breaking down his brothers' smug self-justification. He had to be prosecutor before he could become pardoner.

This gave him no choice but to act very much like John the Baptist as he prepared the way for Jesus! Perhaps you remember how John went about bringing people to a place where they were finally prepared to receive the immense grace Jesus came to bring. He was as in-your-face as a preacher can be! Look what happened when people showed up to hear him:

> "John exploded: 'Brood of snakes! What do you think you're doing slithering down here to the river? Do you think a little water on your snakeskins is going to deflect God's judgment? It's your life that must change, not your skin. And don't think you can pull rank by claiming Abraham as "father." Being a child of Abraham is neither here nor there—children of Abraham are a dime a dozen. God can make children from stones if he wants. What counts is your life. Is it green and blossoming? Because if it's deadwood, it goes on the fire." (Luke 3: 7 – 9, The Message)

That is tough talk. That is...harsh! Still, amazingly, people flocked to hear it! Why would people travel out to a desert just to be scolded? It's because deep inside many of us carry a terrible weight of guilt, and, it can be so oppressive at times that we even find ourselves longing for the relief of getting it off our consciences. One of our deepest needs is face up to the truth about our ugly side, and finally get all that guilt out. And yet, most of us cannot bring ourselves to that point all on our own. Like Peter after his third denial, what we need is a piercing divine look gazing deep into our souls, forcing us to realize just how shameful our behavior actually is. Without that look, we're stuck. We cannot be redeemed unless God himself moves, you could say, *against* us. Often his agent is a wise, brave, honest person who cares enough about us to push against our defenses, wear down our rationalizations, strip away our pride, and boldly say it like it is to us in such a way that it cuts us to the heart and drives us into the position of a supplicant, begging for mercy. Even though he uses human agents, only God can effect kind of surgery on the human heart. Unless He breaks us, we will never be broken. That is why authentic redemption comes so hard, and so very few people, as Jesus taught us in Matthew 7: 14, find it.

So Joseph had his work cut out for him, because his brothers were deep into denial. It's obvious from the get-go. When Joseph interrogated them, what word did they immediately summon up to describe themselves? "Honest!" They said they were honest men (the word shows up five times in chapter 42!) Honest men? Had they not, truth be told, covered up the truth about what they did to Joseph for some twenty two years now? Honest men! Give me a break! Had they not watched their father Jacob's tears and heard his moans all these years, and yet never once breathed a word about how they caused those tears? Honest men! And now their denial was twenty two years old! It was deeply entrenched. It was part of them. It would be a long and painful journey for Joseph to bring them to that a place where they finally came face to face with just how deeply their dishonesty had taken root. Consequently, what they needed, right now, was one tough prosecutor. And now God, the God of all mercy, had brought them face to face with him!

This is as good a place as any in the story to make a critical distinction regarding forgiveness: it is one thing to *be* forgiving, to have a heart of forgiveness towards the person who has hurt us. It is another thing to *extend* that forgiveness to that person. The words "I forgive you" are as sacred as the words "I do" in a wedding ceremony. Those words are some of the most solemn words humans ever utter, and they are never to be spoken lightly. The words, "I forgive you" rise to that level.

Allow me to underscore this distinction because it is just so critical in the process of redemption. You may remember that on the cross Jesus' very first words were a prayer, "Father, forgive them for they know not what they do." Let me ask you: at that moment was Jesus actually forgiving his crucifiers? Here's a hard truth: no, he wasn't. Look again. He was not extending forgiveness to them; he was simply praying that they would (at some point) be forgiven. (And that prayer was answered, 53 days later, but only after Prosecutor Peter's Pentecostal preaching cut them to the heart.)

When our Lord actually extended forgiveness to a person, he would look right at them and say something to this effect, "Your sins are forgiven."

This is what he did to the lame man lowered down through the roof by his friends into his presence. He spoke directly to him and said, "Son, your sins are forgiven" (Matthew 9: 2). He did something very similar to the woman caught in the act of adultery when he spoke directly to her and said, "Neither do I condemn you." He made the same pronouncement over the weeping woman, with a sinful past, whose tears fell on his feet. After she dried them with her hair, and anointed them with a fragrant offering, Jesus explained that act to the skeptics in the crowd: "Therefore, I tell you, her many sins have been forgiven..." (Luke 7: 47a). He made it very plain that she had been forgiven. But Jesus didn't do that as he hung from the cross. He didn't look at the centurion and say to him, "Sir, I forgive you." He didn't say, about the people who had just nailed his hands and feet, "These soldiers have been forgiven." Instead, notice what is actually quite obvious: he prayed that they would be forgiven, which is very different that actually extending forgiveness to them.

That prayer reveals the heart of Jesus—it was full of forgiveness towards his killers. But it also raises this question: when was that prayer answered? If you just keep on reading the story, you will discover it: 53 days later. Fifty three days after Jesus pleaded with his father to forgive his killers, Peter, filled with the Holy Spirit, stood up, on the day of Pentecost and preached one of the fieriest sermons in history. Acting very much like a prosecutor, Peter blasted his audience with these blistering words:

> "Men of Israel, listen to this: Jesus of Nazareth was a man accredited by God to you by miracles, wonders and signs, which God did among you through him, as you yourselves know. This man was handed over to you by God's set purpose and foreknowledge; and you, with the help of wicked men, put him to death by nailing him to the cross!" (Acts 2: 22 – 23)

He ended his sizzling sermon with these piercing words: "Therefore let all Israel be assured of this: God has made this Jesus, whom you crucified, both Lord and Christ." (Acts 2: 36)

And then, what happened? It was as if they had just been stunned with a Taser (at their peak, they deliver 50,000 volts)! They were "cut to the heart and said to Peter and the other apostles, 'Brothers, what shall we do?'" (Acts 2: 37) This is virtually the exact same question the crowds asked John the Baptist after his harsh preaching!

And then, what did Peter say? "Repent and be baptized, every one of you, in the name of Jesus Christ for the forgiveness of your sins" (vs. 38).

That day about three thousand did repent for the sin of crucifying Jesus, and they were baptized. In other words, that day three thousands of them were forgiven. In other words, on that day, for three thousand people, the prayer our Lord made to his father on the cross was answered, and his request was granted. It was as if he himself said to them, through Peter who possessed his very spirit: "I forgive you."

But it took 53 days, the compelling fact of the resurrection, and an in-your-face sermon by prosecutor Peter confronting them with the painful truth of their own wickedness. Finally they came under deep conviction and repented. Only then Peter was able to assure them that the Father had extended to them the forgiveness that Jesus had earned for them and longed for them to receive.

So Joseph's love for his brothers had to begin in a very different place: he had to first "bless them with guilt" (to borrow a curious, but precisely correct, phrase from Scott Peck [Peck, p. 71]) before he could wash them with forgiveness. That meant he had to begin by bearing down upon them like a merciless prosecutor. Watch him!! He is one tough "District Attorney."

Joseph, certain they have not recognized him, cuts them off and roars, "You are spies! You have come to see where our land is unprotected!" That is a most serious charge because spies, if caught, were summarily executed. (This is why Rahab, years later, showed such courage when she actually hid the Israeli spies—if she had been caught, it would have cost her, and them, their lives. You can check this out at Joshua 2: 14). Terror hit them instantly; they knew how serious the charge was and how defenseless they were at the moment to prove it wrong.

So they tried, as best them could, to make their feeble defense, and in the process only ended up confirming their identity all the more to Joseph: "We are all sons of one man." Again, they protested their innocence, saying, "Your servants have come to buy food. Your servants are honest men, not spies." Notice what they did: they uttered one truth ("all sons of one man"), but joined it to one lie ("honest men"). That is what deception looks like. It can be largely truth, but with a small twist of distortion sandwiched inside it.

Joseph is relentless. He repeats the charge, refusing to believe a word they say.

So, they try again, this time revealing a little more information ("Your servants were twelve brothers, the sons of one man, who lives in the land of Canaan. The youngest is now with our father....") but ending with a euphemism covering up the real truth of what they had done twenty- two years earlier to Joseph ("...and one is no more."). They had lived their cover-up so long I wonder if they even realized what a half-truth it was that they were expressing right now.

So now Joseph lowered the boom. He repeated his charge that they were spies and informed them that the only way they could prove that they were truthful men was for one of them to go back to Canaan and return with the brother they claimed was back there, while the rest of them would be imprisoned. Joseph knew full well what would happen when that solo brother returned to Canaan with this demand: it would never happen. He knew his father, and he knew his father would never allow Benjamin out of his sight. And, more to the point, he knew that they knew this too.

So, in effect, he put them into an impossible situation. That is tightening the screws!

He promptly threw all of them into jail to give them some time to stew in their misery, perhaps even into the very prison in which he himself had languished so long, since it was, after all, the prison in which the king kept his convicts (39: 20). Suddenly, they found themselves being escorted, under armed guard down strange streets and into a very dark place. They heard the heavy iron gate slam shut behind them, and just like that found themselves in a position they never expected to be in when they first showed up that morning. There they sat, confined and, restricted. Their world suddenly caved in on them. They ate the meagre provisions of prison food, sitting on a hard, cold floor, eyed by well-armed guards, and not knowing what would become of them. Was it enough to break them? Did they come out with the truth? Hardly! Redemption comes hard because, truth be told, repentance comes hard.

After three days, seeing no evidence of any softening in their hearts, Joseph took a different tack. He showed them (what seemed like) a kindness. He gave them some relief by magnanimously announcing that all of them but one would be released to go home on the mission to return with Benjamin. But this was only turning the screws tighter. For now it would be nine of them facing the agonizing task rather than just one. All nine of them would experience the anguish of trying to pry Benjamin from their father's iron embrace. Nine of them would have to witness their father's misery over allowing Benjamin, his last connection to his beloved Rachel, to be taken out of his sight. Nine of them would watch him wrestle with this terrible dilemma, this impossible possibility. Nine of them would have the opportunity, when they witnessed their father's terrible agony as he had to come to grips with the unthinkable, to finally break down and admit their own terrible guilt. And so he released them all but Simeon, whom he held hostage. The rest would now face torture in Canaan!

As he released them, he used solemn language meant to pierce their hard consciences. He informed them that he was no ordinary heathen. He was a man who "feared God"! What was he saying? That he was a man who also had a conscience, and his conscience could not allow him to be blindly cruel. Fearing God meant that he also needed to practice mercy, and mercy meant letting nine of them go. It was all part of the front, the charade he had to present to them to make them feel they were being shown a kindness. After all, kindness itself does have the power to lead a person to repentance (Acts 14: 17; Romans 2: :4). This is not the first time Joseph would use what would appear to be an act of kindness to pierce their hard hearts. The second one was about to be sprung on them, with even more painful consequences—but that will have to wait until the next chapter.

And so they were released, but not before being forced to witness something meant to intimidate them with the fact that this was a ruler who was not to be trifled with. Joseph arranged for them to witness a chilling sight. While they were forced to look, he had Simeon singled out. They watched as his hands were bound with chains and his feet with shackles. Perhaps an iron yoke was locked around his neck. They were compelled to see one of their own brothers being treated like a common slave. Did this bring back any memories? Had they not, likely, seen this very thing happen before to a brother? Very likely. This just might have been a replay of an old video, was it not? Surely, they had watched something much like this when the Midianites bought Joseph off their hands. We can be quite sure those merchants, having paid good money for him, didn't let him walk free in their caravan! Likely, they bound him securely so as to make escape impossible. Did they remember? And now they're watching a reprise of that scene. This image would torment their minds the whole time they were on their mission to retrieve Benjamin. It would force their hand to force their father to release Benjamin so that Simeon might be released. But would it be enough?

The hammer of Joseph was hitting down hard on the sharp chisel cutting into their granite hearts.

Then Joseph carefully arranged for their consciences to be pricked yet again. He instructed his steward to fill their bags full to the very top with grain and to give them extra provisions as food for themselves and their donkeys for the return trip. It looked as if he was being lavish. But then, the sharp edge of the chisel! He instructed his steward to take the money they had paid for these supplies and place it right at the very mouth of the sack, so that, upon opening the sack, it would lie there, staring them in the face, declaring, "You thief!" And so he did.

They set off, grateful to have been released and comforted to have sacks bulging with grain. Here was some assurance that they and their families would live to see another day. They must have felt some relief. They were on their way home, putting more and more distance between themselves and that nasty ruler. The first evening, one of them went to open his sack to get a little food for his donkey—and there, right at the very top, resting on all that grain, was the pouch containing every shekel of his payment of silver, staring at him. It cut his heart like a knife, slicing into him with the accusation that he had defrauded that man ruling Egypt, that man who had the power to make him pay dearly for such theft. He told the other eight, and the hearts of all nine of them just sunk. Every one of them began to tremble, shaking and quivering inside. A shard of fear pierced their hearts and for the first time in years they finally asked the right question: *"What is this that God has done to us?"*

This is exactly the question Joseph wanted to rise up from their consciences. It is a hard question. It is a rare question. Life has to take a very severe turn to bring such a question out of us. When adversity comes our way, most of us don't seriously consider that there just might be a divine message in it, as if, possibly, God is actually speaking to us through it.

We are usually not listening for the voice of God as we go about our everyday lives. There are so many other voices demanding our attention. This may have prompted C. S. Lewis to make his well-known claim: "God whispers to us in our pleasures, speaks in our conscience, but shouts in our pains. It is his megaphone to rouse a deaf world" (Lewis, The Problem of Pain, 1962, p. 92). He goes on to say, "

> Until the evil man finds evil unmistakably present in his existence, in the form of pain, he is enclosed in illusion. . .. ...no doubt pain as God's megaphone is a terrible instrument; it may lead to final and unrepented rebellion. But it gives the only opportunity the bad man can have for amendment. It removes the veil; it plants the flag of truth within the fortress of a rebel soul" (p. 95).

That is exactly what Joseph has done here. He has planted something in the mouth of that bag that shouted at all of them, "So you are honest, are you? Look here! The truth is, you are nothing but thieves!!" The flag of truth shouts, soundlessly, from the open mouth of a bag of grain!

And this was just the beginning of the misery Joseph had skillfully crafted to keep on exposing their entrenched illusions about themselves. For when they finally arrived home, they had no choice but to report to their father the confrontation which the ruler had had with them, since, after all, Simeon was conspicuous by his absence; otherwise, it is very likely that they would not have said one word until the time they were forced to return by the famine that would not let up on them. So as soon as they showed up at the compound, they had to tell their father what actually happened. "Dad," they said, "he spoke so harshly to us! He accused us of being spies! And then, when he learned we had a brother at home, he demanded that we prove we were not lying by going home and bringing him back with us! Otherwise he will refuse to trade with us, and we will be in deep trouble if this famine continues." And all through their five verse report, one word kept on surfacing . . . three times: "honest." (vs. 31, 33, 34). They were locked into their illusion.

Jacob must have cringed to hear that word. Dishonesty had infected the family for years. Abraham had been dishonest about Sarah being his wife. Isaac had been dishonest about Rebekah being his wife. But the most damaging dishonesty of all took place the day he himself, under his mother's coaching, had put on a disguise, presented himself to his father Isaac as Esau, and stolen the blessing of the firstborn. That one act of dishonesty had driven him from his home for years. He had seen it surface in the next generation. His sons had been dishonest with the Shechemites, and made their family a "stench" to the Canaanites. And now that wretched word repeatedly surfaces all over again!

But even that was not the worst of it. It came time to unload and empty all their sacks. As Jacob watched his sons open them, horror came over all of them—every sack contained the pouch of silver meant to pay for it, pointing a long and bony finger, accusing every single one of them of dishonest dealings. Every one of these tough guys was totally shaken, as was Jacob. The prosecutor just kept right on prosecuting, even long after they had walked away from his unnerving presence in Egypt.

It was all too much for father Jacob. His rage erupted, and now he became the voice of the prosecutor. He leveled a serious charge against his sons, and now it was his accusation that had to sound very harsh:

> "You have deprived me of my children.
> Joseph is no more and . . . . . .
> Simeon is no more and . . . . . .
> now you want to take Benjamin." (vs. 36)

He is laying the blame squarely at their feet. Not only are they robbing the man in Egypt; they are robbing him! And what they are stealing is not just money; they are robbing him of his own children!

Reuben made a pathetic stab at alleviating Jacob's misery. Clumsily, he offered up both of his sons as sacrifices if the boys failed to return from

Egypt with Benjamin on their next trip. But of course, Jacob would never murder his own grandsons! That got nowhere. Instead, it only stiffened has dad's resolve to never, ever allow Benjamin to leave home. And then, as if their frustration with their father was not acute enough, they all heard him say these blatant words of favoritism: "My son will not go down there with you; his brother is dead and he is the only one left." There it was again: Benjamin was now the favored son. None of them really counted. They were all non-sons, as far as their father was concerned. They were the despised offspring of unloved women, accidental children of accidental wives.

And so they were at a stalemate. Dad wouldn't budge. This might have been bearable were it not for another, even more ruthless, reality: neither would the famine! This translates into, "Neither would God!"

Just imagine life there in the tents of the Jacob clan: every day a little more of the grain would be consumed. First one sack, then another, would run empty. And every day, the sun shone hot and the rain never came. Every day their anxiety sharpened. The discipline of God, skillfully orchestrated through Joseph, was silently but irresistibly boring into them. As they watched their hoarded resources slowly but inevitably being used up, they had to suffer a growing apprehension, but not enough to tell the truth.

Why does redemption come so hard? You are looking at the core reason: our hearts are much harder than we ever dare to admit. God is literally turning up the heat, as the sun beats down upon them mercilessly, and still, despite all that pressure, they will not break. One of the hardest truths to recognize is what the Bible says about our hearts before we are redeemed: they are as unbreakable as granite. They are so hard, in fact, that unless God breaks them, they cannot be broken. You and I cannot change our own hearts! (This is also true physically, an obvious fact, which should teach us a deep spiritual truth. A person who needs a heart transplant cannot conduct the operation upon himself. We can remove a sliver from a finger by ourselves, or even set a broken bone if we have to. But no human has ever performed a heart transplant upon their own body.) This truth is foundational to Christianity. You are living in a culture that breezily talks about people having a "change of heart" as casually as people changing clothes. But such changes rarely go deep enough. People may and do have a change of attitude from time to time, and sometimes those changes may even seem transformative, like George Bailey's in "It's A Wonderful Life." But it is one thing to change an attitude or a perspective; it is quite another to change the basic orientation of the human heart. We cannot change our hearts, any more than a leopard can change its spots (Jeremiah Jer. 13: 23).

Consequently, God's approach to our hearts is not to repair them; it's to remove them. It's not to put in a stint here or a new valve there, but to have them out! It's nothing less than a total heart transplant. That is just how radical real redemption is. When David was forced by his pastor, Nathan the prophet, to face up to the depth of his double sin of adultery and murder, he finally came to a very unsettling realization: he needed a whole new heart. And so he pleaded with God to actually create inside of him a completely pure heart. It was one of the largest "asks" he ever made of God. His sin opened his eyes to a very unsettling fact: that, in truth, he had been born with a spiritual heart defect. He put it this way: "Surely, I was sinful at birth, sinful from the time my mother conceived me" (Psalm 51: 5). When a person finally is brought to the point where they begin to wonder if perhaps their misconduct, their addictions, their moral collapses are due to something more than poor parenting, peer pressure or growing up in a tough neighborhood, but actually come from somewhere as deep as their own hearts, it's the beginning of their new life. They are slowly turning onto the road that will lead to their redemption.

But Joseph's brothers have yet to make that slow, agonizing turn. They need tougher discipline. They need to be put through hell itself to guide them onto the path to heaven. So, they will be forced to face that harsh man one more time. If they thought their first encounter was an ordeal, they are in for something far worse. Joseph has been thinking, and he has cooked up (literally) a way to finally slowly break them. The plan he has been given will be so devastating it will finally shatter them. And from those broken pieces, God will redeem this family and craft them into a nation that will, in time, bless the whole world. It's His way. It's a way you never would have guessed.

CHAPTER 14

Kindness: Redemption's Spring

Read Genesis 43

ho would have ever imagined that redemption can spring from simple acts of kindness? This chapter just might open our eyes to its mysterious power. For kindness is a power. It not only surprises our enemies; it disarms them. This chapter invites us to watch the power of kindness at work. It's a hint pointing to a far greater kindness up ahead:

> At one time we too . . . lived in malice and envy, being hated and hating one another. But when the kindness and love of God our Savior appeared, he saved us, not because of righteous things we had done, but because of his mercy. He saved us through the washing of rebirth and renewal by the Holy Spirit, whom he poured out on us generously through Jesus Christ our Savior. (Titus 3:3–6a)

Wherever you find a story of redemption, look for kindness. It's always there.

However, chapter 43 begins on what appears to be a very unkind note: *Now the famine was still severe in the land.* Slowly but surely, the heavy hand of God kept bearing down on the brothers: soundlessly (famines are eerily quiet), and ever so relentlessly. More and more wells dried up. Gaping cracks appeared in the parched ground. Bushes withered. Animals collapsed. Grain sacks ran empty. Finally father Jacob tells his sons to go back to Egypt. He made it sound so easy, so simple: just run this little errand for me over to Egypt, and "buy us a little more food."

But there was nothing quick or simple about it, as he surely well knew. Son Judah stepped forward to burst his bubble. There were high stakes involved in making another trip: a weighty condition had to be met. They would not even be allowed access to "the man" unless brother Benjamin was with them. So Judah gave his father an ultimatum: if you let Benjamin go, we go; and if you don't, we don't. Father Jacob whines, "Well, why did you tell the man you had a younger brother?" Judah patiently explains: "He interrogated us. He demanded to know all about our family. We had no idea that he would require us to bring our younger brother to him!" But Judah could see his father shaking his head. So he stated the case forcefully: if Jacob held on to Benjamin, it most surely would lead to the death of all his sons, all their wives, all of his grandchildren, and even Jacob himself. Almost seventy people would perish, and just for Benjamin?

Moreover, he said, "I will personally guarantee his safety!" Isn't that ironic? He was the one who, twenty-two years earlier, had persuaded his brothers to sell Joseph into slavery! *He* is going to guarantee Benjamin's safety?

But it is possible that Judah had changed as he watched his father grieve all those years. Surely he could see that it very well could slaughter Jacob to lose Benjamin. So, in the strongest terms, he pledged to safeguard the boy: he would take personal responsibility to guarantee his return. That pledge plays a key role in the next chapter. It will lead to one of the most eloquent pleas by one person for the ransom of the life of another to be found anywhere in the entire Bible.

He spoke forcefully because he could see the titanic wrestling match going on inside his father. This is not the first time Jacob wrestled with God in the face of what seemed like certain disaster. Years before, at the river Jabbok, he faced his estranged brother Esau coming at him with four hundred armed men. Dreading the possibility of losing everything he owned, including his entire family, he had spent a full night wrestling with God. He had prevailed then, and his name had been changed from Jacob to Israel, meaning, "You have struggled with God and with men, and have overcome."

There is a little detail worth pondering here: the name change. In chapter 42 Moses called him "Jacob," but in chapter 43, he calls him "Israel." Notice that. By this new name, Israel had been given one of the greatest comforts available to any human being: *it is possible, even when we find ourselves wrestling with God, to experience a kind of "prevailing" or "overcoming" with God.* How can that be? Think wrestling. Is there any sport in which two people grip each other more tightly than wrestling? When we wrestle with God, we are putting a vise grip on God, and that deep clinging to God, strangely, is its own blessing. For is not God himself our greatest good? So Jacob, holding God in an iron grip and refusing to release him, now behaves as Israel: because he will not let God go, he binds himself to God and God to him. As a result of that precious union, he is able, finally, to release his most cherished human treasure.

This is a vital truth; you may well experience it at some point in your life when you lose something you treasure deeply, or sense that you are about to lose it. So often the very people who have found themselves being pushed deeper and deeper into knowing the goodness of God are those who, paradoxically, seemed to have experienced his non-goodness! Why does God allow us to be put in such binds? Strangely, this is his way of curing our anxieties. *Our anxiety is directly proportional to the vulnerability of those things in our lives that bring us our greatest joy.* Jacob's greatest joy right now was Benjamin. No wonder his anxiety spiked over the very thought of letting him out of his sight! God is prying Benjamin loose from Jacob's iron grip, only, truth be told, to give him, the wrestler, an even tighter grip on his one and only truest joy: Himself. God is nudging him back to that level of blessedness he received at Jabbok when he would not let God go!

Forced by circumstances he cannot change and realizing he has no other option, Israel finally relaxes his grip and "sacrifices" his "only" son. I wonder: might he have remembered the family history here? After all, is not this the very same path of sacrifice by which his own father Isaac returned safely home from Mt. Moriah?

Still, notice something utterly pathetic as Israel, always the schemer, tries to appease "the man." He tells his sons to present him with a gift of the best stuff they can scrounge up in their withered land: "a little balm and a little honey, some spices and myrrh, some pistachio nuts and almonds," plus double the silver to prove they were not thieves. Such little things! Such measly amends! This small stuff has no power to atone for the great wickedness of these boys. I am grateful Moses included this part of the story, because it demonstrates the impotence of gratuitous gifts to effect redemption. It also alerts us to a sobering reality: just how pathetic so many of our human efforts at redemption actually are. When we do something as egregious as these boys did to their brother, it's laughable to think that "a little balm and a little honey" is going to make things right! Their redemption will demand something far weightier: ten shattered hearts.

Once they have the green light, they waste no time. They "hurry" down to Egypt and promptly present themselves to Joseph. Joseph was ready. He has already designed the reception he is going to give them. As soon as he sees them in the queue and then notices that Benjamin is with them, his plan kicks into action. He immediately instructs his steward to guide them to his own home, slaughter an animal, and prepare a feast.

Joseph, filled with divine wisdom, sees his measures during their first visit had barely dented their hard hearts. He has been shown the perfect plan for shattering their pride and bringing them to that place of brokenness that will finally enable him to extend to them the forgiveness he has been longing to lavish upon them.

So, just what might it be? What does it take to finally melt hearts, shatter pride, and put us on our knees as supplicants? *This is the great redemption question.* What does it take to finally break us habituated sinners? What does it take to finally strip away all our illusions and compel us to face up to the unwelcome truth about our own profound moral flaws? More harsh talk? More time in prison? More ultimatums? What does it take to lead a guilty person, deep into denial, to finally admit to the truth? How many parents, judges, teachers, and counselors have struggled with that question!

Many answers run along this line: give them a taste of hell. Make life as miserable as possible for them. Throw the book at them. That'll teach them! Unless and until they "hit bottom," they will never turn and find salvation. Make them reap what they have sown. Make life as bitter for them as they made it for others. Perhaps then they will finally "come around."

Aside from the possibility that such an approach is easily infected by our own lust for revenge or, even at best, compelled by the need to honor the demands of justice that offenders pay for their crimes, the question still remains: does this approach actually *redeem* sinners? Does it have the power to break a hardened heart?

I have no doubt that you, my readers, will find yourselves *agonizing* over this question, if you haven't already. People will hurt you. They will let you down. They may even turn on you. *You* will be treated the way Joseph was treated by his brothers. It hurts when strangers hurt you, but it *stings* when friends or family do. The closer your relationship to this person, the deeper your pain will be. More than once David describes this kind of trauma, the worst of all the injuries he ever suffered, in his psalms, such as Psalm 55:

> If an enemy were insulting me, I could endure it;
> If a foe were raising himself against me, I could hide from him.
> But it is you, a man like myself, my companion, my close friend,
> With whom I once enjoyed sweet fellowship as we walked with the throng at the house of God. (vv. 12–14)

How do you turn someone like that around, if you even care to try? Might kindness be the answer?

This was the strategy Joseph devised (or, more likely, was shown): he would shower them with lavish kindness and then, against that backdrop of generous hospitality, help them see their ugliness. He decided to pour all kinds of goodness and favor over them and treat them like dignitaries; then, suddenly, he would expose them as responding like scoundrels and thieves. What better way to finally shame them than to first shower them with lavish kindness? What better way is there to show an evil man the depth of his evil than by exposing it *as a response to a great and beautiful good?* Is not this right at the very heart of what God did on the cross? The cross is the ultimate display of the kindness of God, and that act of immense kindness has the power to break the hardest heart. One hymn writer described it this way:

> Alas! and did my Savior bleed
> And did my Sov'reign die?
> Would He devote that sacred head
> For such a worm as I?
> Was it for crimes that I had done
> He groaned upon the tree?
> Amazing pity! grace unknown!
> And love beyond degree!
> Thus might I hide my blushing face
> While His dear cross appears,
> Dissolve my heart in thankfulness,

And melt my eyes to tears. (Isaac Watts, 1707)
Kindness melts hearts.

And so the brothers, nervously awaiting their turn to meet "the man," are approached by the steward and informed that they were to follow him to the house of Joseph. They were terrified, fearing that once they arrived at the man's personal compound, they would be attacked, overpowered, seized, enslaved, and robbed! Isn't that a case of déjà vu? Perhaps you will remember how they treated Joseph twenty-two years earlier when he had approached them at Dothan. Don't miss the near match here: the action verbs used to describe what they did to Joseph then ("stripped," "took," "threw," "sold") almost perfectly match what they feared would now be done to them ("attack," "overpower," "seize").

Certain they were about to be detained because of a terrible misunderstanding, they went up to the steward and tried to explain that they were not thieves, that they had paid, that they had been as surprised as anybody to find their money in their sacks—the exact amount!—and that they had brought it all back, and that they now had extra money to buy new food, and that they had no idea how that money ever got into their sacks, and that . . . and that . . . and that . . . Oh, how busy they were, protesting their innocence!

They were completely taken aback by the steward's strange answer, along these lines: "What are you worried about? Relax, men. Everything's cool! The money? It must be that your God, the God of your father, decided to give you a special treasure! I got your money! No problem!"

God? The God of our father? Come again? Is this pagan suggesting to us that *our* God was behind all that treasure? He's talking exactly the way we did at the time! How could this steward possibly know that when we ourselves first discovered that money in our sacks our first question was, in fact, "What is this that God has done to us?" He doesn't even know our

God, and yet here he is, repeating what we ourselves said! How could he divine such a thing? (Remember what's coming: a cup of divination!)

But before they even had time to sort it all out, to their surprise and great joy, there was Simeon, released and free! What a wonderful omen! And then they were told that their donkeys would be fed while they were to prepare themselves for a special feast with "the man." Water was provided. Feet were washed. They were ushered into the house. There, they carefully prepared the gifts they had brought to appease him.

At noon, Joseph arrived. They respectfully presented to him the gifts they had carried all the way from Canaan. (Once again, do notice a small detail here: one of the gifts was myrrh, which just might alert you to another time, centuries later, when travelers, also from the east, presented this same gift, fit for a king, to a child who would be king. Might this be a harbinger of that day when the true Joseph would finally appear upon the earth?) Joseph, perhaps to their great relief, accepted their gifts. And then they all prostrated themselves before him.

They had to be surprised at Joseph's demeanor. The harsh tone was gone. Instead, he seemed genuinely concerned for them. He asked them if they were all well, and then, right after that, asked if their father was well. Did they notice the unusual tone of concern when he asked about their father? They assured him that he was not only still alive but healthy as well. And once again, they bowed low to pay him more honor, perhaps trembling with apprehension. What would "the man" do next? Would that harsh voice erupt at any moment? They had to be on edge.

But when they looked up, they noticed that he was gazing at Benjamin. Indeed he was. For there, in his very presence, was his only true brother, the only other son of their common mother, Rachel. It had been twenty-two years since he had seen him last. Joseph was just seventeen at the time, and Benjamin younger than he. Now he was a grown man, likely in his mid-thirties. Joseph's heart began to beat wildly. It was all he could do to restrain his tears enough to ask them if the young man he was noticing was in fact the one they had told him about. He didn't even give them time to answer. He knew it was Benjamin. And he knew too that they all had to be extremely anxious over what might happen to "the boy." Benjamin himself may have been trembling, knowing that "the man" had demanded his presence and that "the man" was not beyond throwing people into jail. What dread had to be in that room! Yet what came out of "the man's" mouth? A blessing! Suddenly, his voice soft and tender, gazing full into his face, Benjamin heard "the man" say to him, "God be gracious to you, my son." Then, curiously, "the man" quickly exited the room. Baffling!

If you could have followed Joseph into his private quarters, Moses tells us that you would have watched a fully-grown man sobbing uncontrollably. Filled with joy at learning that his father was still alive and thrilled at the sight of his very own brother, his tears reveal how precious his entire family was to him, and especially Benjamin. His own mother had died giving birth to him. And now here he was, right under his own roof! It was just too much. And so after a good cry—a very good cry—he composed himself, washed his face, and, once again adopting the façade of a high official, reentered the dining room. With a tone of authority, he ordered that the food be served.

And so it was. Keeping up the charade, he ate in a separate area by himself. But if they had looked closely, they would have noticed a curious thing: he was actually eating *all* by himself. The Egyptians were not eating with him either. Why wasn't Joseph eating with the rest of his staff? If they had been alert, they just might have picked up on the clue and begun to wonder. It slipped right by them.

Joseph had given two secret orders to his steward. One had to do with the seating of his brothers in the dining area. He gave the list of their names, in the order of their ages, to his steward, who then placed them in exactly that order. They stared at each other in mystified astonishment. What are the chances this could have happened accidentally? Baffled, they had to wonder how the steward could have possibly known. The question hung in the air, unanswered. And only later might they possibly have caught on, for the very next day they would learn that this Egyptian ruler had a silver cup he used for *divination!* Could it be that he also learned the order of their ages from that cup? If they made that connection, it would have made them realize that the theft of that cup was grave indeed. Indeed, perhaps Joseph wanted them to make that very connection to terrify them all the more as they may have wondered about the power of that cup: might it have exposed all their secrets? What did "the man" really know?

The second order was that Benjamin was to be conspicuously favored during the banquet: his portions of food were to be five times those of any of the other brothers. Surely you can figure out what Joseph is up to here! He's testing them, even *baiting* them. He's watching to see if this inflammatory display of lopsided favoritism would produce the same revulsion against Benjamin that a richly embroidered coat had triggered against himself all those many years earlier. He is looking for signs of that old enmity against Rachel's brood. If it arose, he would soon know. For he had already designed the perfect opportunity for them to express that resentment by ridding themselves of Benjamin the way they had disposed of him all those many years ago! It would come the very next day.

But, says Moses, there was no immediate sign of the old antipathy among any of them as they watched Benjamin savor his huge portion. Instead, they all began to actually relax and even enjoy themselves. Moses puts it this way: "So they feasted and drank freely with him." Their anxieties melted away as they savored the delicious food and drank their fill of fine wine. The harshness in the ruler seemed to have lifted like a fog burned off by the sun. And with all this kindness being shown to Benjamin, their greatest apprehension—that perhaps he might be held back and even imprisoned, as Simeon had been—began to ease as well. For the ruler even seemed to *like* Benjamin. Surely, he would never think of him as a spy! And so it was that they relaxed all the more. Ah, they may have thought, this just might end up being a piece of cake. Tomorrow we will be on our way back home, Benjamin in tow and donkeys groaning under sacks crammed with food, with a wonderful report for father. I'm thinking they slept well that night!

The beauty of Joseph's lavish kindness had warmed all their hearts. This would now become the backdrop against which the true condition of their hearts would be tested . . . and revealed.

CHAPTER 15

Broken

Read Genesis 44:1—13

L ittle did Joseph's brothers know what was happening out in the barn
area even as they were awakening from their sweet slumber. The steward had been busy. He had been implementing a specific order Joseph had
secretly given to him. Once all the sacks had been packed with as much
grain as they could possibly hold, and (again) all the brothers' silver had
been returned and stashed in the mouth of each of their sacks, a very significant detail was to be executed. The steward was to place Joseph's cup—the
silver one, mind you!—in the mouth of Benjamin's sack. Then, the mouths
of all the sacks were to be tied up tightly and the sacks loaded onto the
donkeys, so that the only thing the men would need to do after breakfast
was to simply be on their way without having to inspect a thing. So it was
ordered, and so it was done.

Morning came. The brothers awoke. Likely they were given a hearty breakfast, and then were warmly sent on their way. Mission accomplished! What
a relief they must have felt as they strode out of Joseph's compound, hit
the road, and briskly picked up the pace to get back home. Whatever fear
they had felt had turned out to be unfounded. The harsh ruler had been
surprisingly kind, even hospitable. Why, they had been his honored guests

and even stayed the night at his own house! And now, at break of day, they were safely on their way home. Simeon was right there with them. Every sack was packed with grain. The donkeys were fresh, ready for the road. And most of all, the risk of possibly losing Benjamin had turned out to be nothing—nothing at all! What wild joy must have filled their caravan that morning as the sight of Joseph's compound slowly receded in the distance. They were flying high!

But what was that cloud of dust fast approaching them from the rear? Could it be a chariot? Why was that horse pulling it so furiously? And who was in that chariot? Why, it was the man's steward, the one who had been so kind to them just yesterday! They recognized him immediately. What might he want? A slight shiver of fear popped their bubble of euphoria as he pulled up alongside them. He wasn't smiling. One look at his face, and it was obvious: he was enraged! And when he spoke, his words were sharp. The tone of his voice immediately reminded them of the harsh tone they had heard from his master on their first trip. Suddenly, a wave of apprehension swept over all of them. Now what?

They didn't need to wait long. The steward had a piercing question for them: "Why have you repaid good with evil?"

Just seven words. But seven words that summed up the core of their great sin against Joseph twenty-two years earlier. Just seven words, and yet they contained an indictment crashing down upon them, I might suggest, from heaven itself.

Think about it. Isn't this the heart of the charge God has with humanity? Isn't this the heart of the charge he issued against Adam and Eve in the wake of their reckless disobedience in the garden of Eden? God had been nothing but good to them, providing them with a banquet of fruit from every tree in the garden but one. The invitation had been generous indeed: "You are free to eat from any tree of the garden" (Gen. 2:16). And yet their response, instead of gratitude, had been a desire for something more. All through the Bible, this is the heart of the quarrel God has with us: he has showered us with good, but our response has often been warped by another desire. In the Old Testament, he led them to a land of milk and honey; they turned away to worship their idols. In the New Testament, it is the argument Paul used to draw the people in Lystra to end their idolatry and turn their hearts to "the living God." Here is the case he made: "In the past, he let all nations go their own way. Yet he has not left himself without testimony: He has shown kindness by giving you rain from heaven and crops in their seasons; he provides you with plenty of food and fills your hearts with joy" (Acts 14:16–17).

In other words: God has been so deeply kind to us, but the power of evil at work within us, fostering simple ingratitude at best to rebellion at the worst, corrupts our response. In the case of the brothers, Joseph's goodwill mission back in chapter 37 to look after their welfare had been met with a brutality that nearly had him killed. That reception is a picture of the one Christ himself received. Though he went about doing immense good, his country's leader slaughtered him. Yes, the question is timeless: Why have you repaid good with evil?

But the steward knows the brothers have no idea why he is making this charge against them. So he assaults them with another question, even more ominous: "Isn't this the cup my master drinks from and also uses for divination?"

This is one unsettling question! The steward throws it out over their heads. It hangs there in the air and slowly begins to settle down on all of them, like particles of dust. They look at each other, totally baffled, wondering, "What might this mean? Cup? Divination? How much does 'the man' really know?"

And then the steward came out with a flat-out indictment, as if there was no doubt about their guilt, as if they had already been weighed in the balances and found wanting—as if, while the master still had the silver cup, it had already revealed to him that a heist by the brothers was in the works, and it would be stolen right out from under his nose! And so, as far as the master was concerned, the verdict was already in and needed only to be read out by the foreman of the jury:

"This is a *wicked* thing you have done."

Wicked? He's saying we've done a *wicked* thing? What a weighty verdict!

And indeed it was. There isn't a more solemn term in the Bible to describe something evil. The word is used only eight times in the entire book of Genesis, but the brothers would likely have recognized it, especially Judah, because it was used to describe each of his two sons, Er and Onan (Gen. 38:7, 10). Their behavior was so "wicked," God himself had immediately executed them. This is a heavy word. The word "wicked" puts an evil act into the gravest of all categories, much like our category "aggravated first degree murder." Joseph had carefully selected this word for his indictment, so that the brothers would be shocked, and suddenly brought up short in the face of a most horrible possibility—that they were being charged with a crime that surpassed all other possible crimes.

Their response was forceful. They flatly denied the charge. They came right back at the steward with a question of their own: "Why does my lord say such things?" They wanted him to know his questions and accusation were totally unwarranted and therefore utter nonsense. To them, it just didn't "fit" them at all. How could the master even conceive of such a possibility? Why, they had just enjoyed all his kindness; how in the world was it even possible that they would turn on him and perpetrate a heist like this? No way! This was bizarre. So much so that, with bravado in their voices, they came right back at him with a forceful claim of complete innocence:

Look here. We would never, ever think of doing a thing like that. Why, look at the record: it speaks for itself. We returned to you the silver we found in our sacks on our first trip here, so it makes no sense at all that we would turn right around and try to steal anything—silver or gold—from your master's house. Why would we do a thing like that? How can you possibly justify a charge like this after the honesty we displayed to you? You tell us!

They didn't even give the steward a moment to answer. They were so cock-sure of their innocence that they came out with a rash verdict for the guilty party, if one was found: "If any of your servants is found to have it, he will die, and the rest of us will become my lord's slaves."

Right here we have the reason why redemption comes so hard. This is a picture of just how deeply entrenched we can be in our illusions of innocence. Self-righteousness is our natural default when our behavior is questioned. It's rare for any of us to quickly admit how we have been at fault. It still is, even at the highest levels of corporate, governmental, or institutional malfeasance. For someone to step forward and immediately admit their wrongdoing is as rare as snow in the Sahara.

Now, to be fair to Joseph's brothers here, they were in fact quite innocent of this specific crime for which they were being charged. They had not stolen Joseph's silver cup; they had been framed. The damning evidence for the charge had been planted in Benjamin's sack; they had had nothing to do with it. But when we broaden out the picture, we see the old history of how they had stolen, not a cup, but a *person*; and they stole it, not from a foreign lord but from their own *father*, by taking from him his one beloved son and selling him off into slavery. The charge being leveled against them is there-fore actually more than justified. This false charge is a minor league version of the true charge, the major league wickedness of the theft of their very own brother from their very own father's embrace. Stealing a cup from a stranger is peanuts compared to stealing a son from a father! What Joseph was doing here was framing their true guilt in such a way that they could now finally be led to see it for the horrific deed it actually was. The "heist" of the cup is a symbol of their ancient sin.

But they were oblivious to their real guilt. Right now their focus was on the gnat, not the camel (Matt. 23: 24). They were so centered on the charge at hand, it never occurred to them that this accusation was merely an illustration, a kind of anti-sacrament of their once utterly graceless act. They just didn't catch on that Joseph was painting a picture for them of that old, old sin.

The steward quickly softened their grandiose offer. It was as if he said, "No, such a severe punishment will not be necessary. My master is not a cruel man, for, as you may or may not remember, he told you he feared God and therefore released all of you from prison during your first trip here. No, he is not a hard and graceless man. His punishment will be much more restrained. He will allow every innocent brother to proceed on home. Only the guilty one will be retained. And even he will not be executed. He will simply be sentenced to serve the Master as a servant. My master has far more grace than you do. He would never treat you the way you just offered to be punished. You don't know him! You don't know him at all."

So we now witness a scene of high drama. The brothers are so self-righteous they actually help the steward in his hunt for the evidence: they quickly lower all their sacks from the backs of the donkeys and set them down on the ground. They even open them themselves, as if to say, "Look for yourself—you won't find a thing." So the steward begins the investigation. And once again, he proceeds methodically, checking each bag in the order of the brothers' ages. He reaches his hand down deep into the grain at the top of Reuben's sack. He feels around, as if he is trying to locate the cup, even though he knows very well it's not there. It's all part of the carefully designed charade meant to clobber the brothers with the greatest impact once the cup is finally exposed. After thoroughly checking every nook and cranny of the sack, he comes up empty. No silver cup. The brothers smile. They knew it wasn't there.

The slow drama plods forward. Next, he goes through the same deliberate process with Simeon's sack, reaching deep down into his sack and feeling all around. He wasn't in a hurry. In fact, he likely was intentionally slow, prolonging the process, building up the brother's illusion of their innocence. He wanted the final revelation to be as shocking as possible for, no doubt, his master had warned him that these were hardened men. And so, after another agonizingly long search, he came up empty. No silver cup. Once again, the brothers smiled. They knew he wouldn't find a thing!

So, on to Levi. Again, the same arduous process. Again, the steward came up empty. No silver cup. Again, the smug smiles. But the steward was in no hurry. He was biding his time. He knew he would find the cup in Benjamin's sack. But the brothers still weren't ready yet for the exposure. He knew that he had to heighten every bit of pride, smugness, and arrogance in the hearts of the brothers so that when he finally shattered it, they would be utterly devastated. And so the agonizing pace of the investigation continued through the sacks of Judah, Dan, and Naphtali. It was all so thorough, so meticulous, so exasperatingly methodical. Then, on to Gad, Asher, Issachar, and finally Zebulun. After perhaps as long as twenty-two agonizing minutes (?!), ten innocent sacks sat on the ground. Each one had been opened. Each one had been thoroughly searched by the long arm of the steward. In each and every case, nothing had turned up. And all this time, the brothers had become more and more cock-sure of the baselessness of the charge that had been laid against them. And now just one sack remained, and they all knew that Benjamin was no thief. Surely, they would soon be on their way, completely exonerated.

The tie around the mouth of Benjamin's sack was slowly loosened. The mouth of the sack was spread open wide. And there, glistening in the sunlight, lay the silver cup! The steward raised it up and displayed it to the brothers. It hung in the air, this damning evidence not one of them could deny, soundlessly shattering all their pride, piercing their consciences, and, without uttering a single word, indicting every last one of them. Every one of them was cut to the heart.

And then the sound of ripping fabric, as each of them began to tear the very cloaks they were wearing. This is how people in that culture expressed their dismay in the face of tragedies that tore up their worlds—they tore up their clothing, as if to symbolize the profound disruption the tragic news had caused. This is how they demonstrated how their worlds were "coming apart at the seams." This is what they had seen their father do when they had presented him with the blood-stained robe they had torn off Joseph twenty-two years earlier—he had torn his clothes while they stood there watching, stone-faced, unmoved (37: 34). And now that same shredding had come around full circle.

There is a great moral principle at work here: what you do to others will most surely end up being done to you. This is an inescapable law. The culture around us calls it *karma*. The Bible puts it this way: "A man reaps what he sows" (Gal. 6:7b). What you do to others will be done to you—for better or for worse. David described this in Psalm 7:15–16: "He who digs a hole and scoops it out falls into the pit he has made. The trouble he causes recoils on himself; his violence comes down on his own head."

That is what we are watching at this very moment in our story. They had stripped Joseph's cloak off from him twenty-two years earlier. Now they are stripping off their own cloaks and tearing them up. It's exactly what we say today: *What goes around, comes around.* The very heart of the gospel, however, is that we are spared the ultimate consequences of our own "bad karma." The Bible describes that gift like this: "God made him who had no sin to be sin for us, so that in him we might become the righteousness of God" (2 Cor. 5:21). Grace upends karma!

The next sentence is the climax of the entire story. You might think the climax comes when Joseph finally reveals himself to them in 45: 3. There's no doubt that verse is the *emotional* climax of this high drama. But the *redemptive* climax is right here: "Then, they loaded their donkeys and returned to the city" (44: 13b).

Repentance is the first sign that redemption is right around the corner. What is repentance? Simply, it is turning around. Repentance begins in the heart, but the proof is in the act—they literally loaded up their donkeys, turned them around, and began the slow journey back to face "the man." No one repents without some kind of reverse over a behavior in their life. The alcoholic drives *past* the tavern instead of turning in. The student hits the books instead of wasting another hour in the coffee shop. The tax evader begins to pay his taxes again, in full, plus the penalty. The great test of all repentance is this: will this person turn their behavior *around*?

That is the great question here. Would the brothers abandon Benjamin? After all, the steward had just told them that only the person in whose sack the cup was found would be detained, and the rest were entirely free to return home with full sacks. This was their chance to finally be rid of the second favorite brother. Had they not just chaffed one more time at seeing him favored over all the rest of them? He had been served five times as much food as any of them. Besides, just before they had left home on this trip, had not their father described him as "the only son he had left"? How galling! Were they not all sons too? Did they not count just as much? No, they didn't, and that hurt. So here was their chance: send Benjamin back, tell Dad the truth (that he had been caught stealing), and just let the chips fall where they may. Finally, they would come into their own as Jacob's legitimate children! It was high time this evil of favoritism finally was given its due!

The fate, not only of Benjamin, Jacob, or even Joseph, but of the entire family hung in the balance. The fate of a nation that would arise out of this family, and which was destined to be a blessing to the entire earth, hung in the balance at this moment on that road a few miles outside of Joseph's compound! This is a critical moment in the entire story of redemption, for, truth be told, the fate of the redemption of the entire world hung on this one moment here on the road from Egypt to Canaan. What would these brothers do?

Wondrously, they turned around! Why? Why was it that, at this moment, they finally broke? *What was it that finally turned the tide*? We will find out soon enough. Judah will reveal it to us. He will be the one who speaks for all the brothers. He will describe the one unbearable cross that had finally shattered all their stubborn hearts. What might it be?

Could it be nothing less or more than breaking the heart of a father, longing for a son to come home?

CHAPTER 16

The Heart of Repentance

Read Genesis 44:14–34

I grew up in a family with eight children. Like all kids, we misbehaved. When my father was gone to work, my mother had the task of bringing us to repentance.

Repentance is painful, much like childbirth; yet its consequences, also much like childbirth, are invariably beautiful. We are about to see how the repentance of Joseph's brother's will not only reconcile them to Joseph—it will heal an entire family! This family, which has been so broken for so long, will undergo an astounding transformation. They will not only be reunited. They will flourish as they have never flourished before. And, in the long run, through them the entire world will be blessed.

Repentance is one of the most powerful forces upon the face of the earth. Hearts broken by repentance can transform a life, a family, a church, a college campus, a corporation, and even an entire country. During the First Great Awakening from 1730 to 1745, virtually the entire eastern seaboard of the United States experienced a much-needed moral cleansing, and it was largely because of the power of repentance. You can watch a video about it, titled "America's First Great Awakening," here: www.youtube. com/watch?v=n-dk4-HBNWQ.

If you have a hard time changing something wrong in your life you know you need to change, very likely the reason is this: you have not truly repented of it.

My mother, Julia Koeman, knew the power of true repentance. Like so many moms, she did all in her power to develop it in her children. One of her main tools was the hallway closet.

Might I describe this repentance factory to you? It was rather small, about four feet wide and six feet long. It was musty because all our coats hung there. It was crowded because the vacuum cleaner and all the brooms rested on the floor. It was dark. There was a light bulb fixture on the ceiling, but no light switch on the wall. The light was turned on by a pull string, and my mother made sure that pull string was so short none of us kids could reach it. Most of all, that closet was lonely. Once that door was shut, we were cut off from everything that made life lively. It was so dead in there! Looking back, I have to think it was something like being put into a grave.

When we did something seriously wrong, she put us in that closet with admonitions along these lines:

> "Now you sit in there and think about those cruel words you just said to your brother, Kenny."
> "You sit there and think about how you just kicked your sister, Kenny."
> "You sit in there and you just think about that 'D' you got in spelling and how you lied about having done your homework, Kenny."

When athletes break the rules, they get benched . . . or worse. When drivers break the rules, they get tickets . . . or worse. When business people break the rules, they get fined . . . or worse. When we broke the rules, we got the closet. There was nothing worse!

Imagine life for a ten-year-old sitting in that closet. It wasn't just the darkness. It wasn't just the smell. It was the isolation. My mother was not a theologian, but she understood one thing about sin: sin distances us from one another. Sin digs a canyon between people. Sin *separates and then isolates*. When a person sins, they turn into a kind of leper; people avoid them. So, she gave us a taste of what it is like to be a leper, right there *inside* the family home.

We would sit in that closet, which was right on the main floor of our house, and in that darkness, with that stinky odor, we would hear all the happy sounds of the family: my sister Mary practicing her piano lessons, my mom humming a tune as she prepared dinner (and, come to think of it, I think she hummed louder than usual), my brothers laughing together as they played Monopoly. And there we sat, hearing it all, but cut off from every part of it.

After a couple of minutes, I'd start whining, "Can I come out now?" Her answer usually was, "No. You need to think some more about what you did." She knew that repentance—authentic repentance—takes time. It is rarely instant, though in some cases it can be. To get to repentance, you usually have to get past excuses, explanations, blaming others, minimizing the offense, even simply feeling sorry for yourself. It's a long journey from simply being humiliated to actually humbling yourself. For some of us, it takes years. My mother didn't have years, but she did have minutes—lots of them. So she let them do their searching, surgical work, cutting into our consciences. She was helped along by darkness, mustiness, and loneliness, her powerful allies. She wanted to help us experience what I mentioned in an earlier chapter: she wanted us to be "blessed by guilt" (Peck, <u>People of the Lie</u>, p. 71). She wanted, quite simply, to bring us to repentance. She knew that if we repented, we would have a shot, a real shot, at truly changing for the better. She was bent on giving us a priceless gift: the power of repentance to transform our rebellious little hearts.

So, after seven minutes, ten minutes, sometimes fifteen minutes, she would come and open the door just a little. The light would pour in. Fresh air too. It was sweet. She would look at us very intently, studying us. She would ask us hard questions: Do you realize what you did? Are you willing to say, "I'm sorry?" *Do you mean it?* What are you willing to change? What are you going to do to keep this from happening again?

She was searching for authentic repentance. She knew it could transform our lives beautifully, to say nothing of the whole atmosphere in *her* house. And only when she sensed some softness in our hearts—that honest guilt, that "owning up" to the truth, even just a small kernel of it (she was so merciful!)—did the door finally swing wide open, welcoming us back home.

Looking back, I have to think that cultivating repentance was one of my busy mother's top priorities. Why? You don't need to be an expert to find out. Open up the New Testament and you'll see it just pop right out at you:

- It was the first things John the Baptist preached: "Repent for the kingdom of Heaven is near" (Matt. 3:1).

- It was the first thing Jesus preached: "From that time on, Jesus began to preach, 'Repent, for the Kingdom of Heaven has come near'" (Matt. 4:17).

- It was the first thing the disciples preached: "They went out and preached that people should repent" (Mark 6:12).

- It was Jesus's final instruction that "repentance and forgiveness of sins will be preached in his name to all nations, beginning at Jerusalem" (Luke 24:47).

I have to think that my mother knew one thing for sure: if any of her eight kids entered adulthood without ever having learned authentic repentance, they were headed for serious trouble in their relationships with their future spouses, coworkers, and neighbors, to say nothing of their relationship with Almighty God.

Authentic repentance, simply put, has the power to restore our intimacy with God and heal the brokenness in our lives and relationships. The Heidelberg Catechism says it is an exercise involving three steps:

1. Becoming genuinely sorry for sin

2. Hating it more and more

3. Running away from it! (Ursinus & Olevianus, 1975) (Lord's Day 33; Q&A 89)

The ancient Christians practiced repentance as a key element in their daily exercise of spiritual hygiene. They would focus on it as intently as we do on our hair and face in the mirror to get ourselves ready for the day. If you wonder why, may I remind you of what the Heidelberg Catechism says about us? Even the holiest of us, it says, "have only a small beginning of the righteousness that God requires" (LD 44; Q&A 114). There is not a person anywhere, including myself, who does not need to repent, deeply and daily. There are real sins in our lives. They are not trivial. They harm us. They harm other people. They make us dangerous to ourselves and to others. As a result, they grieve God, whose heart laments over the destruction and pain we cause one another. *Our sins do real damage!* The only pathway to repair that damage runs right through repentance.

One of the most detailed passages in the Bible describing repentance is 2 Corinthians 7:8–11. In this passage the Holy Spirit first of all warns us that Satan counterfeits repentance. There is fake repentance called "worldly sorrow." He says it brings death. It will kill you. This is the kind of "repentance" Judas Iscariot had, and it killed him.

- Judas felt sorry, yes.

- He admitted he had done wrong, that he had shed innocent blood when he betrayed Jesus, yes.

- He even tried to return those thirty pieces of silver, yes.

But then he went out and hung himself. He committed suicide. Why? Because his was not authentic repentance. He could only look at the painful consequences of his sin in his own life. It made him look bad. It embarrassed him. He couldn't face the other disciples, much less Jesus. He was only thinking about the damage to his reputation and to his own future. We might sum up worldly sorrow as this: we are sorry, but only because of the painful consequences our behavior has done to our pride, and that's as far as it reaches. It is totally self-centered. It is actually narcissistic.

But there is another kind of sorrow, and Paul calls it "godly" sorrow. It leads to life. It leads to salvation. It brings no regret, because it changes our lives, finally, for the better. It transforms us. We are profoundly changed. This kind of repentance looks outward. It sees the hurt we have caused others and the way in which we have insulted God. We see that our sin is always a sin *against* something or someone, be it a spouse, a neighbor, a child, or, as in Joseph's brothers case, a sibling.

Joseph's brothers have taken the first step toward such repentance: they have turned around. The moment the brothers enter Joseph's house they throw themselves down at his feet, and I think it is fair to assume that they were begging for him to show them mercy through real tears as well as torn cloaks. Are they authentically repentant? We'll find out soon enough.

The very first thing that happens once they come into the presence of Joseph is this: they are subjected, once again, to the harsh side of "the man." For the first words out of Joseph's mouth were not spoken with gentleness. Instead, we can be sure his voice was raised in anger as he barked at them, "What is this you have done?"

There's that same question again, only with a sharper point. During their first return from Egypt, when they had discovered the money in the mouth of one of their sacks on the way home, they had asked, "What is this that *God* has done to us?" But now the question was personal: "What is this *you* have done?" Joseph is leading them to the doorway into authentic repentance: "What have *I* done?" Redemption cannot begin until we are compelled to face up to one of the most difficult realities to admit: saying, "It's me. It's nobody else but me. I am the problem."

As Joseph asks this question, they are likely thinking he is only asking about the silver cup, as if he were confronting them with this question: "How is it that my silver cup is found in your possession; i.e., what is this that you have done?" But the question implies so much more. It spans the whole sordid story of the last twenty-two years: the enmity against Joseph as a teen back at home, the attack on him at Dothan, the stripping off of his richly embroidered coat, the cistern, the sale into slavery, the deceitful cover-up, and all those years of silence as they watched their father cry his heart out. All that history is encapsulated in these six words: "What is *this* you have done?"

And then, to drive home the point, Joseph repeats what the steward has already told them on the road, that he has the power of divination! What a shudder *that* claim must have sent through them. He is telling them that he knew immediately that the cup had been stolen and who did it. And if he knew that, they had to be wondering, what else did he know? What else had the cup told him? Did he know *all* their secrets? He knew about the cup; he knew about their birth order! What else?

We all respect the Bible, but did it ever occur to you that one of its greatest benefits to us is its ability to expose us to ourselves, to strip away the lies we tell ourselves? For that is exactly what God's Word has the power to do. Here is what it claims for itself: "The word of God is living and active. Sharper than any double-edged sword, it penetrates even to dividing soul and spirit, joints and marrow; it judges the thoughts and attitudes of the heart. Nothing in all creation is hidden from God's sight. Everything is uncovered and laid bare before the eyes of him to whom we must give account" (Heb. 4:12–13).

Joseph is claiming that his silver cup, much like the Word of God, is so powerful it can reveal all their secrets. That is the tipping point. They now sense that "the man" knows everything. They also know that "the man" has total power over them. Suddenly this "man" has become the single greatest threat to their very existence. By his power of divination, he can "tell all," and, by the power of his position, he can "punish all." It was a terrifying place. It is this utter humiliation that finally reduces them to penitents, pleading for mercy.

All along Joseph had been softening them up for this moment. All along he had patiently turned up the heat. All along he had wisely crafted dilemmas that slowly began to erode their arrogance and plant the beginnings of a fear of God in them. With great skill, he had executed a plan designed to whittle away at their illusions about themselves and, ever so slowly, plant the flag of truth in their rebel hearts.

If you look back at the story, you can watch their journey toward repentance slowly unfold. And, it is fascinating to me that it develops along the lines of the seven marks of authentic repentance that Paul outlines in 2 Cor. 7:10–11, as if they were actually *stages* of repentance, one building upon the other. (They are actually dimensions, or aspects, of repentance, like the facets of a diamond.)

Paul says they are:

1. Earnestness

2. Eagerness to clear ourselves

3. Indignation

4. Alarm

5. Longing

6. Concern, and

7. Readiness to see justice done

Now notice what happens in the story as the Holy Spirit, working though Joseph's carefully calculated measures of discipline, leads the brothers gradually and unerringly into that most blessed of all places, so perfectly described in the first beatitude of our Lord: "Blessed are the poor in spirit, for theirs is the Kingdom of Heaven" (Matt. 5: 3). Look back at how the Spirit of God gradually crumpled the pride of these brothers to the point where they, through their spokesman, Judah, are now "ready to see justice done."

1. Earnestness

The first sign that we are moving towards repentance, says Paul, is *earnestness*. We get serious about what we have long minimized as "nothing."

Remember the harshness at the first encounter. Joseph's tone was sharp and his accusation serious. Then, jail for three days. Suddenly they realized they were in serious hot water! Then the ultimatum: they could not come back unless they took their brother Benjamin with them to verify their "story." At that point those guys, for the first time in years, showed some *earnestness*. They sobered up. "They said to one another, 'Surely we are being punished because of our brother. We saw how distressed he was when he pleaded with us for his life, but we would not listen; that's why this distress has come upon us'" (42: 21).

That's earnestness.

2. Eagerness to Clear Ourselves

At the same time one of the brothers, Reuben, showed that he was farther along into repentance. He was showing evidence for both the second and third dimensions of repentance Paul describes.

The second element, says Paul, is an "eagerness to clear ourselves." This does not mean an eagerness to excuse ourselves or justify ourselves. This part of repentance is marked by a willingness, on the part of the offender, to "own up" to their part in causing the harm and to make whatever reparations are required in order to make things right again.

Notice how Reuben does this. He takes on something of the role of a prosecutor, and he lets them know in no uncertain terms that they are going to have to "clear" themselves. They are going to have to give a full accounting of their behavior: "Now we must give an accounting for his blood" (42: 22b).

The second mark of authentic repentance is simply this: you realize that you need to come clean, and you want to. You want to finally admit what really happened. You are open to giving a full accounting of what you actually did—no fudging, no excusing, no justifying, no minimizing. You want to expose the whole story, no matter how ugly or sordid it is. You may even long for this. You just want to get it off your chest, because the truth is this: unconfessed sin weighs on our hearts like a sack of cement. We may harden ourselves to its weight. But we never quite stop feeling it. No wonder we say, "Confession is good for the soul." It may be hard to do, but carrying the burden of secret guilt is infinitely heavier.

3. Indignation

Where does a person find the compulsion to finally come out with a confession? One possible source of strength to do so is what Paul calls indignation. This is the third dimension of authentic repentance. It is a very real rage at myself for what I allowed myself to do, whether to myself or to another person. It is a holy contempt that the very Spirit of God arouses in me as I grasp how wicked my offense actually was in the sight of God.

Three days in prison aroused Reuben's anger so strongly that he unloaded on his brothers, right there in front of Joseph. Feel the heat behind these words: "Reuben said, 'Didn't I tell you not to sin against the boy? But you wouldn't listen!'" (42: 22a)

That is indignation. Do you feel the rage there? Unless you and I reach a place where we are incensed at ourselves for the sin in our lives, we are not on our way to real repentance. This is why we don't change. *We're not angry enough at our own misconduct.* We're embarrassed, even disgusted, perhaps. But are we enraged? Other people might be enraged at our behavior, but their rage may or may not arouse ours. We may even be enraged at them for being so enraged with us! It is only when we finally see just how egregious our sin is in the light of God's holiness and find ourselves experiencing a revulsion toward it that we begin to move towards authentic repentance.

One Saturday evening many years ago, when I was a young pastor in Albuquerque (I am ashamed to admit this), I was still up late one Saturday evening watching some dumb show on our little black-and-white TV, and my sermon for the next morning still needed work. Suddenly I came under deep conviction, and a storm of anger at myself welled up inside of me. I was so enraged that I took the TV into the garage and smashed it with a sledge hammer into small pieces and stuffed them all into our garbage can.

The next morning my wife asked me, "Honey, where's the TV?"

I said, "It's in the garage."

She went into the garage to look for it but couldn't find it.

She came back and said to me, "I looked all over the garage, and it's not there!"

I said, "Well, honey, it's actually in the garbage can."

She said, "Garbage can? It doesn't fit in the garbage can."

I simply said to her, "Well, now it does."

This was a very significant moment in my life as a holy anger from the Holy Spirit came over me and compelled me to take immediate action to slay this dragon in my life. We didn't have a TV set for at least a year, and we only got one when we both felt it was finally safe again.

That's "indignation."

4. Alarm

You will remember how Joseph, the skilled prosecutor, did something to test for alarm in his brothers. He put all their money into their food sacks to make it look like they tried to get out of Egypt without paying. He was working on shattering the lie they believed about themselves, that they were "honest" men, by making them look like thieves. And this produced the fourth sign that they were moving towards repentance.

Alarm is a sense of apprehension, even terror, over the damage our own behavior has brought upon ourselves or others. It can happen suddenly, as when texting causes an accident. Or it can happen gradually, as when careless spending habits sink a person more and more into debt. In our story, it hit the brothers hard when one of them found his silver pouch staring him in the face from the mouth of his sack: "Their hearts sank and they turned to each other trembling, and said, "What is this that God has done to us?" (42: 28). Then they got a double whammy of that alarm after arriving back in Canaan. They all opened their sacks, with their father watching over their shoulders. Every man's money had been returned. It was horrifying: "When they and their father saw the money pouches, they were frightened" (42: 35).

Here is the fourth evidence of authentic repentance: you say things to yourself like, "I am beginning to sense that what I have been doing is actually dangerous. If I keep on behaving like this, if I stay on this path, there is no telling what I just might end up doing to myself or to people around me that I care about. This sin in my life, which I thought I had kept covered up and under control, could end up exposed to everyone, creating terrible problems for me, for my family, for my company, for my church, for my town. This is scary. "

Alarm is a powerful gift. When alarm comes, good things being to happen: people quit smoking, doing drugs, gambling, or being unfaithful to their spouses because it dawns on them just how deadly the consequences could be to those they love. This is a vital ingredient in authentic repentance, and you can see how Joseph is working skillfully to trigger it at every turn in the lives of his brothers. And, be assured, there is one pivotal moment of sheer terror still waiting for them.

But all of this was still not enough. The brothers were miserable alright. They were unsettled. Their consciences were beginning to prick them painfully. But they were not yet broken.

It was not until the discovery of the silver cup in Benjamin's sack that the brothers finally display the last three marks of authentic repentance. They turn around, retrace their steps, come into his presence, and fall on their faces. The first words out of the mouth of Judah as their spokesman are full of the fifth quality that is always found in authentic repentance.

5. Longing

Longing is an intense yearning, rising up out of the very core of a person's soul, to finally do whatever they can to repair the damage their sin has caused. It is a consuming passion to not only be rid of the sin that has so long held sway, eradicating it once and for all; it is also an all-consuming desire to repair all the damage that it has caused. This is right at the heart of Judah's first words: "'What can we say to my lord?' Judah replied. 'What can we say?'" (44:16a).

Do you feel the longing behind those words? Can you sense the desperation in his trembling voice as he begs Joseph to tell him and the brothers what they need to do to make things right? Are you picking up on his intense desire to somehow clean the slate? This is longing! It is only when we have been brought to this place of passionate aspiration that we have realized this powerful dimension of authentic repentance.

Then Judah, on behalf of all the brothers, beautifully expresses the sixth mark of authentic repentance.

6. Concern

Concern is birthed in the heart of the penitent when they are finally able to see the gravity of their offense. Their eyes are opened to the true dimensions of the damage they have brought upon themselves or others, and it staggers them. This is what we hear from Judah as he makes his desperate plea to "the man."

He immediately repeats to Joseph the offer he and the brothers had made to the steward. He said to him, "We are now my Lord's slaves—we ourselves and the one who was found to have the cup." Already here we see his deep concern: he will never leave Benjamin behind, and if that means all the brothers need to stay behind, then so be it.

Joseph corrects him. He tells Judah that he would NEVER make such a demand. He is not that hard! He is not that rash! (Do these brothers, who thought nothing of slaughtering an entire city full of men for the sin of just one young man, Shechem, not feel even a twinge of shame at this assertion . . . and by a pagan ruler at that?) He is, after all, a man who fears God! And so he repeats what he believes is a reasonable punishment: only the one who was found to have the cup will become his slave and the rest were free to leave—right now, if they wished.

Here it is again: the great test, the decisive moment, the ultimate examination of the hearts of the brothers. They are being given the perfect opportunity to abandon Benjamin just as they had abandoned Joseph so long ago. Here is their chance to finally rid themselves of the last of Rachel's detestable brood, on whom all the favors of their biased father had always been poured. They had never been loved like her sons; not one of them! Hadn't salt once again been poured into their wound just yesterday? As they sat around that table they had to sit and watch as Benjamin was served *five times as much* food as any of them!

But twenty-two years had passed since they had disposed of Joseph. For twenty-two years they had watched as Jacob would repeatedly break out into loud lament and refuse to be comforted. Judah, and all the brothers, know beyond doubt that if they don't come home with Benjamin, their father will die of grief. This is the heart of his concern. So he pleads for Joseph to hear him out. And then he makes an exquisite appeal, not so much for Benjamin, but for the very survival of his aged father. He narrates the whole story for Joseph in compelling detail.

- Benjamin was deeply loved by his father because he was born to him in his old age and was the only remaining son of his mother because his older brother was dead.

- They had told Joseph on their first trip, when he demanded of them to bring Benjamin, that he could never leave his father, and that, if he was forced to do so, it would kill their father to see him go.

- And then, when it was time to return to Egypt for more food, it was impossible for them to come without that boy because without him (as you yourself insisted, sir), they would not be allowed to see Joseph's face.

- Their father had anguished so painfully over this terrible quandary and told them, once again, how devastated he had been when the boy's older brother was torn to pieces by a wild animal. Therefore, if any harm ever came to him, the second son, and he were bereft of him as well, it would bring his "gray head down to the grave in misery."

- Finally, there was no doubt, since the life of the father was bound up in the life of this son, that if this boy also did not return home, the father would most surely die.

This is not only a passionate, eloquent, and most compelling speech—one of the grandest in all of Scripture—it is so much more. It is actually a picture of how deeply God, our Father in heaven, treasures each one of you who are reading this book, as well as every human being on the face of the earth.

For there is so much more here that meets the eye. When you read the Bible, you need to understand that the gospel as revealed in the New Testament is actually concealed in the Old Testament. If you look closely, you can detect beautiful intimations of it! Consider this now: it is *Judah* who is the one son who steps forward and makes this impassioned intercession. Do you know who is "in" Judah? Do you know who it is that will someday descend from the line of Judah? Of course you do. You might for every Christmas you are reminded that Jesus was descended from Judah when you read the story of the wise men (Matt. 2:6), and in the book of Revelation he is described as "the lion of the tribe of Judah (Rev. 5:5). So, concealed here, but revealed in the New Testament, is something truly magnificent: what we are witnessing here at the feet of Joseph is a preview of Jesus interceding for us! Were you aware that this is exactly what he himself does continually for us in order to rescue us from the power of sin in our lives? Hebrews 7:25 describes it like this: "Therefore he is able to save completely those who come to God through him because he always lives to intercede for them."

What you see Judah doing here is an Old Testament picture of the heart of God toward us. He described the heart of Jacob for Benjamin this way: the father's life was "closely bound up with the boy's life." He was telling Joseph that Jacob treasured Benjamin so deeply that his whole heart was wrapped around that boy in an unbreakable embrace. That is also true for you and me. God's very heart is bound up with us—he treasures us that deeply.

Then Judah told Joseph that if, upon their return, Jacob saw that Benjamin was not with them, it would kill him. Did you ever think that God felt that way about you? Did it ever occur to you that, when Jesus "brings many sons to glory" (Heb. 2:10), if you were missing among those "sons," it would break the Father's heart? We are even more precious to our heavenly Father than Benjamin ever was to Jacob.

Finally, Judah comes out with one more statement that will surely remind you of Jesus. It shows us the seventh mark of authentic repentance as well.

7. Readiness to See Justice Done

Judah is finally brought to such a position of total brokenness that he now demonstrates the seventh evidence of authentic repentance. He expresses a complete willingness to bear in his own body the full consequences of the sin that Benjamin supposedly has committed. In other words, he is fully ready to satisfy the demand of Joseph's justice and serve as Joseph's slave instead of Benjamin. This is a glorious place, because when we get to this level of repentance, we just might be completely surprised. We might discover that no payment is even necessary but that instead forgiveness (as the prodigal son was stunned to learn) is, unknown to us, right around the corner, waiting to pour itself out all over us. When we get to this place, we may be awed to find out that all heaven is about to break loose and the angels are on tiptoe, ready to launch a celebration!

Here is what Judah said:

> "Your servant guaranteed the boy's safety to my father. I said, 'If I do not bring him back to you, I will bear the blame before you, my father, all my life!' Now then, please let your servant remain here as my lord's slave in place of the boy, and let the boy return with his brothers. How can I go back to my father if the boy is not with me? No! Do not let me see the misery that would come upon my Father." (vv. 32–34)

What a change of heart! Judah, the one who twenty-two years earlier proposed that Joseph be sold into slavery to the Ishmaelites for twenty pieces of silver, is now prostrating himself before "the man" and pleading to take the place of Benjamin! What a wondrous transformation is that! Let it sink in! Who would have ever imagined such a change in a man who once consorted with a prostitute and was ready to execute his own daughter in law! (You can read this sordid story in Genesis 38.) The very man who once upon a time couldn't get rid of Joseph soon enough now has been so broken that he can't pay a price high enough just to save Joseph's brother. He is willing to let his wife be bereft of her husband and let his children be fatherless rather than see Jacob bereft of Benjamin. He offers everything he has—body and soul—to rescue Benjamin from a sure and certain life of slavery and to spare his father from a sure and certain death.

Oh, what a holy moment this is! Surely, once again, you will see that this is a perfect parallel to our dear Savior, the Lord Jesus Christ, who did the very same thing for us. If he had not stepped in and offered to be a substitute for us, as Judah did for Benjamin, you and I would have no Savior. We would, in fact, be doomed to slavery our entire lives. Jesus made a powerful statement when he once said, "Very truly I tell you, everyone who sins is a slave to sin" (John 8: 34). That was our fate. The very heart of what Jesus did for us is exactly what Judah offered here. Jesus said to God, *"Please, take me instead."* And God did. Jesus became a slave for us. Paul said so in Philippians 2: 7: "He…made himself nothing, taking the very nature of a servant." And not just any servant. He became a servant who was willing to actually offer up his very life in his death on the cross so that we might be spared from having to face the charge that was against us, just as Judah offered up everything he had to give just to spare Benjamin from the charge against him and its certain consequence: slavery for the rest of his life. Judah was offering himself as a *ransom* for Benjamin, which is precisely how Jesus described what he came here to earth to do for us when he said, "For even the Son of Man did not come to be served, but to serve, and to give his life as a ransom for many" (Mark 10: 45).

This is the heart of the gospel, all laid out for us right here in this one gripping, high-stakes moment. What would Joseph do? Would he accept a substitute? Would he set Benjamin free? Would he spare that father this unbearable grief?

All this time, the boys never knew that they were, in fact, in the presence of someone who loved both Benjamin and their father more than any of them. They did not know that "the man" who seemed so dead set against them *was actually for them and had been all along.* This is the great paradox in the story and in the gospel itself—the God we so much dread is actually full of mercy toward us. This is what is so surprising about the gospel. God is not a judge waiting to punish us but a father waiting to welcome us back home, just like Joseph was a waiting brother, waiting for that precious moment when he could embrace his brothers.

And now that moment has finally come. Joseph now knows that the transformation in the heart of his brothers is real. He knows that the last dark stain of their old animosity toward the children of Rachel has been completely laundered out of their hearts. He knows that they have come under the conviction that God has dealt with them most severely for their sin against their one-time brother (who, even now, they think "is no more"), and that they are now determined to never allow themselves to do such a dastardly thing again . . . ever! And as he hears this plea from Judah, he knows, with a sure and certain finality, that all their hearts have been broken.

It breaks his heart. His tender love for them, which he has had to restrain all this time, comes flooding out! He is filled with an irrepressible delight as he sees plainly that the hearts of these hard men have finally been softened! He is overwhelmed at the beauty and sincerity of Judah's love for his own brother. He is deeply moved.

And he is profoundly gratified. The one change in the hearts of his brothers for which he had longed all these years is now, finally, beautifully, and compellingly displayed right at his feet. We never know if our prayers and our tough love will ever produce the fruit of repentance in the hearts of those for whom we care so deeply. He has to be ecstatic with a holy euphoria!

He cannot hold in his secret any longer. Finally, after twenty-two long years, he is free to let his forgiveness wash over all of them. Finally, he is free to gather each one of them in a bear hug and embrace them as tightly as his arms will allow. Finally, he is free to let them know that all along he has been their waiting brother, longing to call them by their names, hold them, kiss them, and assure them that he has never stopped loving them.

He cannot suppress his love for them any longer. It is surging up from within himself, and it has to come out. It is ready to explode! Oh, how he has dreamed and longed for this moment. Finally, he can take the mask off. He can end the charade. He can set aside all the harshness. The "hallway closet" has done its good work.

The grace in his heart that cared enough about them to discipline them is now ready and eager to show them in its grander side: the grace of a pure and complete forgiveness, and then the restoration of a long-lost friendship. The real banquet is now ready to begin. He, and they, have drunk the cup of suffering to its dregs. It's resurrection time! It took so long to finally get here, and the path was excruciating. But now, finally, the long, hard road to redemption has reached its destination. A family is about to dance with the angels!

CHAPTER 17

The Sweetest Thing I Know

Read Genesis 45: 1 - 24

When redemption finally comes, it is impossibly sweet.

All this time Joseph had steeled himself from revealing his great secret. With an iron will, he had waited until his brothers were fully prepared to receive their redemption. He delayed until he saw the compelling evidence of genuine repentance, the contrite heart David said God would never despise (Ps. 51: 17). When he heard Judah plead to take Benjamin's place, he was certain that the hearts of his brothers were truly broken. Then, he just couldn't hold his grace in any longer. It exploded out of him.

Bursting at the seams, he quickly ordered all of his servants to immediately leave his presence. The first moments of reconciliation are deeply personal and almost private. This is a sacred time between the offended and the offender. A moment like this is not for third parties to gawk at. In due time, everybody would hear about it, but right now this was just between brothers.

Once all the assistants left the room, Moses employs a fascinating way of describing the drama of reconciliation . . . from *outside* the room. He places us in the hallways with Joseph's servants. So we *hear* the reconciliation before we *see* it. And what a sound we hear! The servants, who had watched a very efficient Joseph run his operation with the cool skills of a calm executive, hear loud sobs from inside that room like they had never heard before, and there was no doubt that it was the voice of Joseph. The sound was piercing! The noise of Joseph's bawling from the very depths of his soul reverberated down the hallways. People stopped what they were doing. His cries were alarming. They had never heard him like this. Immediately some of them were dispatched to inform Pharaoh that something very serious, maybe even frightening, was going on in Joseph's chambers.

But they did not know, and they could not have known. For the wailing behind those closed doors was a love that had been pent up for twenty-two years bursting out! This was the mighty sound of a long-ripening joy!

Moreover, this joy is the one joy toward which the whole Bible strains to draw us. This is a pointer to the greatest joy fallen humans like us could ever taste. If it were ever to happen that any one of you turned away from the living God, only to eventually come back home to him, then this is the kind of sound there will be in heaven as well as in your house! This is a clear window into just how God and the angels feel when one sinner repents. You cannot imagine the exhilaration that reverberates through heaven when just one sinner turns their heart toward home. This is the tearful exuberance of an ancient love finally free to lavish itself upon a person who, at long last, is ready to receive it. This is the joyful sound of life's greatest homecoming.

If any of you ever have a child who disowns you only, after what seems like ages of silence, to finally turn his heart back to home, then you—if your love for him has not turned bitter—will experience this exquisite happiness for yourself! There is none greater.

Somehow, between all those heaves of emotion, Joseph was able to finally blurt out what he had so long bottled up: *"I am Joseph! Is my father still living?"*

His brothers may have heard the final five words, but it was the first three that stunned them to the core. The shock of those three words charged into them with such force it "terrified" them. This man is . . . *Joseph?* This man is . . . *our brother, Joseph?* This is the very one we . . . .? Oh, no! The very one we almost killed? Oh, no! Suddenly, they realized the danger they were in. Their secret was out, their cover was blown, and they were fully exposed. There was no place to hide. You can just see them fall backward in utter horror.

We need to freeze-frame this moment and feel the sharpness of the panic that grabs these brothers at this instant. This moment is a preview of another just like it, only on a much bigger stage. Virtually at the very beginning of the book of Revelation, we are told about one of the most frightening aspects of the second coming of Christ back to this earth: "Look, he is coming with the clouds and every eye will see him, even those who pierced him, and all the peoples of the earth will mourn because of him. So shall it be! Amen" (Rev 1: 7).

The return of Jesus on the clouds of heaven will fill the hearts of all those who refused him with such shock and awe that they will call for the mountains to cover them. But there will be no fear greater than the fear of those who pierced him—they will be forced to face him very much alive, and it will terrify them. This is what Joseph's brothers experienced the instant he revealed to them who he was. This moment brought them face to face with the very one they had "pierced" now towering over them from a position of absolute power.

Try to grasp the gravity of this moment: here they were, these hardened, cocksure men, who had proudly refused to own up to the terrible gravity of their own history of murder, cruelty, and deceit, trapped in the presence of the very brother they had so heartlessly eradicated out of their lives years before, standing before them in all of his awesome power as second only to Pharaoh. They were fully exposed and utterly defenseless. This is the place to which they needed to be brought if they were ever to receive redemption. And bringing them to that pivotal place was no easy project. This was the climax of a patient, stern divine providence that gradually lifted Joseph to a place of power and lowered them to a place of powerlessness. It had taken over twenty years for the victim to become the judge and the villains to become defenseless.

Back at the cistern twenty-two years earlier, all the power had been on their side. It had been nine against one, and the one was just a teenager. There they had had him completely outnumbered and totally overpowered, free to bully him, abuse him, and finally dispose of him in any which way they wished. Now, horror of all horrors, the tables were suddenly turned—*big time. All* the power of Egypt was on his side. *He* was the aggrieved party, and if he was as resentful towards them (as he had every right to be, and they knew it!) as they had been toward him long ago, there was nothing to stop him from throwing the book at them and making every last one of them finally pay dearly for that dastardly deed of and all the suffering it had caused him. All of this had to suddenly flash into their minds; no wonder they were scared out of their wits.

In his widely read essay *The Weight of Glory*, C. S. Lewis, determined to take the Bible's teaching on the final judgment at face value, puts the matter like this:

> In the end that Face which is the delight or the terror of the universe must be turned upon each of us either with one expression or with the other, either conferring glory inexpressible or inflicting shame that can never be cured or disguised. I read in a periodical the other day that the fundamental thing is how we think of God. By God Himself, it is not! How God thinks of us is not only more important,

but infinitely more important. Indeed, how we think of Him is of no importance except insofar as it is related to how He thinks of us. It is written that we shall "stand before" him, shall appear, shall be inspected. The promise of glory is the promise, almost incredible and only possible by the work of Christ, that some of us, that any of us who really chooses, shall actually survive that examination, shall find approval, shall please God. To please God . . . to be a real ingredient in the divine happiness . . . to be loved by God, not merely pitied, but delighted in as an artist delights in his work, or a father in a son—it seems impossible, a weight or burden of glory which our thoughts can hardly sustain. But so it is. (Lewis, *The Weight of Glory*, pp. 38–39)

Later on in the same essay, he reminds us that this same inspection could result in the most unthinkable of all horrors, which was clearly taught by Jesus in Matthew 7:23, where he said, "Then I will tell them plainly, 'I never knew you. Away from me, you evildoers!'":

There we are warned that it may happen to anyone of us to appear at last before the face of God and hear only the appalling words, "I never knew you. Depart from Me." In some sense, as dark to the intellect as it is unendurable to the feelings, we can be both banished from the presence of Him who is present everywhere and erased from the knowledge of Him who knows all. We can be left utterly and absolutely *outside*—repelled, exiled, estranged, and finally and unspeakably ignored. On the other hand, we can be called in, welcomed, received, and acknowledged. We walk every day on the razor edge between these two incredible possibilities. (pp. 41–42)

Joseph's brothers are right on that razor's edge. What will he do to them? Will he banish them as they once banished him? Are they about to be lacerated with harsh and livid words, laced with contempt? Are they about to get a taste of what it feels like when someone takes out his murderous revenge upon them, the same way they did, years ago, to all the men of Shechem? Are they about to drink the full cup of his wrath? Will they be executed?

Before they can even plead for mercy, they are amazed to hear Joseph say words they never expected. Tenderly, he said to them, through his tears: *"Come near to me."*

What? Near? He wants us to come close to him? We drove him out; he wants to draw us in? He is not going to denounce us, convict us, and sentence us? He wants us, instead, to come close to him? What is *this*? He is actually beckoning for us to get up off the floor and gather around him? How can this be? They could not comprehend this, but, trembling, they honored his invitation and approached him. For they did not know that the man who called to them was not the kind of man they thought he was. Where they feared they were about to face fury, they were about to discover they would find the most unexpected of all possible dispositions towards them: favor! They were about to learn that they were loved.

This is what grace looks like, and it is *always* a surprise, even a shock. It is the last thing the guilty, shamed, broken villain expects. And yet it is so. This is always how it is with grace. It is the living God inviting us in those moments when we are full of fear, brokenness, and shame to come *close* to him. It is God stretching out his hands to us. It is the same God who has been our prosecutor, confronting and breaking us, now *welcoming* us, to our utter astonishment. It is the last thing we would ever expect. It is the one thing we would never have thought could happen. To be full of shame and still invited to come close? How can it be? (This is why, as C. S. Lewis once pointed out, Christianity is a religion we never would have guessed.) Grace always comes as a surprise! Why? It is because a *truly broken sinner* is so absorbed in how undeserving they are of anything good, and how fully deserving they are to reap the full consequences of their wrong, they just cannot imagine any other consequence than justice. This is why the prodigal son returning home fully expected to only be allowed back, if he was at all, as a slave. The thought that he would be welcomed back with a party never crossed his mind. It was unthinkable! And it is unthinkable to any "fair-minded" person. It is even offensive! Grace runs counter to all our notions of justice.

And yet, the brothers did come close. Trembling, fearful, apprehensive, surprised, and certainly curious, they came up close and gathered around this man who claimed to be their brother, only to hear him tell them something sweeter than anything they could ever have imagined. What he had to say to them is truly "the sweetest thing I know!"

The first thing he did was to confirm to them that, in fact, he actually was who he claimed to be. So he used their very crime to confirm his identity! He said to them, "I am your brother Joseph, *the one you sold into Egypt.*" There! It was out! The details are confirmed, and the facts laid bare. Now there is no doubt, for the truth is that this very thing is exactly what happened all those years ago, over in Dothan. Only Joseph would know that detail. And now that dastardly deed was laid right out in the open! What a shard of pain it must have sent through those eight who did it, and what shock to Benjamin, who was hearing that sordid fact for the very first time.

But quickly, Joseph moved to comfort them. Once again, he made it very plain that they had sold him as a slave, but he immediately went on to set their sin into a much larger scheme of things, a context they never could have imagined: the context of *what God was up to.* One of Joseph's greatest virtues was that he saw God's hand behind everything. Nothing was ever just a free-standing event with no meaning beyond itself. He related everything—*everything*—to God. Therefore, everything was significant. Everything, whether good or bad, had a purpose. Whether a promotion by Potiphar and then the warden, or a dream he interpreted, it made no difference. He had always looked for the hand of God in all of it. He had had plenty of time to put the pieces of the puzzle of providence in his own life together and figure out just what God was up to in all of it. But he had figured it out, and now he explained it all to his brothers in a very simple way: "And now, do not be distressed and do not be angry with yourselves for selling me here [there it is again, a second time, that sordid evil!] because it was to save lives that God sent me ahead of you" (v. 5).

What? To save lives? Our evil was part of a greater good, even a massive good? They had to be curious now. So Joseph patiently laid it all out. He wanted to comfort them with an unimaginable consolation: that what they had done, evil as it was, was actually an instrument of God for immense good! God had permitted them to sell him because God had planned to use that very same wrong to do something so very right. To modern ears, this is a new and unsettling thought! God uses evil? God permits something terrible, even atrocious, to effect something tremendous, even awesome in its beauty? Really? How can that be? Evil is *evil*! Most of the time, nothing good ever comes out of it. What good comes out of genocide, or abortion, or so many of the cruelties of history? What good comes out of the blight of homelessness? Look at all the wars of history—what good has ever come of them? This is a preposterous idea.

Yes, it would seem it is. And that is why I ask you to take a second look. Evil is strong, and its damage is indescribably destructive. Look at the misery Joseph himself suffered. Yet here is the very victim of all that evil rising up and saying that the misery evil causes is *never the whole story!* Good and evil are not equal; good has always been greater than evil and, wondrously, will not only ultimately prevail against it, but—and this is the stunner—*use it*. In fact, if you know the bigger story of the Bible you will, once again, see that what Joseph is telling his brothers here is actually a preview of another evil—the worst evil, in fact, of all—being used to effect a good so great there has never been another greater. This is a preview of what God did through the crucifixion of Jesus Christ.

There has never, in the history of the world, been a more evil crime than the crucifixion of Jesus Christ. For, as Peter said on Pentecost, he was "a man accredited by God to you [his own people, the Jews] by miracles, wonders and signs, which God did among you through him, as you yourselves know. This man was handed over to you by God's set purpose and fore-knowledge; and you, with the help of wicked men, put him to death by nailing him to the cross" (Acts 2:22–23). There have been horrific evils in the history of mankind, some on a massive scale, but none greater than this, for Peter was charging the Jews with nothing less than *murdering a God-attested perfect man*. In the light of the full revelation of the Bible, this was, in truth, *the murder of God*. That is why I say it was history's greatest evil. And yet, that self-same evil was the very instrument through which God himself brought about the greatest good that has ever come to the earth since the creation itself. That good is not just our own forgiveness; it is redemption on a cosmic scale. It is the rescue of the very earth itself from the curse that has enslaved it since the fall of Adam and Eve.

And so, said Joseph, you sold me, one person, into slavery; now, thousands of people are, this very moment, being saved from certain death because of what God allowed you to do. The good that has come out of your evil dwarfs that evil.

Then he went on to inform them of just how critical and momentous this strategy of God was for the entire clan: "For two years now there has been famine in the land, and for the next five years there will not be plowing and reaping. But God sent me ahead of you to preserve for you a remnant on earth and to save your lives by a great deliverance. So then, it was not you who sent me here, but God. He made me father to Pharaoh, lord of his entire household and ruler of all Egypt" (vv. 6–8).

Joseph is gently instructing them in the ways of God. And what a lesson it is. It could be titled: "The Earliness of God," and its point could be stated this way: "God is always ten steps ahead of us—always." (Later on this will become even more obvious when the Bible speaks of God as a shepherd. Shepherds always led their sheep; they were always out in front of them. The sheep only ever followed, which is why, when Jesus calls us to be his disciples, he always puts it this way: *Come, follow me*.) Joseph wants to comfort them in their shame by showing them how God has been way out in front of them, *preserving* them long before they ever knew they would need it.

Then he informs them that the famine is not going to let up. In fact, he informed them, the famine was going to last another five years. Five years! They had been right on the verge of starvation already back home. They never would have lasted another five years. Here is Joseph confirming that death sentence: they most certainly would not have made it. And so he tells them that they have been given a "great deliverance."

But Joseph's greatest concern right now is that his brothers, so shattered by their shame and fear, were overwhelmed. Gently he continues to ease their pain by seeking to comfort them in their brokenness by continuing to teach them a different narrative for what has happened the last two decades. Repeatedly, he describes his presence in Egypt as the result of being *sent* there (vv. 5, 7–8). He repeats it over and over. Why? Twice he had described what they had done: they had *sold* him (vv. 4–5). Now he turns right around, and, in the light of "the earliness of God," he does some historical reconstruction. He looks at the very same event and now redefines it, not as a *selling* but as a *sending*. He is now teaching them how to read history in the light of God's providence. There is more to history than what lies on the surface—there is another story underneath the "facts" we all know. When you look at history from heaven's point of view, you discover that something quite different is going on than what first meets the eye. So Joseph is summoning his brothers to return back to that terrible moment by the dry cistern when they handed him over to the Ishmaelites and teaching them that what they thought was *selling*, which it most surely was from a human point of view, was actually something radically different: it was a *sending*, as far as heaven was concerned. What a stunning revelation this had to be to the brothers. Even now, it had to stagger their imaginations as they tried to "get their head around" this strange reality.

So Joseph spells it out for them in even greater detail. He informs them that, in fact, God used their "selling" him to put him into an even more favored position than the one they had so much resented back at home. Their very act of demotion ultimately resulted in a promotion the likes of which they could only barely imagine:

- First of all, I am "father to Pharaoh." This claim would be ludicrous if it weren't for the evidence staring them right in the face. Joseph was claiming that even the mighty Pharaoh looked to him as a father, that is, as both a provider and a guide. In effect he was saying that this is the fulfillment of his second dream as a seventeen-year-old. In his first dream, sheaves of wheat bowed before his sheaf, picturing his role locally, as master over his own family. But in his second dream, all the powers of the heavens bowed down to him, picturing his position on a cosmic scale in Egypt, where the sun is worshiped as a divinity.

- Then he states that he is also chief of staff over Pharaoh's entire household. Pharaoh's children, servants, advisors, officials, and even wise men all looked up to him, he told his awed brothers. The scope of his managerial responsibilities extended far beyond mere food distribution; he was overseeing Pharaoh's entire domestic operations.

- Finally he informed them that he was "ruler over all Egypt." He was not just the man in charge of a small piece of the action dealing with food surplus. He was running the entire country.

All of these claims had to stagger his brothers. They had no idea of just how exalted Joseph's position actually was. At best, they may well have figured he was simply managing the surplus distribution center in the department of agriculture. But now Joseph wants to reveal to them the full extent of his power and influence. He wants them to see the sheer scope of the glory that has come his way, not to boast before them, but rather to make their minds just explode with wonder at what God had done. He wants them to see something you don't see in the mundane work of tending sheep (except on the hills of Bethlehem centuries later!). He wants to show them the glory of God! He wants them to see that their evil deed was used by God to do something unimaginable. He wanted them to see God in all his beauty and show them that one element of God's glory is the way he uses a terrible evil to effect something so grand it takes our breath away.

This is very similar to what Paul does in Philippians 2 when he describes just how high was the honor that came to our Lord Jesus because he became a slave and was obedient even to a shameful death on a cross. He put it like this:

> "Therefore God exalted him to the highest place
> and gave him the name that is above every name,
> that at the name of Jesus every knee should bow,
> in heaven and on earth and under the earth,
> and every tongue confess that Jesus Christ is Lord,
> to the glory of God the Father." (Phil 2:9–11)

You see all the extravagant language there ("highest," "above," "every")? Right here in Genesis 44: 8 you are looking at a preview of . . . *that!*

Then Joseph quickly spelled out for them the next steps they needed to take, steps he had already worked out in advance:

1. Hurry back home and bring Father back, insisting that he does not delay.

2. A place has already been prepared for them, and it was chosen for just one reason: so that the entire family could be *near* Joseph. More important than the fertility of the soil was the intimacy of the family! So Joseph brought up even their grandchildren, and

how important it was for them to be near the person who had actually saved their very lives.

3. They were not to worry about a thing, even though, in fact, they were facing five full years of withering famine. And why not? Because Joseph would provide!

4. Finally, he warned them. He said they *had* to come to the place he had prepared for them and believe his promise to provide for them. If they didn't, they would become destitute.

And then, Joseph paused. He could see that they were still in shock, still trying to grasp the truth that it really was him, Joseph, who was standing right in front of them.

So he backed up a bit. He asked them to take a second look so that they could see for themselves that *he really was Joseph*. In fact, he said, even Benjamin could surely recognize him. Joseph and Benjamin were mirror images of each other as sons of the same mother. Surely, the rest of them could tell by looking at Benjamin that this man had to be Joseph. Note this: Joseph asked to be recognized by having them look at his full-blooded younger brother. Jesus does something very similar today. He is our older brother. His spiritual blood runs through our very heart (which we renew each time we receive the Lord's Supper), and if we follow him, people will surely spot the similarity, just like the Sanhedrin did when they scrutinized Peter and John. It became very obvious; they could see that these men had been with Jesus (Acts 4: 13).

But Joseph was also very eager. More than anything, he longed to see his father. So Joseph commissioned all his brothers to be his witnesses to his aged and anxious father. He insisted that they go back and testify that he was truly alive, that he occupied a position of great honor, that they had seen it themselves, and that they were to bring him down to Egypt. What a wonderful assignment in contrast to the assignment he gave them at the end of their first trip. That assignment meant tearing Benjamin from their father's embrace; this assignment meant bringing Joseph into their Father's tight embrace. This is what redemption does: instead of savagely severing people apart, it softly sutures them together.

And then, once again, the love in his heart just overflowed for all of them. He had just mentioned Benjamin's name, and his affection for the brother he had not seen for twenty-two years just poured out of him. He went to Benjamin, threw his arms around him, and just wept and wept. Benjamin started weeping. The other brothers could only watch in wonder and, no doubt, with deep shame: two brothers, barred from embracing as brothers for twenty-two years because of *their* terrible deed, now poured out a love that had been bottled up inside of them all those years. What a mixture of relief and shame they must have felt.

No doubt, Joseph sensed that watching this tear-filled embrace had to make them feel a touch of exclusion but worse, a very keen sense of self-loathing. So, one by one, Joseph went to every one of his brothers and kissed them, embracing them and weeping over them just as he had with Benjamin. The old dividing lines were gone! They were brothers again, sons of the same father, equally loved, equally cherished. The ground beneath them was level once again. No one was better, and none worse. The grace and goodness of God had fallen on every one of them, and when that happens, all human distinctions and differences are leveled out, transcended by love.

And then came the sweetest thing I know: brothers who were once ene-mies, alienated from and hating each other, now sat down and had a long, long visit . . . *together!* What a simple but precious sentence it is that describes it. It is short. It is even plain: "Afterward his brothers talked with him" (45: 13b). Picture that! The tension is eased. They become more and more relaxed. They start catching up. There are questions. There are sto-ries. No doubt, there are fresh apologies, more confessions. But there are also eye-opening insights, breakthroughs in understanding, epiphanies! I can imagine one of them telling Joseph, "Those dreams you had as a kid! I *never* imagined they meant *this!* But they were *true!*" Then there were all the stories: stories from Joseph about Potiphar and his wife, the years in prison and the butler who ignored Joseph's plea, Pharaoh's dream and his sudden rise, and then meeting Asenath, Manasseh, and Ephraim. There were stories from back home, perhaps even a confession of the bloodied coat they had presented to their father, and his inconsolable grief. But there were stories too about their families and all the children that had been born to them in the land of Canaan.

By this time the word finally got out that the men in Joseph's presence were actually his brothers. When Pharaoh got word, he was delighted. His affection for Joseph immediately spread out over all his brothers. He immediately wanted to be a benefactor for the whole family of the man who had been such a benefactor to his entire empire. His largesse knew no limit. He told Joseph to lavish his family with the very best that Egypt had to offer and assured him that he was welcome to bring the whole clan to come and live in the best part of the country; indeed, the "fattest" part! His magnanimity just kept tumbling out:

- Take carts back with you so that your wives and little children, and especially your aged father, don't have to walk here.

- Forget your stuff back home. Come back with just your people; we have everything you need! And so it was that when Jacob's family first arrived in Egypt, and then, four hundred years later when they finally left Egypt, two million strong, they were loaded down on both occasions with the best of Egypt, a picture of our Father's sure provision!

- So, he told them, don't worry about what you will eat, or even about what you will wear. Does not this sound familiar? (Matt. 6: 25). Here is a brand-new wardrobe for each of you! Their common shepherds' garments were replaced with the finest fabrics of Egypt. And so it was that the favor once shown upon Joseph when his Father adorned him in that richly embroidered robe (37:3), and then again when Pharaoh fitted him with robes of fine linen (41:42) now *overflowed* out onto all of his brothers. This is a hint of what the New Testament will trumpet forth loudly when it says, "all of you who were baptized into Christ have clothed yourselves with Christ" (Gal. 3:27). In Christ we received a completely new wardrobe. Such is the transformation his redemption brings into our lives!

Then Joseph, as directed by Pharaoh, did something that helped them see even "favoritism" in the light of simple love. He favored Benjamin with a financial windfall of three hundred shekels of silver and five sets of clothes as Joseph's full brother. But this time, not one brother resented it, for they were all highly favored with one gift after another. Besides, in the abundance of grace that every one of them were now savoring, the old feelings of jealousy were helpless to rise again! Grace makes us all so rich, all the old comparisons evaporate. This is why it is said, "The ground is level at the foot of the cross."

Finally, Joseph prepared a special gift of love for his father. He organized two pack trains of ten donkeys in each one. The first train carried an immense assortment of all the finest things that could be found in Egypt, and the second was loaded with all the grain and bread his clan would need on their trip to Egypt. When Jacob had sent his sons back on their second trip, you may remember that he sent gifts with them; however, considering how impoverished the family had become, those gifts were trifling indeed: *a little balm and a little honey, some spices and myrrh, some pistachio nuts and almonds.* Why, all of that could barely fill the bottom of one sack! But now, look at this! Once redemption came, once sin was forgiven, once grace flowed into the family, the treasures that came back to Jacob in its wake far surpassed even the finest gifts he could cobble together. The wealth that flows *out* of grace—these are the true treasures, and compared to them our honey, spices, myrrh, and nuts look paltry indeed!

When those two trains arrived back in Canaan and entered Jacob's compound there, for the second time in his life (the first was the elaborate parade of gifts he prepared to pacify Esau back in chapter 32: 31 – 21) Jacob would see that his human attempts to get himself out of a jam looked ludicrous compared to all the wealth to be found in the mercy and grace of his covenant God, waiting for him *right around the bend*. Now that the sons of Jacob had been brought to their end by way of the cross Joseph had compelled them to bear, just as their Father had been brought to his end at the River Jabbok as he bore the cross of wrestling with God, so too now they were all being brought into the glorious riches of their faithful, covenant-keeping God.

Joseph rounded out all these blessings with one last note of kindness: as he bade a fond and, I suspect, tearful farewell to his brothers just before they departed for home, he gently urged them to make sure they did not *quarrel* on the way back. He knew how easily recriminations could surface between them if they accused each other of the ways each of them had treated Joseph in the past. He knew how Reuben, especially, could have acted superior and blamed them all over again. He knew that perhaps even Benjamin could have expressed his own outrage at the others for having deprived him of his one true brother for all those years. He knew how hard it would be for them to *let bygones be bygones*. Grace is something new. It cleans away guilt, but it neither erases old memories nor changes old habits overnight. The transforming effects of grace take time to settle in. This is why Romans 15:7 pleads with us: "Accept one another, then, just as Christ accepted you, in order to bring praise to God." It is one thing to receive grace; it is quite another to practice it! And so Joseph gently admonishes them: behave yourselves! Don't allow old hurts to loop back and ruin all your joy. If old hurts pop up, *drop them!*

And so they left, forgiven, reconciled, welcomed, honored, enriched, but most of all *redeemed!* Their redemption had come hard, *but it had come.* God is never thwarted in his redemptive purpose. Look back over this amazing chapter and review again just how far ahead of these brothers God was as he was working out his purpose to redeem them:

- You saw how, the moment they showed up in Egypt, Joseph recognized them. There's the first instance: *Joseph knew them before they knew him.*

- You saw how often Joseph wept for them (42:24; 43:30). There's the second instance: *Joseph loved them before they loved him.*

- Then notice all the ways that God, through Joseph, broke them down. He spoke harshly to them, imprisoned them, demanded they bring Benjamin with them, returned their silver in their sacks, and then charged them with the theft of his silver cup. There is the third instance: *Joseph was actually effecting their salvation before they even knew they needed it.*

- Finally, when he revealed his true identity to them, and urged them to come near to him, they were terrified. There is the fourth instance: *Joseph was reaching out to them even while they were terrified of him.*

In all of these ways, Joseph portrayed Jesus, who knew us, loved us, and worked out our salvation long before we knew him, loved him, or even realized our need for salvation. And even if we had tried to run from him, his grace would have drawn us in because it is, simply, irresistible, as was Joseph's. All through the story, Jesus shines through Joseph.

This is a compelling picture of just how deeply Jesus loves us. It is a picture of how he is able to save us in spite of ourselves. Consequently, if there is one thing that's obvious, it's this: our redemption is *not about us*. It is *all of Him*. He is the one who leads us to repentance and then redeems and restores us. These brothers did nothing; Joseph did everything. It is just as Paul described it in Romans 5: 8: "But God demonstrates his own love for us in this: while we were still sinners, Christ died for us."

CHAPTER 18

Could It Really Be True?

Read Genesis 45:25—28

"Hope deferred makes the heart sick, but a longing fulfilled is a tree of life." (Prov. 13:12)

hen a broken relationship is redeemed, it's like breaking a piñata open. Blessings gush out on everyone. Once that pivotal event occurred at the feet of Joseph, once the brothers were broken and then washed with grace, a cavalcade of sweet gifts cascaded into the family of Jacob. It was blessing upon blessing, grace upon grace, treasure upon treasure. It reminds me of that extravagant description John wrote in the prologue to his Gospel when he described the Joseph of the New Testament, Jesus himself: "From the fullness of his grace we have all received one blessing after another" (John 1:16).

Jacob may be a patriarch, heir to blessing upon blessing. But grief has parched his spirit much like the famine has withered his pasturelands. Worse, his clan (God's chosen people!) has been infected with a long-hidden scandal that has never come to light. And yet, because of the grace that has been poured upon them by God through Joseph, this deflated man is about to experience a renewal so wondrous it will take his breath way. His would be an ecstasy like that of the exiles when they finally returned back to Jerusalem after seventy long years of banishment. It's described this way in Psalm 126:1–3:

> When the Lord brought back the captives to Zion,
> We were like men who dreamed.
> Our mouths were filled with laughter, our tongues with songs of joy.
> Then it was said among the nations, "The Lord has done great things for them"
> The Lord has done great things for us, and we are filled with joy.

This is a major theme in Scripture: redemption ends our exiles and returns us to our true spiritual home. Here it begins with the healing of a family. You could, in fact, call it a family reunion—a *real* family reunion. When family members who may not have seen each other for several years catch sight of each other for the first time at a reunion, get out of the way! They will run to each other, shout each other's names, grab each other in a hug, cry for joy, and refuse to let go. It's one of life's sweetest moments. It's even sweeter when a husband or wife returns after a tour of duty in a war zone and are greeted by their spouse at an airport or a military base. And then there are those best of all, surprise reunions, often headlined by the media, when a military mom or dad secretly sneaks back into the country and shows up at their child's school, catching them completely by surprise and sweeping them up into their arms!

Without redemption, reunions are not so sweet. Old sibling rivalries, nursed grievances, and relationships simply gone cold over time can infect a reunion with guardedness, cold looks, and unspoken tensions. People keep their distance, greetings are perfunctory, and glances are avoided. For some whose old hurts can flare up just at the sight of a family member who failed them, it's a triumph just to remain civil and keep their mouth shut.

But what we are going to see here is the finest and most rare kind of reunion—where old conflicts have finally been resolved, where confrontation, contrition, confession, forgiveness, and reconciliation have done their healing work, and family members, once alienated, are enemies no more. This is a reunion of people who once stared at each other with looks that could kill; now, wondrously, their faces are soft, their smiles are tender, and when they hug, they cannot stop weeping. It is simply phenomenal! Redemption comes hard, but when it has done its healing work, the result is a family reunion the likes of which this world rarely witnesses!

It reminds me of Christmas Eve, 1914, during World War I, when something so rare and wondrous took place it was forever enshrined in the minds of those who were there. It was eventually brought to life in a 2005 movie called *Joyeux Noël*. For one brief evening, German and Allied (British, Scottish, and French) soldiers in their trenches, separated by a narrow and deadly no-man's land, heard each other across that lethal space singing or playing the familiar sounds of Christmas carols. They began blending their voices across that divide, each side singing from their trenches. Then, one of them tentatively stepped out as he sang, holding a lit Christmas tree. The other side held their fire. Then, more soldiers stepped out from their trenches. They approached each other, declared a truce, and for a few precious hours, ate, drank, sang, and even shared wine and cigarettes with each other. It was so rare it arrested the world with disbelief when it was reported. The brightness and beauty of the birth of the Redeemer in the context of Christmas 1914, so darkened by a wretched war, shone through nonetheless. Just like the skies over Bethlehem, the battleground was suddenly flooded with a holy light.

This is what we are about to see here in the wake of the redemption God brought to Joseph's brothers. It is, once again, a preview of a reunion on a far more massive scale. This family is both the ancestor and prototype of the ultimate new family: the church of Jesus Christ. Because of the redemptive work of God through our savior Jesus, the kingdom of heaven is populated with people who were once just like Joseph's brothers, who "hated him and could not speak a kind word to him." Paul describes us before we were redeemed in Titus 3:3 when he says, "At one time we too were foolish, disobedient, deceived and enslaved by all kinds of passions and pleasures. We lived in malice and envy, being hated and hating one another." Then the "kindness and love of God our Savior appeared" (v. 4a) and transformed us. In this story it transformed alienated brothers into embracing brothers.

All of that enmity is now being swallowed up by what Scripture calls *shalom:* the vast, all-encompassing peace of God that, in the wake of redemption, can remove the cacophony within a person, a family, a community, a country, a government, and even creation itself, and replace it with a harmony no one ever thought possible. The longing for that shalom has filled the hearts of men ever since the fall, especially in the wake of devastating wars, divorces, and even church splits. It has led to the creation of everything from simple armistices to the United Nations itself.

That shalom, slowly healing all the old griefs and enmities, is what the rest of our story is all about.

Joseph's brothers wasted no time getting home. Their brother had told them to move quickly, and they did. After all, they were now, you could say, missionaries of the gospel: the gospel of reconciliation! Their hearts were beating with news so good they couldn't wait to announce it. And so, in a matter of just a few days, they were running up to their aged father and pouring out the good news: "*Joseph is still alive! In fact, he is ruler of all Egypt.*" It just exploded out of them. First one, then another—their voices tumbling all over one another—told the story. Excitedly shaking their heads up and down, they kept on assuring him it was really true.

Jacob, says Moses, was just stunned! Of course! He had long given up Joseph for dead; he was only too relieved that they had brought Benjamin back alive. But to hear that Joseph too was not only actually still alive but ruling the entire country of Egypt was just too much to take in. It was simply too good to be true. In a sense, it was ridiculous! On the surface, this at first had to seem even foolish! Who would believe a story like that? This made no sense! He had seen the blood-spattered garment himself, and probably still had it as his only tie to his long-dead son. This just didn't *fit*. It didn't line up with what he had long believed were the facts of the case. And yet, here were the rest of his sons, even Benjamin, testifying to him in perfect agreement. It had to blow him away, and once again he found himself wrestling with his own spirit, struggling between complete disbelief on the one hand and daring to entertain the remote possibility that this report just might possibly be true on the other.

God graciously nudged his beloved patriarch into faith. The brothers kept on telling him more and more of what Joseph had said: of how he had become a father even to Pharaoh, of how there were yet five more years of famine, and of how Pharaoh had announced that they could come to Egypt and would be given the best of the land. One revelation built upon another. The story kept on filling out as the blanks were all filled in.

That is what happens when you finally "catch on" to the beauty of the gospel, of what God has done for you in Jesus. For, truth be told now, this is everything you learned in Sunday School about Jesus: how he suffered, then how he rose from the prison of death, then how he was elevated to being put in command of all things under his Father, and then how, from that place, he pours out one blessing after another upon us, rescuing us from the famine of our self-absorbed lives and bringing us into his own land of Goshen, the kingdom of heaven, the place we could call Bountiful! When you finally "catch on," see it for yourself, and take it into your own heart after all these many years of having been told about it, it just takes your breath away.

The good news that our creator loves us so deeply that he has found a way, despite our own deep shamefulness and incredible pain for himself, to bring us back into his embrace is invariably just so stunning that once we finally see it for what it really is, it almost seems foolish to actually believe it. And that is where Jacob was: for him to believe a story like this almost made him look like a fool. And yet, how do you ignore that many witnesses all saying the same thing? And how do you ignore all of us who have told you these things: your parents, your aunts and uncles, your grandparents, your Christian school teachers, and all those good people you knew in the churches where you grew up?

Try to envision this scene in front of Jacob's tent: there they all were, pushing in close to him, each one in turn massaging the oil of this wonderful message into the leathered skin around his embittered soul. Then they showed him the carts that Joseph had sent back with them. Those carts, those fine Egyptian masterpieces of workmanship, just waiting to carry the whole family to their new home, stood like silent testimonials there in the middle of the encampment, assuring Jacob that this report, unbelievable as it seemed, just had to be true.

It is hard to absorb bad news, but it may be even harder—especially for a jaded person like Jacob whose years of life have been "few and difficult" (which is how he describes them later 47:9)—to absorb good news. Invariably on such occasions, people say, "I can't believe it." People like Jacob, made skeptical by a life of cruel disappointments and devastating losses, could easily get to a point where they decide, in the spirit of "getting real," that it is just too risky to ever get your hopes up again. Once that spirit of resignation settles in and slowly suffocates our aspirations, it is no easy thing *to dare to believe again*. Faith has to work its way into our hearts through layers of accumulated callouses of learned skepticism. But then, God drops a dozen carts in our camp, beautiful carts obviously made in Egypt. We stare at them. And finally a small seed of faith sprouts, our hopes revive, and we slowly make the journey back to daring to believe once more. No wonder the Bible teaches that faith is a gift from God. That makes sense. The good news is just that hard to embrace.

Consider this: for Jacob to believe meant so much more than just finally accepting their report as true. It meant being uprooted! It meant leaving his true home, Canaan, the land promised to him through his grandfather Abraham by God, and pulling up stakes—literally. It meant doing the very thing Jesus always called would-be disciples to do: *Leave . . . and follow.* For Jacob to believe meant that his whole world would be disrupted. It meant packing up—lock, stock, and barrel.

And yet God gave him the faith to believe the report of his transformed sons enough to take a step as daring as Peter did when Jesus called him to "get out of the boat." And so he said, "I'm convinced! My son Joseph is still alive. I will go and see him before I die" (45:28). Might I wonder now about something reported much earlier in the story? When Joseph first reported his dreams as a seventeen-year-old, everybody scoffed. Even his parents questioned him, but then we read this pregnant phrase: "but his father kept the matter in mind" (37:11b). Is it possible that all these years Jacob had harbored the memory of those dreams in a small corner of his heart? And now, being told that Joseph was even a father to Pharaoh himself, it might just be that the memory of that dream came rushing back, finally convincing Jacob enough to conclude, "*This has to be true! This is exactly what he told us would happen over twenty years ago.*" Perhaps, in this moment, Jacob saw that God had prepared him to believe right now through a dream all but he had forgotten. Perhaps.

There's something else worth noticing here: a message like the one with which the brothers came home to their father, which is unbelievably good and indescribably sweet, is why the Bible says that even the very feet of the messengers who bring such good news are, simply, beautiful: "How beautiful on the mountains are the feet of those who bring good news, who proclaim peace, who bring good tidings, who proclaim salvation, who say to Zion, 'Your God reigns!'" (Isa. 52:7).

This time the brothers' feet were lovely because they ran home to tell Jacob, "Your son reigns!" And that son was a preview of the real Son, who reigns even now from the right hand of God. I have been privileged all these years to be a minister of that gospel, to live with a pair of beautiful feet! There have been times I have been privileged to watch what happens when people to whom I've told the good news finally catch on and see it for themselves for the first time. One woman once left my office saying she felt like she was walking on air! And she was!

There is one question you might have: did they finally tell him the *whole* story? Did they finally 'fess up to what they had done all those many years ago? Did they finally tell Jacob that they had actually sold Joseph into slavery for twenty pieces of silver? Surely Jacob would have wondered how in the world Joseph, whose blood-smeared robe he had personally inspected and was sure had been killed, ever survived in the first place, much less ended up in Egypt—much less ended up *ruling in Egypt!* Surely, he must have said to his boys, "How can this possibly be?" Did they finally tell him? Did they recount the dark part of even this latest chapter in the story, the missing silver cup found in Benjamin's sack, and the brokenness they all felt?

We don't know. However, it does appear that Jacob eventually did learn the whole story. If you run ahead a minute to chapter 50:17, you'll notice it suggests that Jacob may very well have known the whole story (even though it is possible Jacob never did ask his sons to beg Joseph's forgiveness, as they claimed he did). We still don't know for certain that Jacob knew everything, but I have to believe that it is more likely that they did confess everything in time.

This is why: once grace finds us—once we are broken, once we finally admit to the truth, once we have been washed clean—*we are free to come out of hiding.* Broken people stop covering up to save face. Grace actually frees us to keep on coming cleaner and cleaner because we are now in a very different place. So much of our pride has finally been shattered. This grace is what enabled St. Augustine to write his *Confessions*, and Charles Colson his *Born Again.* We have entered the true reality of sin in our own lives and discovered that, in spite of it all, God still treasures us! This sense of being beloved, even in our sinfulness, is actually the spring from which the boldness finally surges up within us to dare to come completely clean and admit to more and more. Grace, strangely, kindles confession! Covered as we are with the favor of grace and the blessing of having been forgiven, we finally dare to uncover what has long been covered up, *because we know we'll not be condemned.* We're already past condemnation, says Romans 8:1, when it announces, "Therefore, there is now no condemnation for those who are in Christ Jesus." But, regardless of how forthcoming they actually were, we do know this: they did exactly what Joseph told them to do. They told their father everything he told them to say. They were faithful "missionaries!"

It appears that Jacob wasted no time. The very next verse, which starts chapter 46, says, "So . . . " Jacob was told the good news. At first he was stunned. Gradually he believed. And then: "So . . . " Simple as that: "So . . . "

"So" . . . he packed up and moved out. At this point it was full steam ahead.

Once we believe, the paralysis is over. Momentum returns. Faith restores traction. And once again, life becomes an adventure.

CHAPTER 19

Why Worship First?

Read Genesis 46:1–7

Jacob believed. He believed enough to actually uproot himself and his entire family from the very country he knew was meant to be his permanent home. He left real estate that belonged to him and had been promised to his descendants for generations. He walked away from the home place! That took faith.

Then he headed down to Egypt, and that took faith as well. To him, it was not only a foreign country, but a dangerous one at that. It was a pagan country. The faith of his grown sons had never been strong, as evidenced by all the ungodliness in their behavior. He had every reason to be concerned that their hearts would soon be ensnared by the attractive gods of Egypt. After all, the people who worshiped those gods had developed a culture that was one of the most advanced in the world. Egypt was populated with experts in mathematics, architecture, agriculture, weaponry, and astronomy. It was affluent. It was another manifestation of Babylon, the glorious kingdom of this world (Rev. 18). It was magnificent, enticing, and even seductive. He had good reason to fear that it would sabotage the flickering faith of his children, who lived in tents and endured a mundane life as ordinary shepherds.

Moreover, he knew a frightening chapter in the history of his family regarding Egypt. His grandfather, while he was still named Abram, had been compelled to go there. A severe famine in Canaan had coerced him to leave the land of promise for the Nile-watered farmland of Egypt just to survive. But that journey had also exposed him to a dangerous risk because his wife, Sarai, was very beautiful. Fearing that the Pharaoh would simply kill him off and seize her to be his wife (Gen. 12:10–20), he lied, claiming she was his sister. Pharaoh took her into his palace, paying Abram handsomely. But God stepped in and inflicted serious diseases on Pharaoh and his entire household. So Pharaoh summoned Abram in for questioning. Then, after a stiff lecture, he ordered Abram, Sarai, and the entire company out of the country. That is the unnerving history that now had to give Jacob pause.

And so it was that Jacob took measures to protect his family. He stopped and worshiped. At the final oasis between the promised land and Egypt, the very place he had grown up, a spot named Beersheba, he stopped the entire procession . . . to worship.

Beersheba meant roots. It was grandfather Abram's home. Abram had signed a major peace treaty there with a Philistine king named Abimelech. Later, perhaps as a sign of that treaty, he had planted a single tree of a particular species known to survive famines and even provide life-saving shade from the hot desert sun for both animals and humans. It was a tamarisk tree, and it very well was still there. Jacob wanted his family to see that tree and sit in its shade. In addition, Beersheba had also been the home of his father, Isaac, where he had dug a well that had been a source of life for his family and his flocks for years. But most important of all, this was Jacob's childhood home. Jacob had grown up by that tree and that well.

This was the place he had resorted to a deceitful ruse to steal the birthright from Esau. You can read all about this shenanigan in Genesis 27. When Esau learned he had been cheated, he vowed to murder Jacob as soon as their father Isaac died. Jacob, terrified, fled Beersheba, and there is no record that he had ever returned to it until this moment.

The very first night of his flight, after he had stopped at a place (which he later named Bethel) because the sun had set, God came to him in a remarkable dream. He saw angels gliding up and then back down a giant stairway, like an escalator. The base of the stairway was right next to him, and the top of it was high in the heavens, where he could see God. The effect was electric! He felt vividly *connected* to God, as if those active angels were carrying all his fears up the escalator to God and then carrying back down to him all the assurances of God designed to calm those fears. The promises the angels carried down that escalator to him as he lay on that hard ground with his head on a stone for a pillow were staggering. To this frightened young man, God, after clearly identifying himself as the God of his grandfather Abraham, and his father Isaac, made six massive promises that were pivotal for this moment as he was about to exit the land of promise:

1. He would give to him and his descendants the entire country all around the spot on which he was lying.

2. His descendants would become so numerous they would be as countless as the particles of dust in the ground, and they would spread out from this very spot in every direction . . . for miles.

3. He and his offspring would be so blessed, the whole world would benefit from God's favor upon them.

4. God would be right there with him every step of the way.

5. God would surely bring him back home, for this land was his true home.

6. God would never leave him until every single promise had been fulfilled. In other words, God would never leave him . . . for the rest of his life.

He could see how those promises were beginning to come true. God had been with him all during his time in Haran. He had returned very rich. His family had grown. He had settled in the promised land. Now he had learned that one of his own children was fulfilling the third promise. Joseph was saving not only him and the family nor even the entire country of Egypt, but all the countries around Egypt. God had indeed been with him every step of the way since that dream he was given on his flight from Beersheba.

He was back home, but at a very different stage in his life. He was 130 years old now, father and grandfather to a company of seventy people. But once again, he was about to launch out into totally new territory. As a young man, he went west; now, he's headed east. As a young man he was running away from his brother; now he is running to his son. But he has never been to Egypt as far as we know. He is about to begin a whole new chapter in his life—something old people rarely do. Young people like you feel completely free, and welcome adventure into unknown places. You're not afraid to pull up roots and try something totally new; most old people like me can hardly imagine it, though you should know that your grandmother and I, at the ripe old age of 24, went off and lived in a slum for an entire year, ministering to people of a totally different color and culture than us. We thought nothing of it; today, at seventy five, we'd think twice . . . or more.

So Jacob stopped the entire caravan . . . for worship. This final outpost on the border was their last chance to worship in the promised land. Who knew if, or when, they would ever return? Jacob wanted his family to remember that *Canaan* was their true country, their spiritual home.

If you and I could have attended that "worship service" there, what might it have been like, "going to church" with that family? We have a good idea, based on a previous "worship service" Jacob had held at Bethel (Gen. 35:1–15).

First, it likely was a time of confession. Previously, after the slaughter of the Shechemites, as he assembled his family for worship at Bethel, he had told them to "purify themselves and change their clothes." And so, once again, assuming that the terrible truth of what the sons had done to Joseph twenty-two years earlier had now come to light, it is very possible that he, as the leader of the family, humbly confessed to God the truth of his children's deep sins.

Then, it is also likely that this was a time of thanksgiving. He had been overwhelmed with unbelievably good news. He was going to see Joseph one more time before he died. His family was going to find a shelter from the famine. And all of them would soon be together after years of separation. They all had to be just overflowing with sheer gratitude for the sweet turn of events that had come their way.

Then, it is also likely that this was a time of fear-filled prayer, pleading for God to go before him and protect both him and his family. Egypt was full of pagan deities. The Egyptians worshiped a whole pantheon of gods, says James Montgomery Boice:

> Osiris, Hapimon, and Tauret were gods of the Nile; Nu was the god of life in the river. Geb was the god of the land. There were Nephri, the grain god; Anubis, guardian of the fields; Min, deity of the harvest and crops. There were gods in the form of animals: Apis, the bull god; Hathor, the cow goddess; Sekhmet, the lion; Khnum, the ram; Sobek, the crocodile; Thoth, the ibis; Horus and Month, the bird gods. Nut was the sky; Shu, the atmosphere. Greatest of all was Ra, the sun god, thought to be embodied in the reigning Pharaoh. Their gods remind me of the all the animals we worship in American today (and we do, don't kid yourself!), from the Chicago *Bears* to the Washington *Huskies*, from the Seattle *Seahawks* to the Detroit *Tigers*.

We worship our sports teams and we proudly wear clothing adorned with their mascots! (Boice, *Genesis, Part 3*, p. 207)

We are told that during the sacrifice Jacob offered there, he called upon the name of the "God of his father Isaac." No wonder. His sons had actually met their grandfather Isaac, since he was still alive when the entire family returned from Paddan Aram. Isaac lived to be 180 years old, so there very likely were many occasions when they visited with him and heard him speak about all that God had done for him. Then, they had all gone to his funeral when he died (Gen. 35: 27–29). It is very likely that they knew all about Isaac's faith in the one true God, as well as the promises God had given through Isaac (Gen. 28: 3–4) to bless the entire world through Jacob's family.

Now Jacob was calling upon the only God his children knew, the God of their grandfather. He wanted to anchor the faith of every one of those seventy people in that God before they found themselves awash in the idolatry of Egypt. I can understand why Jacob was so concerned for his family; it's one of the reasons I feel compelled to write this book for you. I want you to know the God I have known all these years, and one of the finest displays of him in the Old Testament is as the God of Joseph. This is a God you can trust!

Then, once again, Jacob received a revelation straight out of heaven! As he slept that final night before leaving the promised land, Jacob heard God call his name, "Jacob! Jacob!" It was as clear as the voice a little boy sleeping in a temple centuries later was to hear three times over: "Samuel! Samuel!" God does call us, as it were, by our own name, in the privacy and quietness of our bedrooms when it's just him and us. God knows our names, and he also knows the plans he has for us. He is able to reveal them to us.

Once again, God met Jacob just as at Bethel (Gen. 28:10–22), in Paddan Aram (Gen. 31:3), at Mahanaim (Gen. 32:1), at Peniel (Gen. 32:22–32), and again at Bethel (Gen. 35:9–15). Never doubt that God is fully able to engage you at pivotal moments in your life. God is able to come to you when you are facing a major decision or about to embark on a new venture. Sometimes he uses your readings in the Bible. Sometimes he uses wise mentors. Sometimes he gives people dreams, even today, just as he did here for Jacob. Sometimes he speaks through circumstances, revealing opportunities or closing doors. Sometimes you hear his still, small voice in the quietness of your own prayers. But this much is still true: God is able to speak into our hearts. Jacob was a fearful man, most of his life, and yet God repeatedly spoke to him and encouraged him. He can, and he will, do the same for you.

And this time, what a message! The first thing God told him was to not be afraid to proceed, with his entire family, right on down into Egypt. God knows when we are afraid; again and again God, often quite gently, assures us that our fears need not paralyze us. Over eighty times in the Bible we are told, "Do not be afraid." God commands us to not fear! But how does a person not fear when he is facing something truly fearful? The only way I know to overcome fear is *by cultivating an even greater fear*. I have always feared being poked for a vaccination. But I fear the flu, or pneumonia, and especially shingles so much more. That fear overcomes my fear of the needle. The cure for all fears is cultivating the far greater fear of failing to trust the one who says to us, "Don't be afraid." Fearing God always frees us from the fear of man. This is where all lasting boldness is birthed.

Then God told him why he had nothing to be afraid of:

1. God promised that it would be in Egypt, of all places, that the old promise already given to Abraham years earlier would finally be fulfilled: that his descendants would grow into a nation numbering in the millions. And so it came to be.

2. The second announcement must have calmed every last tremor of fear left in Jacob. God promised to be his personal escort every step of the way into this strange and forbidding country.

3. The third announcement must have answered one of Jacob's most heartfelt yearnings. The last thing he wanted was to end up not being buried in the family plot by the oaks of Mamre, where grandfather Abraham and father Isaac and their wives were all buried. He dreaded the thought of being buried outside of his true home, the land of promise. So God made him a sure promise: he would receive a right and proper burial in his one true home. In fact, said God, it will be the very hands of your own beloved son, Joseph, that will close your eyelids at the moment of your death. What a tender and consoling promise. It's been said that "All's well that ends well," and now God is assuring this frail old man that he will be in the presence of his own son Joseph when he dies, and he will be buried in the only place worthy of the name "home." What a consoling word of assurance to a man leaving the only true home he ever knew.

What a worship service! Jacob led his family sacrificing to God, and God responded with words of such power Jacob had everything he needed as he was propelled into *the rest of his life!* This is what worship is meant to do for us. It is meant to be nothing less than an encounter with the living God, reaching deep into our hearts, settling us in his grace and promises, and empowering us to step up into whatever he directs us to do. Not all worship experiences may do this for you, but this is their purpose. If you make it your habit to regularly assemble with other Christians, pray with them, listen to God's Word together, celebrate the sacraments, and leave under his benediction, you are exposing yourself to a practice that, over the long haul, has the power to keep your heart focused on the adventure up ahead where God is sending you. There have been times when God encountered me in a compelling way in church, and I have no doubt he will do the same for you. But you have to "go" to church in order to "go" into life! And so it was that Jacob and his family left "church" under a powerful benediction and headed straight to Egypt.

Finally, we are treated to quite a riveting sight (vv. 5–7): a long procession of carts holding entire families and all their stuff—along with braying donkeys, bleating sheep and goats, and other assorted animals—slowly crawling toward the east through the desert on their way to the green river valley of the Nile, all of them filled with expectancy. Can you see them, this caravan of the chosen ones, making their way from home to a foreign land, knowing only that up ahead, waiting for them at the end of their pilgrimage, is a sure redeemer?

That is a picture of all Christians today, on our way to the new heaven and the new earth, which will come down from heaven. There we will find our true home in the heavenly city, whose builder and maker is God himself. And even now, that heavenly city, the kingdom of God, is taking shape all around us as we devote our lives to bringing every square inch of this earth under the control of him who is redeeming all of it into our eternal home.

CHAPTER 20

He Knows Your Name

Read Genesis 46: 8–27

When I was a child, my dad read a portion of the Bible at the end of every meal. He just went right on through from Genesis to Revelation, didn't skip a word, and when he got to the end, he started all over at the beginning. It took him several years each time. There were ten of us around that table: two parents and eight fidgeting kids, stomachs full, eager to finish so that we could go out and shoot baskets or play fast-pitch softball. Sometimes we didn't get to our game until the second or third inning!

When he came to a passage like this one, with all these names in it, we figured he'd just skip over it. What's a bunch of names, anyway? They meant nothing to us. But no, he insisted on reading every single one of those names, struggling mightily to get the pronunciation right. Sometimes he had to make three or four runs at one of those names to finally get it right, setting off smirks and giggles all around. Sometimes he even had to laugh at himself! But he was determined. If those names were in the Holy Book, and God saw fit to put them in there, well then, best read every last one of them. You skip over nothing.

I remember barely a single one of those names, but I never forgot the point my dad made in reading them. And I don't want you to forget it either: *names count. Your* name counts. So I'm not going to skip over these six-ty-six names here in chapter 46 because there's real treasure to be found here. But it is hidden treasure. Let me help you dig into it!

Here's why. Soon enough you may decide to find a church for yourself or your family. If you decide to join a church, I want to warn you in advance: *you will be disappointed.* You will discover in that company of God's very real people individuals *like you and me,* who are flawed. Some of their names will be tainted with bad reputations. You'll find opinionated talkers and poor listeners. You'll find people who are highly judgmental and to you may seem terribly narrow minded or too broad minded. You'll find whin-ers. You'll find some who've been known to drive some very hard bargains. Truth is, you'll find some of them to be just plain insufferable! It's even possible you might find yourself thinking, *If this is what real Christians are like, I don't want to get anywhere near them.* In fact, you may very well discover nicer people among your unchurched associates at work or in the neighborhood.

C. S. Lewis, in his book <u>The Screwtape Letters</u>, a collection of letters from a senior devil (Screwtape) to a junior devil (Wormwood), tells the story of a young man assigned to Wormwood whom he protected so poorly from the Enemy (Jesus) that the young man actually became a believer! He even started going to church! But Screwtape assured Wormwood, despite the fact that he had bungled the case so badly, that there was still hope of bringing him back to the dark side *because of the very fact that this new young believer had started attending worship services at the local church.* In his slippery way, Screwtape masterfully directed Wormwood on just how to use the church to win this new convert back:

> One of our great allies at present is the Church itself. Do not mis-understand me. I do not mean the Church as we see her spread out

through all time and space and rooted in eternity, terrible as an army with banners. That, I confess, is a spectacle which makes our boldest tempters uneasy. But fortunately it is quite invisible to these humans. All your patient sees is the half-finished, sham Gothic erection on the new building estate. When he goes inside, he sees the local grocer with rather an oily expression on his face bustling up to offer him one shiny little book containing a liturgy which neither of them understands, and one shabby little book containing corrupt texts of a number of religious lyrics, mostly bad, and in very small print. When he gets to his pew and looks round him he sees just that selection of his neighbors whom he had hitherto avoided. You want to lean pretty heavily on those neighbors. Make his mind flit to and fro between an expression like "the body of Christ" and the actual faces in the next pew. It matters very little, of course, what kind of people that next pew really contains. You may know one of them to be a great warrior on the Enemy's side. No matter. Your patient, thanks to Our Father below, is a fool. Provided that any of those neighbors sing out of tune, or have boots that squeak, or double chins, or odd clothes, the patient will quite easily believe that their religion must therefore be somehow ridiculous. . . . Work hard, then, on the disappointment or anticlimax which is certainly coming to the patient during his first few weeks as a churchman . . . if the patient knows that the woman with the absurd hat is a fanatical bridge player or the man with squeaky boots a miser and an extortioner—then your task is so much the easier (The Screwtape Letters, C. S. Lewis, pp. 15–18).

That is why this list of sixty-six names here is worth a second look. At this point in history, *this is the church!* What a disappointment! Look at some of those names:

- First off, you've got Reuben listed. Well, you know the sleazy part of his story: he slept with one of his father's wives. He disgraced his own father!

- The next verse mentions Simeon. You know how treacherous he was. You read all about it back in chapter 2.

- Next up is Levi—he was the co-conspirator with Simeon in the slaughter of all the men of Shechem. Another scoundrel!

- Then you have Judah. Moses told us his dirty little secret back in Genesis 38, where he ended up going to bed with a prostitute who turned out to be his own daughter-in-law. Judah is exposed there as a man who makes a promise with no intention of keeping it.

- Finally, as you read the rest of the names, you will very well remember what most of them did to Joseph.

The point is this: most of the older adults in this list have a terrible history. And yet, if you "went to church" at this time in history by joining them on their journey into Egypt, these would be the people in the pews with you. This bunch was not just a church. This was *the* church. This was the whole "body of Christ," right here. There was no other.

This list serves you with a fair warning: if you think you are too good to join yourself with a group of people, many of whom have a really dark past, all of whom still have plenty of flaws, and none of whom have their act completely together yet, then you are in for one huge disappointment. For truth be told, *every church* is like this family. Listen to the horrible backgrounds of some of the saints in the church in Corinth:

> Do you not know that the wicked will not inherit the kingdom of God? Do not be deceived: neither the sexually immoral nor idolaters nor adulterers nor male prostitutes nor homosexual offenders nor thieves nor the greedy nor drunkards nor slanderers nor swindlers will inherit the kingdom of God. And that is what some of you were. But you were washed, you were sanctified, you were justified in the name of the Lord Jesus Christ and by the Spirit of our God. (1 Cor. 6: 9–11)

So were these people. What you are looking at in this list is a group of people, many of them with a very sinful past, who have been confronted, broken, forgiven, and redeemed! That is what a true church is: a gathering of people, all of whom (some more scandalously than others) are tainted but nonetheless have been washed clean in baptism and even now, despite some ongoing, serious flaws, are on a journey to enter even more fully into their redemption, just as many of these sixty six named people were. *This* is your real family, right here. *This* is the real church. If you are too good for people with a history like this, you are not ready to be part of any church. You'll never fit because a church is much more a hospital for sick people than a sports team of the finest and the fittest!

There's a second treasure in this list of names: the very fact that the Holy Spirit inspired Moses to write out the name of every single person on this journey is God's way of impressing upon us that no matter how unknown we might be or insignificant we might feel, *we count.* You are not just a nameless face in a crowd; you are a person who is *noticed, recognized, and addressed by name.* God is a God who calls out names. There are billions and billions of stars in our vast universe, and yet, because God is so intimately involved with each part of his creation, even that part that seems to be so vast and impersonal is not so to God: "He determines the number of the stars and calls them each by name" (Ps. 147: 4). There are millions of Christians in the world today, but the Bible says this about how Jesus, the good shepherd, reaches out to every one of them: "He calls his own sheep by name and leads them out" (John 10: 3).

These names are so important to God that in our future home, the new Jerusalem, every gate will be inscribed with one of the names of these twelve sons of Jacob, etching in pearl forever just how deep their redemption ran and how eternally it endured.

There is a deep longing in each one of us to be known as a real person and to be called by a real name. You love to be called by your name, especially by someone who still remembers it after not seeing you for a very long time. Your name is *you*. It is key to our humanity, central to our dignity, and basic to our identity.

Cheers was an American sitcom that ran for eleven seasons between 1982 and 1993. Perhaps you've seen a few episodes. The unique quality of that bar in Boston, from which the show took its name, is that people mattered there! The theme song of the show was, "Where Everybody Knows Your Name." This was a place where the bartender and the customers all knew each other *by name*. That theme song captured just how deep this longing runs in every one of us.

Is there any fate worse than to be known by no one?

There's a third treasure in this boring list! When you survey chapter 46 and read those strange names, not only are you looking at flawed people or people who count: you are looking at real flesh-and-blood people who could very well have perished in the famine. This could have been a list of casualties; instead, it is a register of the rescued, the survivors, the redeemed! Ten brothers committed the crime, but these were the people whose lives were on the line. If that redemption for which Joseph fought so hard had not succeeded, these people would very likely have perished. Seventy people would have died for the one sin that took place all those twenty-two years ago. What we are looking at here are the high stakes in this redemption story! So this is a list of *beneficiaries*—people, many of them children, some even grandchildren (and perhaps some twins? I'm curious about Arodi/Areli; Ishva/Ishvi; Muppim/Huppim!), all of whom were carried on the coattails of the ten redeemed brothers out of a deadly famine into a fertile new home where one blessing after another would cascade into their lives. One redemptive movement can end up rescuing and blessing an entire family, or a college campus, or even a nation.

The Great Awakening in the early part of the eighteenth century began in Massachusetts, but it spread through all of New England and even beyond.

The whole region was transformed. This simple list of strange names is a testament to the powerful ripple effect of any moment in history when God makes his move, redeems a broken family, and then lets the "good infection" of his grace spread health far and wide. Consider this: if you experience the redemptive work of God touching your life in any way (someday perhaps healing your marriage, liberating you from an addiction, lifting you out of vindictiveness, or any of a dozen other emancipations), who knows how many people will directly benefit down the line? It could be in the hundreds! You are not an island. You are a real person with a real name who counts not just to God but to dozens and maybe even hundreds of people around you.

I'm glad my dad read those lists of names, because there is one final benefit to be learned from such a list. It tells us a vital truth: *redemption gives us a name that lasts.* The record of these names is as old as the Bible itself. This list points to another book, filled with millions of names, and every name counts. That book is called "The Lamb's book of life." Revelation mentions it no less than six times. To have your name recorded in that book is more to be prized than seeing it on Facebook, in a major publication, on the letterhead of a Fortune 500 company, in a history book, or even on an impressive building. It is more valuable than having a street, or a scholarship, or even a spot on the moon named after you!

What will finally be put on our gravestones? Our names. Like the thief on the cross, we long to be remembered.

We will be, forever. Our names are written in heaven. Once, upon returning from a mission trip, Jesus's disciples were ecstatic. They announced to him that even demons had submitted to them when they invoked the name of Jesus, and they were thrilled by the demonstration of the power of his name. Jesus concurred that they had indeed won a huge victory over Satan himself, but then he announced something even grander: "do not rejoice that the spirits submit to you, but rejoice that your names are written in heaven" (Luke 10:18c).

So Genesis 46: 8–27 isn't just a listing of strange names after all. It's the joyful account of the names of all the fortunate beneficiaries of a hard-won redemption (except for Er and Onan), and it's only the beginning. From them will emerge a nation of close to two million who will one day be redeemed out of slavery in Egypt and finally brought back to their true home, the same land of Canaan they are now leaving for the time being. But there's even more to the story, for that small land of Canaan is the prototype of our eternal home here on the new earth. The whole earth will be Canaan. In that new Canaan, God himself will come to live right here on planet earth with us, and there, in that new community, he himself will call every one of us, to our everlasting joy, by our new names. And not only this; everybody else there will know your new name as well, and you theirs. All will be remembered, and none ignored.

CHAPTER 21

Son and Father

Read Genesis 46: 28–30

And now, events can't happen fast enough. In this little section of just three verses, there's an overtone of *speed*. Why? Because up ahead awaits the shining glory, the fruit of the entire redemptive enterprise. It is the moment when Joseph, his redemptive mission accomplished, eagerly runs up to his father and is embraced in the arms of the only one he ever lived to please. This moment of greatest joy deserves your most thoughtful attention, for it is, once again, a preview of a far grander and more cosmic moment when another Son, having accomplished his redemptive mission, "hands over the kingdom to God the Father after he has destroyed all dominion, authority and power" (1 Cor 15:24).

You may remember how Joseph longed for this moment. He had no more than revealed himself to his brothers and he was urging them to "hurry back to their father" and then give him this message: "Come down to me. Don't delay." (45: 9) If his father was truly alive, nothing was more important to him. And it was no different for his father. As soon as he was convinced that Joseph was really alive, his very next words were, "I will go and see him before I die" (45: 28b). Both of them are quivering with anticipation at this delicious prospect!

231

So, the caravan of the seventy has no more than left Beersheba, when Jacob singles out Judah to speed on ahead of them to get clear directions to the land of Goshen. Why did he pick Judah? The fact that Jacob selects Judah suggests to me that the sons had told their father how Judah had been the one to step forward, plead for Benjamin, and offer to take his place. Judah had not only proved his loyalty to Benjamin; he had also demonstrated just how deep that loyalty ran: he was willing to pay any price to make sure Benjamin was not lost to his father. I point this out because our own Redeemer came from the line of Judah, something the Gospel writers remind us of again and again. Judah, the intrepid "Savior of Benjamin," determined that he would never lose that younger brother entrusted into his care, is as vivid a picture of Jesus's determination to rescue us, his younger brothers, from the enslaving power of sin as you will find anywhere in the Old Testament. Listen to our older brother: "And this is the will of him who sent me, that I shall lose none of all those he has given me, but raise them up at the last day" (John 6: 39). If you want to see just how deeply entrenched this same determination was embedded in the heart of our Lord, it keeps on surfacing in John 10: 28, 17: 12, and 18: 9.

So it was Judah who raced down to Egypt while the slow caravan plodded on, hindered as it was by all those animals and little children. It was Judah who raced back again and led them unerringly to their new home.

No sooner had they arrived than word reached Joseph informing him that his family was now in Goshen. Joseph didn't waste a second. He ordered his chariot to be made ready, and in minutes one of Egypt's fastest horses was yanking that chariot down the road at breakneck speed. In very short order, Joseph arrived. As soon as he saw his father, the two of them ran towards one another, wrapped themselves in one another's arms, and wept and wept and wept. Tears of joy gushed out of them unrestrained. There is no more exquisite joy! Can you even begin to fathom the rapture of that moment? It is not just that they had not seen one another for twenty-two years, though surely that would have been enough all by itself to bring on such gladness. It was so much more than that. It was that both of them were reveling in the pure goodness of God. Jacob was not just hugging a son; he was embracing an honored son, an elevated prince who was saving his entire family, to say nothing of a whole nation and all the countries around. And Joseph was not just hugging his dad; he was embracing a father he knew he had pleased in the most excellent of ways—he had rescued everything Jacob held dear from certain extinction. Here is a preview of just how rich it is for Jesus, and for us, when redemption—hard-fought-for, slow-in-coming, tortuous-in-the-making redemption—has finally accomplished its mission! That hug, that tight embrace, those tears of pure joy—that is the capstone, the peak, the very apex that made all the pain, grief, and loss in the redemptive enterprise so worthwhile.

If you look back through this long story, there is a solid steel thread running through it from the very beginning: *Joseph lived for his father.* What gave him the courage to be a whistleblower way back in chapter 37? His loyalty to his father: "he brought their father a bad report about them" (37: 2b). What gave him his sense of honor? It was the richly embroidered robe *from the father.* Why did he go and check on his brothers at Shechem and then, when he couldn't find them, persist in his search all the way to Dothan? *His father sent him.* Joseph lived to please the eye of his father.

This longing to win the approval of a parent is deeply embedded in the heart of every child. It's embedded in you too. Let me tell you a couple of stories.

Surely one of the highest honors to which entertainers aspire is to be chosen as the featured star of the half-time Super Bowl show. In 2017, that honor went to Lady Gaga. Lee Cowan interviewed her for CBS's *Sunday Morning* a few weeks before the big event. In that interview, this woman, a star to millions and worshiped around the world, opened up a rare picture into her heart of hearts. 110 million people would celebrate her musical genius in a first-rate Super Bowl halftime show. But, she flatly informed Lee, that was not what brought her the greatest joy of her life. So what was it? In imperfect English, here's what she announced:

> "Making your dad happy is, especially for an Italian Catholic girl, I'll tell you, it feels really good," she said. "And I feel that today. You know, all the awards in the world, you can get into all the nightclubs, they'll send you the nicest clothes. [But there is] . . . nothing better than walking into your dad's restaurant and seeing a smile on his face and knowing that your mom and dad and your sister are real proud of you. That, for me, is real success." (CBS Sunday Morning, Nov 27, 2016)

110 million people watched her on that stage, but she performed for only one pair of eyes—her father's. If he was pleased, it would matter little who was displeased. His joy in her was what made her joy perfectly complete. For she well knew that the crowds will, in time, drift away, mesmerized by a new talent that finds its way onto the stage. But a father is there . . . forever.

A second example: after the game, marked by a shocking come-from-behind win by the New England Patriots against the Atlanta Falcons (who led 28–3 in the third quarter), the MVP of the Super Bowl, Patriot quarterback Tom Brady said virtually the same thing. He said their victory was for his dad and his mom. Earlier in the week, he had declared for the whole country to hear, "My dad is my hero."

Joseph was the second most powerful man in all of Egypt, and there is no doubt that he was determined to serve Pharaoh as best he could. But Pharaoh was not his father. In fact, he told his brothers it was quite the opposite; God had elevated him so highly that he was a father to Pharaoh! For Joseph, there was only one father; there was no greater ambition in his heart than pleasing that one father. So what is truly happening in this tear-filled moment is more than just a reunion. For Joseph, this was an exquisite moment of celebrating how he had pleased his father as a redeemer for the whole family. Twenty-two years earlier, Jacob had sent Joseph out to look after his brothers, and, more than either ever imagined, he had done just that in the finest possible way: he had been God's agent in the complete redemption of hearts imprisoned in deceit and a family on the brink of annihilation.

Take another look at this son-father relationship. Joseph had a wife who came from an elite family. He had sons who, no doubt, he cherished. He worked for the top ruler of the country. He had servants. He had colleagues in the government. Joseph moved in the power circles of Egypt, and no doubt he had plenty of friends in high positions. In contrast to all that, his biological father was not all that impressive. His farming operation was not large. His name was not well known. He was not rich. He was a common shepherd. But Joseph never allowed his advance into the top strata of Egyptian power and prestige to hoist this anchor and leave his father behind. His relationship with his father was the very linchpin of his life. You could surely say that Joseph lived every day just to please his father, even though he was miles away. His father was the invisible monitor of his activities, the secret object of his aspirations. Joseph lived by, under, and for his father. No wonder he yearned for him! When the brothers returned to Egypt on their second trip, Joseph's first question of them was, "How is your aged father you told me about? Is he still living?" (43: 27b). Even more revealing is what Joseph blurted out the moment he disclosed his identity to his brothers. You will remember that he shocked them with the announcement, "I am Joseph!" But right on the heels of that statement, this is what burst out of him: "Is my father still living?" And from then on, his focus was his father:

- "Now hurry back to my father" (45: 9).

- "Tell my father about all the honor accorded me in Egypt" (45: 13a).

- "Bring my father down here quickly" (45: 13b).

- "And this is what he sent to his father" (45: 23).

As players on a team constantly keep one eye on their coach all though the game, so Joseph, during all those twenty-two years of separation, never stopped living out his everyday life before his father's eyes.

Doesn't this remind you of someone else? For as you learned in your youth, the one and only purpose in the heart of Jesus was to please his Father. When he was just twelve years old—having been reprimanded by his mother for staying behind in the temple, listening to and questioning the teachers there—he respectfully challenged her justified irritation (she and "father" Joseph had been searching for him for three days!) with a question that completely baffled both of them: "Why were you searching for me? Didn't you know I had to be in my *Father's* house?" (Luke 2: 49) At just twelve, Jesus's heart was aimed in precisely one direction: the house of his Father.

Then, at the very end of his life, as he summoned up one last mighty breath before he died, what were his final words? "Father, into your hands I commend my spirit" (Luke 23: 46). Between those brackets, his entire life was centered in just that one relationship.

- It defined who he was. He put it this way: "I live because of the Father" (John 6: 47).

- When he spoke, he claimed that it was actually his Father *speaking through him* (John 8: 28; 12: 49).

- When he performed any action, especially his miracles, he claimed that he himself was not doing it at all: *it was his father, acting through him* (John 14: 10).

- The relationship was so intertwined he put it this way: "I and the Father are one" (John 10: 30).

In that light, can you even imagine what it had to be like for Jesus to be reunited with his Father when he ascended into heaven? None of us can even begin to conceive of the joy in the heart of that Son as his Father welcomed him home and then honored him with one laurel after another, giving him a name above every name (Phil. 2: 9), elevating him over every power and authority (Col. 2: 10), seating him at his right hand in the heavenly realms (Eph. 1: 20), and putting everything under his feet (1 Cor. 15: 27).

Let's put this in terms of your own experience. I know how hard all five of you ran in cross country. What propelled you through all that pain? What made you push yourself when every muscle was screaming at you in pain and every cell in your lungs was crying for you to stop? Was it just that ribbon, or that trophy, or that first place spot on the awards stand? It was that, but so much more. It was the joy it would bring to your mom and dad. It was knowing that you had made them proud! It was being an ingredient in their parental joy.

And yet, that is just a taste of the real thing. It's only an appetizer. It's an elemental form of the greatest fulfillment any of us humans could possibly taste. But as I lead you on to that joy, get yourself ready for it. I am about to tell you something that, at first reading, will seem to contradict everything you ever were told about your attitude towards your parents. This could come as a shock to you. You may have bumped into it already in your studies in the New Testament.

When Jesus invited people to follow him, he told them to leave their fathers and mothers. Seriously leave them. In one case, a man asked permission for a short delay in following Jesus because he had to first bury his father. Jesus curtly told him to skip the funeral and "let the dead bury the dead!" Can you imagine not even taking the time to honor your father by giving him a decent burial because of a situation where putting Jesus first demands your absence? But Jesus talked even more severely. He said that he came

to turn a man against his father,
a daughter against her mother,
a daughter-in-law against her mother-in-law—
a man's enemies will be the members of his own household. (Matt.
10: 35–36)

He spoke even more strongly than that. He said, "If anyone comes to me and does not hate father and mother, wife and children, brothers and sisters—yes, even their own life—such a person cannot be my disciple" (Luke 14: 26).

Once when Jesus was teaching inside a very crowded house, he was told that his mother and brothers were outside, calling for him. [They had come to "take charge of him, for they said, 'He is out of his mind'" (Mark 3: 21).] Jesus's curt response, once again, seemed utterly disrespectful toward his mother: "Who are my mother and my brothers?" he asked. Then he looked at those seated in a circle around him and said, "Here are my mother and my brothers! Whoever does God's will is my brother and sister and mother" (Mark 3: 33–35). At that moment Jesus *redefined family*. He was teaching people not to break the fifth commandment but to transcend it. His purpose was to show us that in the heavenly kingdom we *graduate* from our earthly family into that perfect eternal family where our only final allegiance is to the one God and Father of us all. Why? For our even greater joy! For if it thrills the heart of a child to have pleased an earthly parent, imagine the joy of pleasing the very God who formed us with his fingers for himself in the wombs of our mothers!

In his often-quoted essay *The Weight of Glory*, C. S. Lewis attempts to describe what a joyful Joseph-Jacob moment it could be if you and I should discover that we have pleased not just a mom or dad but the living God himself, our one and only "Father who art in heaven":

When I began to look into this matter I was shocked to find such different Christians as Milton, Johnson, and Thomas Aquinas taking heavenly glory quite frankly in the sense of fame or good report. But not fame conferred by our fellow creatures—fame with God, approval or (I might say) "appreciation" by God. And then, when I had thought it over, I saw that this view was scriptural; nothing can eliminate from the parable the divine accolade, "Well done, thou good and faithful servant." With that, a good deal of what I had been thinking all my life fell down like a house of cards. I suddenly remembered that no one can enter heaven except as a child; and nothing is so obvious in a child—not in a conceited child, but in a good child—as its great and undisguised pleasure in being praised." (Lewis, The Weight of Glory, pp.36, 37)

You will have many delights over the years. You may very well savor the deep pleasures of a great marriage, children, promotions, honors, grand achievements, adventurous travel, exciting sports, terrific health, and even, someday, grandchildren of your own. But look one more time at this moment in the life of Joseph, running up to his father, throwing his arms around him, and experiencing his father's embrace. No wonder he wept for a very long time.

That is as vivid a portrait as you will ever see of life's greatest possible joy: living your life in such a way that a day will come when you will find yourself in the very presence of your one and only true Father, feeling his embrace and hearing him say to you, "Well done, good and faithful servant." That will infinitely fulfill and transcend any medal you ever earned.

CHAPTER 22

Redemption's Bounty

Read Genesis 46:31–47:31

─────────────────

At the very beginning of this book, I told you that redemption comes hard. There are some situations that are so broken they appear completely unredeemable.

When I was a kid, I picked blueberries every summer in John De Vries's perfectly cultivated blueberry farm about three miles south of Graafschap, Michigan, the little village where I grew up. That blueberry farm was pristine—every plant was perfectly pruned, spaced, and fertilized, and there was not a weed in sight. We pedaled our bikes the six-mile round trip to pick his thirty acres of immaculate bushes, and the farm produced tons of this perfect health food years before any of us even knew what antioxidants were.

But that patch has fallen on hard times. It changed ownership, and now it's been completely neglected. Not only weeds but full-grown trees have grown up among the bushes. The processing shed, half collapsed, is so overgrown with wild vines it's virtually invisible. The farm has been abandoned. To redeem it back to its former glory would require a person with very deep pockets and even deeper resolve. It could take years and cost thousands. It would demand grit in the face of a frequent sense of futility. It could fail.

Our first instinct when faced with a damaged part of our broken world tends toward head-wagging skepticism. To most of us redemption looks foolhardy. Sounding wise and realistic, we turn away with well-known justifications:

- That would be pouring money down a rat hole.

- They are so set in their ways, they'll never change.

- It's been that way for years now.

- Other people have already tried to fix it; nothing works!

- You can't teach an old dog new tricks.

- The two sides are just too far apart.

- There is too much water over the dam.

You will face broken relationships, impasses, stalemates, and situations that appear unredeemable. You will find them everywhere—in government agencies, corporations, churches, neighborhoods, and families. You will be powerfully tempted, in the name of realism, to tell yourself, "It's not even worth the effort." Your reluctance will be understandable. True redemption is invariably costly.

But now you are about to see the benefits! This is the wondrous "rest of the story," to quote Paul Harvey's famous tagline. The blessings far outweigh the cost. After his tearful and tender reunion with his father in Goshen, Joseph went right to work to secure all the benefits of the redemption of his family.

The First Bounty (46:31–47:6, 11–12, 27): Property

Although he had already promised them that Goshen would be their new home (45:10–11) since it was near where he lived, and Pharaoh had also assured Joseph that his family would be given "the best of all Egypt" (45:20), it appears that the fine print wasn't finished.

So Joseph announced to his family that he himself would go to Pharaoh and serve as their advocate. He would use his highly favored position in the power corridors of Egyptian government to secure legal ownership of the finest piece of real estate in the entire country just for them! To use a common metaphor, this family would come into property *on Joseph's coattails*. This was their only hope. They were unknowns to the Egyptians. Because of their occupation as shepherds, they were even despised by Egyptians. Egyptians wouldn't even sit down with Hebrews for a meal (43: 32). So, they had three strikes against them: they were poor, they were foreigners, and worst of all, they were shepherds. If it had not been for Joseph, their advocate, their prospects were zero.

It's vital that I point out to you the parallel here to Jesus, who is presented to us as our advocate: "My dear children, I write this to you so that you will not sin. But if anybody does sin, we have an advocate with the Father— Jesus Christ, the Righteous One" (1 John 2:1).

Our Lord had no more than won our redemption by his death and resurrection than he became our advocate in the heavenly court. He ascended into heaven, took his place as God's "right hand man," and began "lobbying" for us in order to secure one blessing after another from the Father. He asked that we be forgiven by the father on the basis of his sacrifice. He secured our adoption by the Father into the new humanity he has launched as the second Adam. He secured our inheritance as heirs of eternal life. He asked that the very Spirit by which he lived out his life of perfect obedience, compelling teaching, and powerful works would now be poured out upon us. He ensured that our names were written in the book of life. He locked in the final benefit: that death would not have the last word over our bodies but that we would conquer our graves just as he did, rising with bodies just like his resurrected body: imperishable, glorious, powerful, and spiritual (1 Cor. 15: 42–44). He asked for the works!! And he got it, all for our sake. Colossians 2: 9, 10 describes these vast benefits this way: "For in Christ all the fullness of the Deity lives in bodily form, and you have been given fullness in Christ, who is the head over every power and authority." All of that is illustrated here. Joseph began to win vast benefits for his family.

Joseph personally appeared before Pharaoh and informed him that his family had finally arrived. He told Pharaoh something Pharaoh may not have known, and which could have been a serious liability to their being welcomed. He told Pharaoh that his brothers were shepherds! Since, as I said, shepherds were detestable to Egyptians, this was a whole new wrinkle. Would he allow a group of people who were not only despised Hebrews, but whose occupations were loathed among his own subjects, to actually come and live among his own people? This was a delicate situation!

So Joseph selected just five of his brothers for presentation to Pharaoh and coached them on *exactly* what to say to Pharaoh. They were to confirm everything Joseph had already told Pharaoh about them, and, when he asked them about their occupation, they were not to use the term "shepherds." Instead, they were to say, "Your servants have *tended livestock* from our boyhood on, just as our fathers did" (46:33).

You will notice that Pharaoh never engaged the brothers in conversation. It is very likely that their occupation was so detestable to Egyptians, the very fact that they were even allowed into his presence in the first place was a rare exception. He spoke *only* to Joseph. But Joseph was all they needed. Pharaoh made his royal pronouncement and even threw in an unexpected bonus! He gave them exactly what they wanted, the land of Goshen as their home, and then even informed Joseph that if any of his brothers had special ability with livestock, they would be welcomed into managing even his own herds! It was a bonanza, more than any of them had even dared to imagine! They were not only given a welcome into the land; despite their occupation, they were given *stature!* They walked out of Pharaoh's presence with their "detestable" heads held high. They strolled out like millionaires! They had been handed the works! It was fantastic! No wonder they prospered. Genesis 47: 11–12 and 27 sums up their abundant new life this way: "So Joseph settled his father and his brothers in Egypt and gave them property in the best part of the land, the district of Rameses as Pharaoh directed. Joseph also provided his father and his brothers and all his father's household with food, according to the number of their children. . . . Now the Israelites settled in Egypt in the region of Goshen. They acquired property there and were fruitful and increased greatly in number."

Finally, the promise God gave Abraham that his seed would be as numberless as the sand of the seashore and the stars of the sky began to be fulfilled. It had taken a very long time. God gave Abraham just one son to keep his promise. Decades dragged by. Finally he gave Isaac just one son. More decades crawled along. Even for Jacob, after 130 years (and, now, three generations), his clan numbered a mere seventy. But now, finally, the babies started to come—by the hundreds! A tiny clan that could have been wiped out by the famine in Canaan is now, instead, relocated to a land of such abundance and transformed into a community so productive that in just four generations (a generation is considered one hundred years in Genesis), they will become over two million strong. That is the bounty of redemption. It blesses thousands who come after us.

Now there was no way Joseph could have known that this would be the outcome of his redemptive calling that day, some twenty-two years earlier, when he was dragged off to Egypt as a shocked seventeen-year-old. He was not afforded the vision of this glorious payoff as he bore up under all his sufferings. He drank his cup simply because he had been given a dream, confirmed by a second one, that someday he would rule over his brothers. That's all he had to go on. He embraced his journey in simple, sturdy faith—just like Jesus did for us, and just like any redeemer has to do. We are only allowed to see the bounty in the way the great heroes of faith in Hebrews 11 viewed them: *from a distance*. But this picture is meant to do one thing for us as we face situations that look unredeemable: it is meant to challenge us to believe that if God calls us to be an agent of redemption in a situation that appears unsalvageable, he is able to do far more than we can even begin to imagine. The New Testament pushes us to believe this! Listen: "So do not throw away your confidence; it will be richly rewarded" (Heb. 10: 35).

The Second Bounty (47: 7–10, 13–26): Prosperity

When God first called Abraham to follow him by leaving his home in Haran and going to a place he would be shown, he not only promised to bless *him*. He promised to bless *the whole world through him*. He put it this way: "and all peoples on earth will be blessed through you" (Gen. 12:3c).

The second fruit of Joseph's redemptive work is one of the earliest demonstrations of that astounding promise. All the people of Egypt ended up being rescued from certain starvation by Joseph, and, in that process, Pharaoh himself ended up becoming both fabulously wealthy and much loved through benefactor Joseph. It all was triggered by a momentous event: Joseph presenting Jacob to Pharaoh. "Then Joseph brought his father Jacob in and presented him before Pharaoh. After Jacob blessed Pharaoh, Pharaoh asked him, 'How old are you?' And Jacob said to Pharaoh, 'The years of my pilgrimage are a hundred and thirty. My years have been few and difficult, and they do not equal the years of the pilgrimage of my fathers.' Then Jacob blessed Pharaoh and went out from his presence" (47: 7–10).

It was a very short visit, but with long consequences! You will notice something: *twice* Jacob blessed Pharaoh. It was the first thing Jacob did the moment he came into Pharaoh's presence, and it was the last thing he did as he left Pharaoh's presence, as if to impress upon Pharaoh that this blessing was first and last, the most important business of that meeting. That blessing bracketed a very short conversation.

Imagine this! Here is a very old man, likely dressed in shepherd's plain garb, with wrinkled face, stooped posture and, we know, poor eyesight. He is the very picture of a weathered old codger, tottering into the presence of the most powerful man in the country. Pharaoh was vigorous in health, resplendent in his royal robes, seated on a majestic throne, and surrounded by finely dressed officials. It would seem that it would be the old man who would seek some favor from the mighty monarch. But things are not always as they appear! In fact, the most powerful man in that grand, imperial throne room that day was this aged saint who spoke twice of himself as a pilgrim and summed up his 130 years as "few and difficult," unequal to the years of his fathers. He is presenting himself as a person who has suffered much in his all too short journey through life. But he knows who he is. He is the honored father of an esteemed son who has rescued this Pharaoh's entire country from a terrible fate. Moreover, he is the blessed son of Isaac, the blessed son of Abraham.

Without a doubt, Jacob knew why he had been brought into the presence of that country's leader: to assure him that the presence of that son, and now that son's entire clan, would in fact continue to bless Pharaoh and his country in ways that he could not even begin to imagine. It is not just Egypt that is benefitting Israel; Jacob wants Pharaoh to know that it is Israel that is benefitting Egypt! It is as if he is saying, "Pharaoh, you have no idea of just how favored you are to have this blessed and blessing family move in among you. Just watch. In just a few years you will be richer than you ever could have dreamed, and even better, your people will love you as they never loved you before." A monarch's dream! As aged Jacob shuffled out of his throne room, Pharaoh must have wondered what that blessing might possibly mean for him. He had seen the very Spirit of God in the son (41: 38); it was very possible it was in the father too! He didn't have to wonder long, for Genesis 47: 13–26 spells it all out in fascinating detail.

Here's what happened: as the famine persisted, the people in Egypt as well as Canaan ended up using their last dime to buy food. After two years, they were broke. Their savings had all ended up in Pharaoh's bank (47:14). So when the time came to buy the food they needed to survive during year three, they were at a loss. But Joseph suggested a way out. He offered them the option of bartering their livestock for food. That was a no-brainer, and they knew it. It was far better to hand over a few animals than to watch your children starve to death! They gladly brought in their horses, sheep, goats, cattle, and donkeys; received food in return; and, gratefully, managed to survive for another whole year. But the famine was still less than halfway through the seven years it had been predicted to last. So, as year four arrived, the people came to Joseph and offered to him all they had left: themselves and their property. They volunteered their own bodies and their land in exchange for their survival for the rest of the famine's duration. They *begged* Joseph to accept their offer because, once again, this was a no-brainer: slavery was far better than death. Now think of this: they believed that the best bargain they could strike for survival, for life itself, was turning over their final asset, their land, and turning in their most precious possession: their very bodies! They believed bondage was better than death. In fact, bondage was the key not just to survival but to a future. And then they asked for one more gift: seed, for the time when the famine would end, so that they might "save" the land from utter desolation (v. 19).

Not a few people have read this story and faulted Joseph severely for what he did to these helpless people. And, in truth, he does appear to be an opportunist, seizing this desperate situation as a chance to ingratiate himself to

Pharaoh! It seems he has no heart! Instead, he hatches a clever scheme to generate a huge windfall for Pharaoh which certainly wouldn't hurt his and his family's futures! This looks completely self-serving! It seems he is utterly lacking in compassion. He seems to have turned into a tyrant! Does this expose a dark side to Joseph?

Take a second look. Notice the benefits this policy brought not just to Pharaoh but to the people themselves.

1. The people were filled with gratitude to Joseph. They said to him, "You have saved our lives" (v. 25). They did not feel defrauded; they felt delivered!

2. Second, notice how this policy shaped their tax obligations once the famine years were lifted: *it placed them in a 20 percent tax bracket* (v. 26). This is a considerably lower tax rate than you will likely ever pay in your lives, if you consider not only the federal income tax but all the other taxes you will pay. In 2016 the Tax Foundation set Tax Freedom Day in the United States as April 24. This is the date by which the nation, as a whole, will have paid up its total tax obligation (national, state, and local) for the entire year, which represents *31 percent* of all our annual earnings. Compare that with what Joseph was able to secure for these Egyptians.

3. Third, consider this: Joseph saved countless thousands, perhaps millions, from sure and certain death.

4. And finally, consider that this fulfilled the very blessing Jacob had pronounced over Pharaoh. Here it is in all its glory: people are saved, a monarch is loved, and the future of a country is ensured. This is an early picture of "the blessing of Abraham."

But there is another dimension that is even more wondrous: this is a picture of the blessed life of every fully devoted follower of Jesus. St Paul was very straightforward about his status as a follower: he was a slave, a *doulos* (Greek), of Jesus Christ, and he was honored to be one for the very same reason the Egyptians were glad to become slaves of Pharaoh: it is a life-saver. No one can be a true follower of Jesus without being his willing "slave" just as he, in turn, was fully obedient to his own Father *as nothing but a servant* (Phil. 2: 7). Even more to the point here: the truth is, there is no such thing as *absolute* freedom. You will be a slave to something or someone. You will be the slave to *whatever you love with all your heart.* You may be a slave to your own ambition. You may end up enslaved to money, pleasure, power, or fame. These are alluring masters, but they are also cruel. They will drive you mercilessly until you will have spent your last energies in their service, but they will never satisfy you. To choose to be a slave of Jesus is, paradoxically, the only way I know for you to actually find your true freedom. For this is what that slave Paul said of his life under the master: "It is for freedom that Christ has set us free" (Gal. 5: 1a). This is such a paradox! George Matheson (1842–1906) captured it so well in his old but grand hymn, *Make Me a Captive, Lord*:

> Make me a captive, Lord, and then I shall be free;
> force me to render up my sword, and I shall conqueror be.
> I sink in life's alarms when by myself I stand;
> imprison me within thine arms, and strong shall be my hand.
> My will is not my own till thou hast made it thine;
> if it would reach a monarch's throne, it must its crown resign;
> it only stands unbent amid the clashing strife,
> when on thy bosom it has leant, and found in thee its life.

That is true freedom. And that was the second bounty flowing out of Joseph's ordeal as a redeemer.

The Third Bounty (Gen. 48): Posterity

When Jacob knew his time had come, he was far more focused on his grand-children's future than on his own departure. There were two grandchildren in particular he was determined to bless before he died: Joseph's sons.

A day came when Jacob fell ill, and Joseph learned about it. He immedi-ately went to see his father, and, since this could have been the last time his two sons Manasseh and Ephraim might see their grandfather, Joseph made sure to take them along. When Jacob heard that Joseph had arrived with his boys, it was so enlivening to his spirit that he rallied his strength enough to sit right up in bed and welcome them. Joseph may have thought that this was going to be a simple visit; it turned out to be far more than anything Joseph could have possibly expected.

As you can imagine, Joseph was concerned about his boys. The other grand-sons, like Reuben's four (46:9), Simeon's six (46:10) or even Benjamin's ten (46:21), had all grown up with grandfather, Jacob. They knew their history and had been trained to worship and sacrifice to the one true God. But Joseph's sons were half Egyptian. They had been raised in a pagan culture and only lately had come to know their grandfather. No doubt, Joseph had taught and trained them well in their heritage, telling them all about the God of their great-great-grandfather Abraham and great-grandfather Isaac. Still, immersed as they were in Egypt's schools and culture, he had to be eager to expose them to their true roots as much as possible. So you can understand how important it was for Joseph to take them along for what might have been one of their final visits with their revered grandfather.

The first words out of Jacob's mouth came right to the point. Jacob told Joseph (again) that *El Shaddai* ("God Almighty," or "Lord of Hosts") had given him a surefire promise in a brilliant vision back when he was just a young man running from Esau, spending a night at Luz (the older name for Bethel), and sleeping under the stars with a stone for a pillow. God had solemnly promised him that he would bless him with many children and propagate his family into an entire community of peoples (which became the twelve tribes) and, moreover, that he would give him the land of Canaan as an everlasting possession. Here was aged Jacob, far from Canaan, sitting on the side of his bed in Egypt, assuring Joseph that the God of the armies of heaven would surely keep his word.

Joseph listened with deep reverence. He knew this story and these promises. His sons had to be entranced to hear that their grandfather had actually seen the living God. Then came the big surprise. Though Jacob had not yet detected the presence of the boys right there in the room because he was almost totally blind, he announced to Joseph that he had decided to treat Manasseh and Ephraim as if they were his own sons, on par with all his other sons. He said he was going to elevate them to a status equal to that of Joseph's own brothers. If Joseph had other children, they would be treated as grandchildren, but not Manasseh and Ephraim. They would be considered bona fide sons of Jacob on a par with all his sons, endowed with all the rights and privileges their uncles were entitled to. This meant title to real estate in the promised land. It was a stunning announcement. But this is how Jacob was determined to honor Joseph as the redeemer of the family: he was going to elevate Joseph's sons to Joseph's level!

Once again, this is also true for Christians! Hebrews 2:11 says, "Both the one who makes people holy and those who are made holy are of the same family. So Jesus is not ashamed to call them brothers and sisters."

Just as Manasseh and Ephraim were elevated to the status of being brothers to their own father—he had redeemed them too—so also Jesus is not ashamed to consider us his full brothers and sisters because he has redeemed us. That is honored status indeed!

As a result, if you study a map of the land allotted to the ten tribes, you will see that close to one third of the entire territory of Canaan was apportioned to Manasseh and Ephraim! What a magnificent gift!

Just then Jacob actually noticed the shadowy figures of the two boys with Joseph and asked him, "Who are these?" When Joseph told him that they were, indeed, Manasseh and Ephraim, Jacob invited him to bring them very close to him so that he might see them better and then place a blessing upon them.

Jacob took each of the boys onto his lap, held them in his arms, and kissed them tenderly. He was overcome with emotion. Full of wonder, he said to Joseph, "I never expected to see your face again, and now God has allowed me to see your children too" (48:11). As Joseph stood there watching his father holding his sons, treating them as equal to all the other brothers, might Joseph have thought about the cistern, the being sold, the slavery, the lie of Potiphar's wife, the unjust imprisonment, the twenty-two long years of separation, the hard work of prosecuting his brothers and bringing them to brokenness? None of that ordeal could begin to compare to the joy of this moment. *The bounty of redemption is so immense, it dwarfs the pain of winning it.* Jesus compared it to the pain of childbirth (which is real enough!) to the joy of holding a newborn (which is indescribably greater) when he said, "A woman giving birth to a child has pain because her time has come; but when her baby is born she forgets the anguish because of her joy that a child is born into the world" (John 16: 21).

But this was just the beginning! Jacob had asked Joseph to bring the boys close *so that he could bless them.* So Joseph gently extracted them from Jacob's embrace, bowed low with his face to the ground as an expression of his deep reverence for his father, and then arranged for the boys to stand properly before their grandfather. He positioned Ephraim as the younger before Jacob's left hand and Manasseh as the older before Jacob's right hand so that Manasseh could receive the blessing of the first born and Ephraim the blessing of the second born.

But it was not to be that way. Jacob had decided to "put Ephraim before Manasseh" (v. 20b). We are not told why, but if you look closely at the blessing Jacob gave to Joseph and through him to his sons, you may see why. That blessing is found in vv. 15–16:

> Then he blessed Joseph and said,
> "May the God before whom my fathers
> Abraham and Isaac walked faithfully,
> the God who has been my shepherd all my life to this day,
> the Angel who has delivered me from all harm
> —may he bless these boys.
> May they be called by my name
> and the names of my fathers Abraham and Isaac,
> and may they increase greatly on the earth."

Jacob is doing nothing less than giving his own joyful personal testimony here. He is informing these tender young boys and their father just how wondrously blessed *he had been all his life.* He told them that God had been his own personal shepherd and, besides that, had protected him like a mighty angel from any kind of harm. Moreover, he insisted, his was the third generation for whom this was true. This was his grandfather Abraham's experience. This was his father Isaac's experience. And now, this had been his experience too. And so he declared that this same high level of protection and blessing would also be the experience of Joseph through his two sons, so that people call these boys blessed—*just like Abraham, Isaac, and Jacob.*

As Jacob savored that blessing, the Spirit of God, I believe, reminded him of the fact that this enormous blessing was given, in only one case, to a firstborn, Abraham. He was the firstborn son of Terah. But Isaac was not Abraham's first-born son. That was Ishmael, who had not received the blessing. Instead it had been bestowed upon the second born, Isaac. Moreover, he himself was not Isaac's firstborn son. That had been Esau, who had despised his birthright and sold it to Jacob. Two of the three ancestors were not firstborns. God had sovereignly decided to bypass the firstborn and favor the second born. He had experienced this firsthand for himself. And now, having tasted that blessing, he felt compelled (I think, by the Holy Spirit) to pass it on not to firstborn Manasseh but to second born Ephraim.

Even though later on in Israel's history, Moses was to codify in law the honor of the firstborn as belonging to God (Exod. 13: 1–2; Num. 3: 13; 8: 17), Jacob wanted to perpetuate, in Joseph's family, the blessedness of the second born. If you look further down the line, you will discover many people whom God blessed mightily who were not firstborns: Moses was not a firstborn (Exod. 6:20). Neither was Gideon. Neither was David.

And did not our Lord himself remind us that many that are first will be last and the last, first? In the kingdom of heaven, birth order, important as it may be in human development, is transcended again and again. Three of you grandchildren are not firstborns, which is so inconsequential in God's kingdom as to be utterly insignificant!

So Jacob extended his arms and then surprised Joseph by crossing them, placing his right hand on Manasseh and his left hand on Ephraim! Joseph was sure this was a mistake, and in a moment of displeasure tried to correct his father by grasping his right hand and transferring it from Ephraim's head to Manasseh's head. It wouldn't budge. Jacob firmly resisted him. This was no mistake. Jacob was resolute. Moved by the sovereign Spirit of God, who has mercy on whomever he chooses, he had decided give the greater blessing to second born Ephraim. He assured Joseph that there was no cause for concern. Manasseh would not be shortchanged, for he too would become great and produce numerous descendants. But Ephraim would be greater, and his descendants would actually become a whole group of nations.

And then, to enrich Joseph all the more, Jacob announced that he viewed him as head of his brothers (v. 22), confirming that the dreams he had as a seventeen-year-old, dreams Jacob had "kept in mind," had truly been fulfilled. As proof, he specifically bequeathed to him a ridge of land that he himself counted as one of his own personal conquests, for he had "taken it from the Amorites with his sword and his bow." He was assuring his one truly beloved son that he had already prepared a place for his descendants in Canaan, just as Joseph had prepared a place for him, for the time being, in Egypt. It was an announced guarantee that the day would surely come when Joseph himself, along with all of his descendants, would finally come to their hearts true home.

The Fourth Bounty (47:28–31; 49:29–50:14): Place

At the very beginning of this story, in Genesis 37:1–2, Moses tells us that Jacob lived in the land where his father had stayed, the land of Canaan. This was Jacob's true home, his settled place on the planet, his roots. Moses then tells us that everything that follows is "the account of Jacob." This seems strange because from that point on, the story hardly mentions Jacob at all. It seems completely focused upon Joseph. But Moses wanted us to know something: even though Joseph occupied center stage, if you look deeper, this is really a story of God's tenacious faithfulness to *Jacob*. This is a story of how God redeemed the alienated family of *Jacob*. But even more personally, this is a story of how God carried Jacob himself through decades of heartbreak and a long, dark valley of unrelenting grief. God then pulled him up out of the other end of that valley into a place of such euphoria it really does look like a fairy-tale ending! The last seventeen of his 147 years of life were indescribably sweet, regardless of the fact that he was slowly going blind. To borrow C. S. Lewis's description of his own conversion, Jacob was "surprised by joy." Joseph was not the only one who was thrown into the pits of a dry cistern or a dank Egyptian prison, only to be redeemed out of them. This was Jacob's story as well.

Now it was Jacob who was finishing strong. All of you ran cross country, and you know well how vital your final kick was to a well run race. You carefully paced yourselves so that during the final stretch, when your competitors were wobbling from exhaustion, you could explode in one final burst of power and dash to that finish line with such blazing speed it would fill us with awe. You beamed if people said to you, "What a finish!!" So you can well appreciate the timeless saying: "All's well that **ends** well." It's the finish that counts.

Now I know you are young, and I am pretty sure that the last thing on your mind is your death! I don't want to get morbid here, but I want to challenge you to think about your life the way you think about cross country. As we look at this fourth benefit of redemption, it moves me to challenge you to live your lives *focused on how you want to finish*. It has been well observed that no one is truly ready to live unless they are first ready to die. Wise people, like smart runners, live their lives *with the end in view*.

There is no grander finale than coming to the end of your days upon this earth and finding yourself filled with joy, not so much over your accomplishments (which will, soon enough, be forgotten by men), but rather over God's surprising goodness to you. That is a panoramic vista so gratifying, it will move you to take your final breath whispering praise. Some 470 years after Jacob breathed his final breath, a diviner named Balaam was so envious of God's goodness to Jacob, he poured out this admiring jealousy: "Who can count the dust of Jacob or number the fourth part of Israel? Let me die the death of the righteous, and may my end be like theirs!" (Num. 23: 10).

What a beautiful death Jacob experienced! This man, who at one time was certain he would end his years in gloom, with a heart full of mourning for his son (37: 35), instead crowned his years with a heart full of worship as he leaned on the top of his staff (47: 31). What a wondrous way to arrive at the finish line.

Once again, there's more here. Jacob died not only with a heart of worship but with a garland of dignity wrapped around his burial. Jacob knew his true home, and so he issued detailed instructions regarding exactly where his body was to be entombed. Even in death, he was determined to honor the faith of his fathers, for he knew that he owed his blessed life to the legacy of faith he had seen in them. So he insisted that he not be buried in Egypt (47: 29). He wanted to impress upon his grown children that Egypt was simply not their true home, so he made Joseph not only promise but swear to him, by placing his hand under his thigh, that he would not allow him to be buried in Egypt. This was a most solemn moment. When Joseph put his hand under his father's thigh, he was placing it near his organ of procreation, the organ that gives a man a future by producing children. It may have looked like Jacob was focused on his funeral; instead, he was focused on his *future*. By locating his grave in Canaan, in a small plot of land his grandfather Abraham had purchased as a cemetery, and in a cave on that property where Abraham, Sarah, Isaac, Rebekah, and Leah had all been buried, he was announcing to all of his descendants: *Egypt is not your true home! Canaan is!*

Joseph never forgot that reality. When he himself approached death, convinced that a day would come when the entire nation of Israel would leave Egypt, he left strict instructions that his body was to be embalmed but left unburied in a coffin. His bones were to be delivered out of Egypt on that day when God's mighty arm would come to their aid and bring them all back home. Both Jacob and Joseph are impressing a vital truth upon us: the ultimate destination of our lives is simply not on this earth in its present form, no matter how lovely our "Goshen" may be. We are pilgrims, and our ultimate destination is everything Canaan represents: a home on this earth when it is finally redeemed from its curse and fully renewed. Then, in our resurrected bodies, we will finally have "arrived," for onto that new earth God himself will come down out of heaven and live with us forever (Rev. 21: 1–4). God's redemption will end up being as immense as the earth itself . . . and much more.

To demonstrate the dignity of Jacob's death, Moses describes it in detail. Much like Jesus, Jacob decided when to take his last breath. He had just issued his last will and testament, specifying precisely what the future held for each of his sons (49: 1–28), issuing a blessing to each one appropriate to their character. He held a kind of final judgment, issuing perfect justice to each of his sons, predicting precisely what would become of each one of them. Finally, once again, in the hearing of all of them this time, he told them exactly where he was to be buried. Then, having run his race and finished his course, he simply drew his feet up into the bed, laid himself down, and freely exhaled his final breath. He released his spirit, just as Jesus did at the end of his six hours upon the cross. This is how he was "gathered to his people," a beautiful phrase teaching us that he now belonged to the ageless ones in eternity, but the heirloom of his faith belonged to his descendants.

Still, the moment of death always stings. The moment Jacob died, Joseph just broke down. His love for his father, the anchor of his life, was so deep he threw himself upon his father's lifeless body, weeping and kissing it over and over again. It moves me to tears just to write about it. Joseph was not afraid to let his emotions out. And now, as death tore his father and his friend from him, he responded just as Jesus did at the tomb of Lazarus: he wept. When my father died, my mother lay her head on his chest and sobbed, "Oh Don, how I loved you." Rarely have I seen a more sacred moment.

The last opportunity most adult children will ever have to honor the fifth commandment is the manner in which they conduct the funeral of their parents. Joseph made sure to honor his father as magnificently as his position would allow. And the Egyptians, deeply grateful for the son of such a father, were eager to follow Joseph's detailed funeral instructions to the letter. As a result, we are allowed to witness one of the most magnificent burials to be found in the Bible. It rivals even the most dignified ceremonies honoring the death of a head of state. The Egyptians took forty days to embalm the body. Then they publicly mourned him another seventy days. These are perfect numbers, representing total respect. Then Joseph approached Pharaoh, much like Joseph of Arimathea many centuries later would approach Pilate, informed him of the promise he had solemnly sworn to his father, and asked permission to transport his father's body to the very grave his father had, as a young man, dug for himself in the land of Canaan. Pharaoh honored Joseph's request, and why wouldn't he? Jacob had blessed him twice, a blessing that had enriched Pharaoh with unimaginable wealth. And he knew how his people must have felt as well, for the eyes of many in Egypt had been awed at the generous kindness the Hebrews' God had poured into their lives through the magnanimity of Joseph.

Consequently, we are privileged to be eyewitnesses to a most solemn and touching event: a royal retinue of pagan officials who had tasted for themselves just how good the God of Abraham, Isaac, and Jacob was, gladly joining the family of Jacob on pilgrimage to their spiritual birthplace and their ancestral roots. It was a long journey made by a very large company: a massive operation! When they finally arrived, they lamented again, and their wailing was so loud the Canaanites living in that area couldn't help but notice. They sensed this death was so momentous that they actually gave the spot a new name, Abel Mizraim ("mourning of the Egyptians"). Then they watched as Jacob's sons solemnly carried their father's body into the cave in the field of Machpelah near Mamre. There in that cemetery (a word related to "semen," meaning seed), they planted him as a man who believed God's promise that all of Canaan was his and his descendants' home. Pagans witnessed the funeral of a saint!

None of this would have happened if Joseph had refused to drink the cup. Redemption brings unimaginable rewards and benefits, and wondrous consequences none of us can even dream. There was a time Jacob would have thought such an honored death unthinkable. But this is what really happened—and it is meant to teach us that if we are willing to embrace our task in life as agents of God's redemptive work, what God may choose to do through us could turn out to be beyond anything we could have ever dreamed.

Wow.

CHAPTER 23

Really?

Read Genesis 50:15–21

You would have thought that the story was over. Joseph and his brothers have been reconciled. The entire clan of Jacob has moved to Egypt and settled into the lush land of Goshen. Seventeen beautiful years had gone by. Jacob had died a happy man and had been given an honored burial by all his sons. You almost expect Moses to say, "And so they all lived happily ever after." Not so fast.

Here comes a strange epilogue. Once the funeral was over, we discover a major crisis in Joseph's brothers: they question their redemption. It's the final battle redeemed people face: they question the reality of their own redemption because it is just too good to be true. They ask just one word: *Really?* The brothers had always feared that a day would come when Joseph would execute reprisals against them for the dastardly way they had treated him. For the time being they had felt safe because they knew he highly respected their father and would never execute his vendetta under dad's watchful eye. But now that dad was dead, they felt frightfully vulnerable. They were sure he would lower the boom and finally mete out the justice they knew they deserved. What was to stop him? He had all the power on his side. He could just obliterate them if he wished. They were sure their days were numbered. Any day now they expected knocks at the door by Joseph's officials, arrest, imprisonment, and then who knows what?

Fearing for their lives, they tried to save themselves. They came up with a plan (a ruse, really) to save their skins. Their strategy was to contrive this message for Joseph: *While he was still alive, dad instructed us to tell you, "Don't hurt your brothers for what they did to you. You need to forgive them."* They were so afraid they first sent this plea to Joseph via a messenger. Perhaps it was Benjamin. That would make sense since he was innocent, and Joseph had a warm place in his heart for his younger brother. Surely he was the best advocate they had left. But we don't know that for sure. Then, right on the heels of the messenger, all of them would arrive, throw themselves at his feet, and beg for mercy. Perhaps, just perhaps, they thought, this might get them off the hook.

They had no idea that when he first heard their plea from the messenger, it had saddened him so deeply that he broke down and wept.

All along I have been suggesting that redemption comes hard, and it does. And now for the final lesson: when it does come, *it is not easy to believe that it is for real. Perhaps that is the hardest part of all.*

Grace is shocking. You can be sure that the prodigal son could not believe his ears when his dad welcomed him home with hugs and kisses, put a ring on finger, dressed him in a brand new robe, and then threw a party for him. Grace is the last thing we expect. It is not easy to trust that the grace extended to us is bona fide. There isn't a catch somewhere? Grace is simply abnormal.

Zaccheus, perched in his tree, could hardly believe that a good man like Jesus would actually want to come into his house. Elizabeth could hardly believe it when the mother of the unborn Jesus showed up at her front door. The repentant thief on the cross had to be stunned when Jesus informed him that on that very day the two of them would be home in paradise. Events like this don't happen every day! No wonder Charles Wesley composed his famous hymn celebrating his own redemption with these first words, "And can it be . . . ?"

There are two realities that are the most difficult for us to believe: *evil at its worst and goodness at its best*. People could not believe that the Gestapo would murder millions of Jews during World War II or that the Japanese would attack Pearl Harbor—those kinds of atrocities were just unimaginable. But then again, they could hardly believe it when the war was finally over and won. That too took days to finally sink in.

One of the hardest steps to being redeemed is the final one: daring to believe that it is for real, finished, done, and accomplished—a final fact that will never be undone! The faith to believe that this is the new normal is so difficult to muster up, much less sustain, it requires constant assurance and reinforcement, which is why Jesus gave us the sacraments.

Do not be surprised if you find yourself doubting your salvation at some point in your life. You will have a lot of company, especially among older Christians who can find themselves tormented as they approach their final years with fresh uncertainty that they have truly been forgiven and will, in fact, be welcomed into God's holy presence. Take it from a pastor: this is much more common than you might imagine. A day may come when you may have to fight this final battle against, not unbelief, but simply *disbelief*. The truth is: the gospel is just so good it will seem too good to be true.

If you study the brothers, you'll see why. It always takes time for us to see the true dimensions and the enormity of the evil in our own hearts. The day they had sold Joseph off, they felt barely a twinge of guilt; instead they were relieved to be rid of him—that spoiled brat, that pest, that whistle-blower. But then they watched their father grieve, inconsolably, for over twenty years while they kept their guilty silence. That took its toll! Then they learned the truth of how much Joseph had suffered for years in Egypt—the slavery, being innocently framed, the imprisonment, and being forgotten. All of this had enlarged the enormity of their deed. And then there was that horrifying moment when he finally revealed himself to them—that had terrified them. True enough, it seemed he had forgiven them and even showed them kindness, but why? Did he truly love them, or was it merely to please their father?

Now dad was gone. Plus, they knew how they themselves had acted when they were crossed. They well remembered how they had deceived and then slaughtered the men of Shechem for the rape of their sister Dinah. Moreover, they had been told about the vendetta in the heart of Esau when their father had stolen Isaac's blessing and how he had bided his time to get even, patiently waiting until after Isaac would die. This was their history. This was their family narrative. This was their *reality*. This is how they saw life:

> Justice will come looking for you.
> You will get what you've got coming to you.
> The chickens always come home to roost.
> Nobody gets by with anything forever.
> Your sins will surely find you out.
> *You will get caught, and you will pay!*

That was the only narrative they knew. And that is why it was so difficult to believe that redemption, when it happened, was for real. When grace visits you, it is shocking because *that is just not how it is in the real world.*

And so it was, as they lay there prostrate on the floor before Joseph, begging for mercy, that they heard what has to be the most surprising words desperate sinners could ever imagine falling upon their ears: *don't be afraid.* Twice Joseph spoke those soothing words: when he began, and then when he ended his response to his brothers: *don't be afraid.*

But Joseph loved them so deeply, he knew he needed to help them over-come their disbelief. So, once again, he urged them to center their attention neither upon themselves as villains nor upon him as victim. He insisted that they move themselves to the margins of the story because none of what had happened was really about them at all. They were *not* the main characters in the story. "Am I in the place of God?" he asked them. Look again, he urged them. Look! Set me aside. This is not about me. The ques-tion is, and always is: "Do you see God? Do you *see* him? Do you see *him*?"

And then he told them all over again what he had told them three times that day almost twenty years earlier when he had first revealed his identity to them: God had used them to *send* him to Egypt (45: 5–8). And then he told them the deep truth of the whole story, the real narrative: that while it was very true that they fully intended to harm him, something else was going on. Some One else, as is always the case, was at work behind it all, orchestrating their evil for the great good he planned for them. And then he opened up to them the greatest, most glorious reality of redemption: that God actually takes evil and *uses it*, not by turning it into something good (it is and will always remain evil), but by employing it, in all its hor-ror, to accomplish good on a grand scale. In this case that massive "good" was saving many lives from starvation.

That is the very heart of redemption: using evil for good. What you are seeing here in the story of Joseph is, in fact, a prophecy. It is a preview of the ultimate redemption when the Messiah, God himself, willingly allowed the powers of evil and death to do their worst with him and then used that evil for the greatest good the world has ever known. He turned it all into an atoning sacrifice by which he paid the penalty for our sins, satisfied the justice and appeased the wrath of God, earned for us true righteousness and life and reversed the curse, restoring the kingdom. And it is out of that deep spring there flows one of the firmest convictions Christians live by, no matter how much evil crashes into their lives—as it surely will in yours. In the light of Calvary, we are now finally convinced that "in all things God works for the good of those who love him, who have been called according to his purpose" (Rom. 8: 28).

In the light of that stunning metanarrative, that overarching reality, Joseph went right ahead and confidently assured them that they had nothing to fear, for he would never cease to provide for them and their children everything they could ever possibly need.

Unbelievable! But so it was, and in Jesus, so it is. The great redeemer is still at it, using both good and evil to work out his perfect purpose right in the drama of the hurts in our own lives.

The story does have a "and they all lived happily ever after" ending. Joseph lived to be 110 years old. He lived to see his children's children. He assured his descendants that the day would surely come when God would bring them all back home. And then he died, insisting that his body not be buried until that day finally dawned. He was sure that the perfect and final redemption would come. And it did.

When you get hurt, as you surely will, and are caught up in the brokenness of this world, I hope you will see that alienation, chaos, enmity, and shattered relationships need not be the end of the story. **Nothing is beyond redemption**. It will come hard, but never doubt: it can come.

Introduction

The purpose of this study guide is just that: to challenge you to drill down deep into the Joseph story. I wrote the book to draw you into the raw drama of this ancient saga. I hoped you would feel the tension in his family, taste his panic in the cistern, imagine his loneliness in that Egyptian prison, wonder at his sudden rise to power, struggle with his severe treatment of his brothers, and finally savor that exquisite moment when he shocked them with the truth of who he was, and then showered them with warm, cleansing grace. Oh, it is quite the story, and I wanted you to live right into it and feel every part of it.

But now, I want so much more for you, if you have an appetite for it. This story is like an onion: it becomes more pungent as you peel the layers away. I wrote this study guide to lead you into the story underneath the Joseph story. There's a cosmic drama going on here.

Underneath, above, and all around the characters in this story are a tangle of competing spiritual powers, good and evil. What you see is NOT what you get. Look deeper. Look higher. Look wider. The real forces here are NOT flesh and blood. They are spiritual. You saw the cold deceit of his brothers as they took their revenge on the Shechemites. You felt the sharp edge of their hatred as they casually munched their lunch, ignoring his pleas from that cistern. You felt the callous hardness of their hearts as they watched their father weep for years, and never told him the truth. And you saw how encased they were in illusion when they presented themselves to the "man" ruling Egypt as "honest men." What's really going on here? The powers are at work!

You will encounter these powers all through your lives, though they are so thickly veiled it will take sharp discernment even to detect them. On the surface of life, you will bump into ordinary people. You may not suspect a thing. Then, in some cases, as you get to know them better, you may discover something that makes you feel uneasy, even guarded. You'll sense that Bill is not truthful. You'll sense that Abby might be using you. You'll discover how enslaved your boss is to the bottom line. You'll slowly discover what women in Hollywood realized about Harvey Weinstein, or gymnasts learned about Larry Nassar: they were in the presence of monsters. Eventually it will stagger you to learn that the ordinary person you rent from, or commute with, may actually have a sinister side. Painfully, you will realize just how naïve you have been.

Then deep reality will dawn on you: you are up against something far more evil than you ever imagined. You'll hear the ring of truth in Paul's words, "For our struggle is not against flesh and blood, but against the rulers, against the authorities, against the powers of this dark world and against the spiritual forces of evil in the heavenly realms (Ephesians 6: 12). Your eyes will be opened to the REAL "real world." It will leave you horrified, shaken, confused.

This study is designed to awaken you to the subtlety, immediacy and potency of these powers. They are right in front of you, hidden behind smiling faces, appealing invitations or enticing opportunities. Do you know what you are up against?

A simple and basic way of understanding them is this:

1. They are named "principalities" because of the immense range of their influence, much as a prince once ruled an entire territory, which then became known as a principality. There are individuals, companies, institutions, agencies, families, neighborhoods, even governments, where their influence has become so endemic they have a virtual lock on the entire culture within them. For example, consider the range of control Jim Crow practices once held as they insured segregation in the South before the civil rights movement finally took them on under the inspiration of Martin Luther King, Jr. He and his indomitable allies were invading a "principality."

2. They are named "powers" because they are just that: dominant. They are so mighty they invariably appear *almighty*. They refuse to budge when initially confronted. They are entrenched. Their grip on a person or institution appears inviolate. As a result, it's not uncommon for despair to set in when a person or group attempts to confront them. Just think of the frustration so many have felt when attempting to modify the gun laws in America to make this country safer in the wake of an epidemic of mass shootings, especially in our schools.

The purpose of this study is to help you recognize them as the real forces at work in the Joseph story. I want you to see their faces, learn their names, watch how they work, and be appalled at the damage they wreck. I want to strip away your naiveté about what it is that *you* are up against.

But there is a deeper purpose as well. This IS a story of redemption, after all. To every assault of the dark principalities and powers, there is a counter-measure from the Real Power, either directly, or through a human agent. That Power is the very real and ever present power of a living God, whom we confess to be "God, The Father, ALL-mighty." He is always right there, whether noticed or not, executing his good purpose even in the tragic side of life.

There is more: Joseph is a prototype of Jesus, the Christ. (In the book, I alert you along the way to some of the dead giveaways that clue you in to this life-giving link.) The New Testament insists upon informing us that the principalities and powers finally met their match when God Himself showed up on the planet in the person of Jesus of Nazareth. Demons shrieked at his presence, then fled as he evicted them. However, it appears they made a powerful comeback at his crucifixion. They attacked full force, employing the powers of betrayal, denial, abandonment, false witnesses, spit, scourging, an unjust sentence, a crown of thorns, and finally, the ultimate humiliation at the hands of the imperial power of Rome: the shame and embarrassment of a public crucifixion. Six hours later, he was dead, and it appeared that the powers had triumphed, using death itself as their final ace in the hole.

Then came the resurrection and the truth of what had really happened finally began to dawn on his heart broken disciples: something ELSE had happened on that cross, invisible to the naked eye. They slowly realized that on the cross Jesus had actually absorbed the powers of evil into himself, nailing them to the cross and carrying them down into death, in effect, putting them to death in his own death. (One might compare it, somewhat loosely but still credibly, to what happens to the dreaded power of a cancer when it kills its victim. The cancer kills her all right; but in her dying the cancer dies too. In gleefully destroying its victim, the cancer discovers, too late, that it has also, stupidly, killed itself.) When God raised Jesus from the dead, he was making a divine announcement: the principalities and powers had been disarmed and defeated at the cross. They had met their match. A new reality was established on planet earth: the powers no longer held unbroken sway.

All of this finds one of its many Old Testament previews in the beloved story of Joseph. This study guide is designed to take you above the fray, behind the scenes, to the "heavenlies" where the REAL story is unfolding, the REAL battle is raging, and the REAL powers are locked in a fight to the death. It's like Ken Burn's documentary on the Vietnam War; he took us to Vietnam all right, and showed us the carnage. But he made sure to bring us to another place as well, a place rife with lying, deceit, inaccuracies and illusions. It was called the White House. This study invites you to do just that with the story of Joseph. Look behind the scenes. See what's REALLY happening. Examine the demonic assaults and divine counter measures in this pitched battle. This is not just Joseph's story. This will be your story. You will experience elements of this story right in your own story. Best of all, this is Jesus' story, which gives hope to all our stories, convincing us that redemption, though hard in coming, can come.

STUDY 1

Assault: Jealousy

BOOK CHAPTER ONE: CATFIGHT

Genesis 29: 1–30: 21

---

*Jealousy: Hostility toward a rival or one believed to enjoy an advantage: envious.
"His success made his old friends jealous." (Mirriam Webster online dictionary)*

1. Where does jealous explicitly erupt in this chapter?

2. Describe the degree of the damage it caused to Rachel's three
   key relationships:

   a. With Jacob (30: 1, 2)

   b. With God (30: 6)

   c. With Leah (30: 14 – 16)

3. How does God temper it in the life of Rachel? Since Rachel saw
   her barrenness as a "disgrace," (30: 23), might the birth of Joseph
   possibly be an act of divine grace?

4. Was it enough? (30: 24) (What does this say about eradicating jealousy?)

5. How virulent did this infection remain in the history of the family? (See Acts 7: 9)

6. Where have you detected the presence and power of jealousy so far in your experience? What damage have you noticed flowing out of it? Why is overcoming jealousy a critical practice for your own spiritual hygiene?

7. Read 2 Corinthians 12: 20 and Galatians 5: 20. Notice the cousins of jealousy, the kindred demonic spirits with whom it keeps close company. What toll have you seen it take on the health of the Christian community?

8. What does coddling a spirit of jealousy say about our true spiritual condition? (I Corinthians 3: 3)

9. Does God's "grace" to Rachel give you a clue to how an entrenched spirit of jealousy might be overcome? How might you see this "grace" at work in your own heart?

10. When considering how deadly this particular spiritual power is, ponder the role it played in triggering the crucifixion of Jesus. (Matthew 26: 18)

11. How does the sacrificial death of Jesus have the power to overcome our normal bent towards jealousy? Close your study by slowly reading Titus 3: 3 – 8 three times and then inviting each person in the group to respond to this question.

Assault: Revenge

BOOK CHAPTER TWO: THE BALD FACE OF EVIL

Genesis 34

———

We will study them. We will find their secrets, learn their weaknesses. Death is too good for them. They must suffer as I suffered. They must see their world, and all they hold dear, ripped from them as it was ripped from me. (The Count of Monte Cristo)

1. Jacob and his family have nicely settled down in a verdant place. All seems well. Then suddenly, seemingly out of nowhere, comes this shocking event of raw revenge. Does this surprise you?

2. How have you seen such raw revenge erupt in your own experience? Did you discover that you did not expect it to be so vicious? Why might that be?

3. Why is the spirit of revenge particularly dangerous?

4. How did God restrain revenge in the Old Testament? Read and ponder Leviticus 24: 17 -20.

5. How did Jesus command us to restrain the spirit of revenge even further in the New Testament? Read and ponder Matthew 5: 38 - 42

6. Think back to an occasion when the spirit of revenge inflamed you, perhaps as a child. What triggered it? How did you respond?

7. Jacob's feeble protest fell on deaf ears. What does this tell you about the degree to which the spirit of revenge is almost impossible to restrain?

8. How does a personal taste of the grace of God in the cross of Christ equip us to face a powerful surge of vindictiveness rising in our hearts? Read Romans 12: 17 – 21 out loud in your group three times. Then discuss these two questions:

    a. Have you ever seen this practiced?

    b. Do you see an estranged relationship in your own life calling you to practice this?

Countermeasure: Pilgrimage

BOOK CHAPTER THREE: PILGRIMAGE

Genesis 35

Blessed are those whose strength is in you, who have set their hearts on pilgrimage. As the pass through the Valley of Baca, they make it a place of springs; the autumn rains also cover it with pools. They go from strength to strength, till each appears before God in Zion. (Psalm 84: 5 − 7)

1. Have you ever experienced a pilgrimage, an intentional journey to a shrine or monument? How did this experience affect you?

2. Why are pilgrimages so appealing that millions make them annually?

3. Why did God direct Jacob to go on pilgrimage to *Bethel*? Why did God choose this step as a countermeasure to the atrocities of chapter 34?

4. Grandpa Koeman describes household gods as "habituated evils that have become domesticated." Does this ring true to you? What might such "household gods" look like in your house, office, neighborhood, company or city?

5. Have you ever experienced or seen anything like the dramatic purification ritual Jacob required of his family in vss. 2 – 4? Why is this excising exercise so essential before embarking upon a pilgrimage? Might it be compared to runners stripping down before a race?

6. How can the "terror of God" (vs. 5) actually be a timely gift of divine protection? Is it found elsewhere in Scripture? (Consider Matthew 21: 46 and Luke 20: 40) Have you ever experienced its protecting power?

7. How have you witnessed, in your own experience or in those of others, the truth of "Israel": that in wrestling with God we actually gain more of Him?

8. How do the cosmic promises God makes to Jacob at Bethel demonstrate that the scope of redemption is far grander than "going to heaven when we die?"

9. In terms of your spiritual roots, is there anything similar to the Bethel stone pillar in your world? Why are such places or monuments so stabilizing for our pilgrimage through life? Would you consider an athletic trophy, an educational degree, even an endorsement, as functioning in a similar way? How is the Lord's Supper the ultimate Bethel stone?

10. Have three members of your group read Psalm 84: 5 – 7 slowly
and attentively. What might you hear God saying to you as you
meditate on it?

Countermeasures: Character and Clothing

BOOK CHAPTER FOUR:
"JOSEPH'S FIRST ACT:
COURAGEOUS WHISTLEBLOWING"

BOOK CHAPTER FIVE:
"THE CLOTHING OF REDEEMERS"

Genesis 37: 1 — 4

Chapter Four:

1. From referees to government watchdogs to Old Testament prophets, whistleblowers are rarely a welcome voice! Why is this?

2. Why is the courage to speak up in the face of wrong a critical countermeasure in our battle against the principalities and powers?

3. Does the author present a plausible case against the idea that Joseph is just a tattler?

4. Few qualities in a child are more highly prized (and assiduously cultivated) in their children than integrity. What birthed this excellence in the character of Joseph? How might this affect your parenting in the future?

5. Why is it impossible to redeem any broken situation without first exposing the truth? Why does this make redemption so hard?

Chapter Five:

1. How have you experienced or witnessed the transformative power of mere clothing?

2. The author argues that this was not a case of favoritism. How do you see it? Was Joseph truly the only eligible recipient of this designation as first among brothers?

3. Why was this simple, though elegant, piece of clothing so critical to Joseph's lifework?

4. Why is knowing that we are dressed up "in the beloved" (who is Christ) essential for true human flourishing? How have you observed the difference between driven and beloved people?

5. How is the transfiguration of Jesus anticipated in Joseph's coat? Why was his transfiguration indispensable to his redemptive work on the cross?

What is our truest and finest wardrobe? Describe a person you have known who is beautifully dressed up in Christ.

Countermeasures: Dreams

BOOK CHAPTER SIX: "DREAMS"

Genesis 37: 5 — 11

1. What is the difference between the dreams given to Joseph and those that drive human ambition? Why is this difference so crucial to our human flourishing?

2. Why was it important for Joseph to reveal his dreams? In your judgment was he being arrogant in reporting them?

3. Why were there two dreams instead of just one? Reflect on the significant differences between them. Is it correct to conclude that his dreams have both a local and a cosmic significance? Why would that be in terms of the scope of God's redemptive range?

4. The dreams are actually mentioned only one other time in the entire story, in 42: 9, when Joseph's brothers first appeared before him as ruler and bowed down to him. How did that moment of fulfillment shape Joseph's treatment of them from that point on?

5. Consider the parallel the author draws between the dreams given to Joseph at the beginning of his journey and the divine endorsement given the Jesus at his baptism before he launched his ministry. What does this reveal about the radical difference between divine unction vs. youthful ambition? (What is the difference between a "called" person and a "driven" person?)

6. Why are visions and dreams from God essential to our redemptive task? How do they function as "countermeasures"? Consider the number of times God used visions and dreams in the early church to empower believers in the face of daunting new challenges:

   a. Ananias (Acts 9: 10 – 12)

   b. Peter and Cornelius (Acts 10)

   c. Paul being led into Europe (Acts 16: 9)

   d. Paul struggling in Corinth (Acts 18: 9)

   e. The entire future of planet earth (Rev. 1: 9)

7. Discuss with your group the dreams or visions you believe you may have received. Why is it important to report them, as Joseph did, to your family and fellow believers? Invite your group members to discuss the dreams you've received, and pray for you.

STUDY 6

Attack: Eviction into Exile

BOOK CHAPTER SEVEN: "WHEN EVIL HITS HOME"

Genesis 37: 12 — 36

1. Joseph was sent on this mission by his father (vs. 13). Jesus repeatedly explained his presence among us by claiming that he was "sent." How significant was this conviction in the life of Jesus? See John 4: 34. How might this transform our understanding of our vocation in life?

2. What is the significance of the fact that Joseph was on a good will mission when he was attacked? How does this make his experience especially painful? Read Psalm 54: 12 – 14 as you attempt to grasp the unique nature of Joseph's ordeal here. Might there be a parallel to the agony Jesus expressed in Matthew 23: 37?

3. In vss. 14c – 17, Moses makes sure to note Joseph's tenacity in his determined search to find his brothers. It seems a small detail that could easily have been skipped. Why do you think Moses

285

included it? What does this tell you about the nature of love? Consider Song of Songs 3: 1 - 4 and John 13: 1.

4. Notice the suddenness in the brutality of the brothers. Why does evil use the sudden ambush as a key strategy for its attack? Consider this in the light of the next episode of a sudden attack on Joseph in Genesis 39: 12 and in Scripture's choice of the animal that best illustrates this device of evil (See Psalm 10: 8, 9).

5. In what ways have you observed that "the veneer of civilization is very thin?" How have you seen it break through the civility in your world?

6. The author argues that in the light of Reuben's possible ulterior motives, Joseph was utterly friendless in the pit. Why is suffering alone far more intense than any other?

7. The author points out four ways in which God protected Joseph during this deadly assault against him. How might the memory of his narrow escape from death have factored into Joseph's sense of his redemptive purpose in Egypt? (Consider chapter 45: 5, 7, and 50: 20)

8. As you conclude this study, consider any experience you have had which could be called your "Dothan day." What two realities sustained Joseph at the time of his eviction? Were they enough? What are the deep realities that keep believers from collapsing into utter despair during such seasons in their lives?

Countermeasure: Divine Favor

BOOK CHAPTER 8: THRIVING IN EXILE

Genesis 39: 1 — 6b; 20 — 23

---

1. Try to imagine the experience of exile for Joseph. Name two or three of the strongest emotions he may have felt as he began his life as a slave.

2. Have you ever felt a sense of exile in this world? Should you? (Consider I Peter 1: 1 and Hebrews 11: 13). Is it accurate to call Christians on planet earth today "resident aliens"?

3. Why can we be fairly certain that Joseph was no slouch in exile? (Consider the clue Moses give us back in 37: 15c – 17.) How should we live in exile? (Consider Jeremiah's instructions to exiles in Jeremiah 29: 4 – 7.)

4. How many times does this passage reference the Lord?

5. Why is Moses so insistent upon linking every part of Joseph's success to the Lord's favor? Why is this a critical perspective for

upwardly mobile millennials? (Consider Psalm 75: 6, 7 as you weigh your response to this question.)

6. What is the balance between the spirit of human enterprise and God's favor as we seek to flourish? (Consider Ecclesiastes 11: 4 and Psalm 127: 1, 2 in your response.)

7. What did Potiphar soon enough notice (39: 3)? What is the significance of the fact that it was a pagan who attributed Joseph's success to God?

8. Is there such a thing as the haphazard fluke of good fortune in the success of certain people? (You may wish to reference Outliers, by Malcolm Gladwell, and also consider Ecclesiastes 9: 11.)

9. Is there any evidence that Joseph himself recognized the link between God's favor and his success? (Consider his reference to God in vs. 9.)

10. Joseph fell out of favor with Potiphar even faster than he fell into favor with him. What warning is embedded in this easy-come, easy-go aspect of the story? How did Jesus view his "success" in John 2: 23, 24?

11. The Heidelberg Catechism (Q&A 27) insists that "prosperity and poverty--all things, in fact, come to us not by chance but from his fatherly hand." How does this part of the Joseph story demonstrate the truth of that claim? What major difference does that make (See Q&A 28)?

Attack: Sexual Seduction

BOOK CHAPTER 9: THE TEST

Read Genesis 39:6b—20a

1. Describe the most recent case of a national figure disgraced by sexual misconduct. Why are such events not at all uncommon?

2. Name at least two Biblical characters whose lives suffered lifelong damage by their own sexual misconduct.

3. Notice the rhetorical questions in Proverbs 6: 27 – 29 and the severe language of Proverbs 7: 24 – 27. Does history support such weighty warnings?

4. Given the statistics the author cites, have you seen enough evidence to conclude that we are living in a more sexually permissive culture than those of previous generations?

5. Why is sexual immorality more serious than other sins? (See I Cor. 6: 18 – 20.)

6. Why can physical beauty be a burden? How have you observed this to be true?

7. What factors contribute to creating an "opportune time" for sexual sin?

8. Discuss the four walls of protection God had erected within Joseph against seduction. What role can their presence (or absence) play in preserving (or losing) one's sexual purity?

9. Weigh the four different lines of reasoning Joseph used in his attempt to dissuade his seductress. In your judgment, which carries the most weight? Why did they fail to stop her?

10. Why are distance and flight vital disciplines in maintaining sexual purity? Why is humility foundational to practicing them?

11. This is now the third time that Joseph's rectitude made his life much more miserable. Ponder this in the light of the health and wealth "prosperity" gospel being promoted today.

12. Both Joseph and Jesus were subjected to intense temptation at the launch of their life's work as redeemers. Recalling Adam's succumbing to temptation, is overcoming temptation a necessary prerequisite to serving as a redeemer? Consider Hebrews 4: 15 – 16 as you ponder this.

STUDY 9

Attack: Forgotten!

BOOK CHAPTER 10: THE DARKNESS DEEPENS

Genesis 40—41: 1a

1. The story of Joseph includes three sets of double dreams. Why are there always doubles? (Consider Matthew 18: 16 and Genesis 41: 32)

2. In your judgment, was it fitting for Joseph to request the butler to remember him to Pharaoh?

3. Why is it so painful to be forgotten (Consider Isaiah 49: 15)?

4. Imagine being utterly forgotten for "two full years." What can happen to a person when their deepest longings are stymied for such an extensive period of time? (Consider Proverbs 13: 12)

5. Why is hope such a dangerous thing? What is the difference between a wish and a hope?

6. What do you think sustained Joseph's hopefulness during his dark night of the soul? Should such a season come your way, what will protect you from capitulating to despair?

7. During this season in his life Joseph was effectively sidelined from his great redemptive task. In your opinion, is it possible to understand why God allowed this attack of being forgotten?

8. What role did injustice play in exacerbating the pain of Joseph's being forgotten by the butler? By this time in the story, how many instances of injustice has Joseph experienced? Why is experiencing injustice usually an element in the rise of a redeemer?

9. Name as many other key Biblical leaders as you can think of who were also "sidelined" and spent a significant season of their life in a wilderness or other place of solitude. You should be able to mention at least six. In each case, reflect on how this molded their character or deepened their focus on God.

10. Why is the desert experience (literally or symbolically) powerfully formative in the life of a spiritual leader?

11. What has been your closest experience to living in a desert? How has it shaped you?

STUDY 10

Countermeasure: Resurrection

BOOK: CHAPTER 11: THE DIVINE MAJESTY

Genesis 41: 1b — 49

1. Unlike his promotions under Potiphar or the warden, Joseph's promotion under Pharaoh was not gradual; it was so sudden it was virtually instant. Is this worth pondering as typical of how God makes his final moves in his redemptive enterprise? (Consider Luke 2: 13, Luke 24: 4, Matthew 28: 9, Acts 2: 2, and I Thessalonians 5: 1 – 4)

2. Why is it significant that not one of all the magicians and wise men in the entire country of Egypt were able to interpret Pharaoh's dreams? Consider vss 16, 25, 28, and 32, as well as Isaiah 29: 14 and 48: 11 in your reflections.

3. What most impressed Pharaoh about Joseph (even more than his convincing interpretation of the dreams), was the clear evidence that inside of him was "the spirit of God" (vs.38). How was this so plainly evident in Joseph? How is it that this "unction" is imparted to certain humans? (Consider I John 2:

27 in your response.) Would you agree with the author that this quality is as essential to becoming a person of influence as learned competencies or honed character?

4. Joseph knew God and now he was observing the divine majesty behind his summons, the dream, and the interpretation he was given. Then he took another step: becoming a self-appointed royal advisor. Describe that bold step. What gave him the chutzpah to stick out his neck and take the risk to do so? How have you seen this quality manifest itself in your own life?

5. What is a "defining moment"? Have you witnessed or experienced one?

6. How does the elevation of Joseph anticipate the resurrection and ascension of Jesus? Why does God choose the weak things of the world to shame the strong?

7. Why is power essential for a redeemer to accomplish their task?

Countermeasure: Prosecution, Part 1

BOOK CHAPTER 12: "A QUALIFIED REDEEMER

BOOK CHAPTER 13: "FORGIVE? NOT SO QUICK"

Genesis 41: 50 — 42: 38

8. How did the famine finally coerce the brothers towards their redemption? What does this imply regarding our capacity for self-redemption?

9. In the NIV there are 94 references to famine, frequently as a means of discipline meant to lead to redemption. Besides this famine, name one or two other biblical famines with a redemptive outcome. What are the great famines of our day? How have you seen "famines" such as school shootings or the hidden consequences of cohabitation serving a redemptive purpose?

10. How can we be sure that Joseph was fully prepared to prosecute his brothers without a trace of personal vindictiveness? How do

the names Joseph gave his sons demonstrate that he was ready to be their redeemer?

11. What other factors may have deepened Joseph's compassion towards his brothers?

12. When people felt the famine, and cried out to Pharaoh, what did he tell them to do? What did Jesus tell famished people to do? (See John 6: 53 – 58) What is the worst possible form of famine (See Amos 8: 11)? What does this look like (see Matthew 13: 14)?

13. What is the difference between "*being* forgiving" and "*extending* forgiveness"? Is it actually possible to extend forgiveness to a person too soon? What condition must be met before a victim can say to an offender, "I forgive you" (Luke 17: 3)?

14. When is guilt a blessing?

15. Why did Joseph know that his demand that one of the brothers go back home and return with the youngest brother would pierce their hearts? What was he testing here?

16. Describe each stage of increasing misery Joseph crafted to break down his brothers. What does this slowly developing unease of conscience tell us about the journey into repentance?

17. What does the stoic silence of the brothers witnessing the misery of their father in 42: 36 – 38 reveal about the depth of hardness in human hearts?

Countermeasure: Prosecution, Part 2

BOOK CHAPTER 14: "KINDNESS: REDEMPTION'S SPRING"

Genesis 43 — 44: 12

God whispers to us in our pleasures, speaks in our conscience, but shouts in our pain; it is his megaphone to rouse a deaf world. No doubt Pain as God's megaphone is a terrible instrument; it may lead to final and unrepented rebellion. But it gives the only opportunity the bad man can have for amendment. It removes the veil; it plants the flag of truth within the fortress of a rebel soul. C. S. Lewis, The Problem of Pain, p. 93, 95

1. What is the heart of Joseph's strategy as he "prosecutes" his brothers in these two chapters?

2. Why can wrestling with God be spiritually beneficial?

3. What finally convinced Israel to let Benjamin go (43: 8)? Is there a parallel here to what moved God to give up his son for our salvation? (Consider Isaiah 9: 2 and Luke 1: 78, 79)

4. Joseph surprised his brothers with kindness. How is the Christian gospel a story of divine kindness? Why is kindness so powerful (See Romans 2: 4)?

5. What do Joseph's tears tell us? How do they anticipate the tears of Jesus? (See Luke 19: 41 – 44)

6. Describe the role that divination plays in these chapters. Since Joseph's brothers were largely godless men, why is this a smart prosecutorial strategy?

7. The author suggests that Joseph kindness was meant to create a backdrop against which Benjamin's "theft" of the silver cup would appear to be a horrific crime. Was this a set up? If so, why did Joseph use it?

8. Why was the pain Joseph caused his brothers through his steward on the road so necessary to their redemption?

9. What single act demonstrates that the brothers were now broken men?

10. How does the fact that extreme measures (famine, lavish kindness, divination, framing Benjamin) were needed to finally break the brothers, square with the notion of the innate goodness of the human heart?

Redemption, Part One

CHAPTER 15: BROKEN
CHAPTER 16: THE HEART OF REPENTANCE

Read Genesis 44: 1 — 44

1. The author argues that the steward's seven word question ("Why have you repaid good with evil?") is at the very core of the divine indictment against humanity. What does this tell us about the true source of our misconduct?

2. Why would Joseph select the silver cup as the one item he would use to expose his brother's guilt as deep wickedness?

3. Why did the steward take his time searching for and exposing the cup? Was this for mere dramatic effect, or does this tell us something more?

4. When the cup was uncovered in Benjamin's sack, the brothers immediately tore their clothes. Why is that singular act so fitting as an expression of true brokenness? Looking far ahead, what is

God's redemptive response to our shredded clothing? (Ponder Luke 23: 45b)

5. What moved the brothers to return to the city? Why can there be no redemption without some expression of vs. 13 in our own lives? What is the most powerful incentive for turning around?

6. Why is the experience of authentic guilt one of life's greatest blessings? If you are comfortable doing so, speak about how such an experience was transformative in your own life.

7. Why is repentance the doorway into the kingdom of heaven?

8. Why is worldly sorrow ultimately impotent as a force in human transformation?

9. Which facet of authentic repentance (godly sorrow) has been most liberating for you?

10. What convinced Joseph that his brother's hearts had finally been broken? Why is the willingness to take the punishment upon ourselves paradoxically the only way to be spared from it?

Redemption, Part Two

BOOK CHAPTER 17: THE SWEETEST THING I KNOW

BOOK CHAPTER 18: COULD IT REALLY BE TRUE?

Read Genesis 45

1. Why were Joseph's brothers utterly terrified when he revealed his identity?

2. Where is the real surprise in the story?

3. How does Joseph's explanation of God's purpose behind their selling him give us a uniquely hopeful perspective on evil?

4. How do the tears and kisses of vs. 14 impact you? Why do they invariably accompany redemption?

5. Read Colossians 2: 9, 10. How does the largesse of Pharaoh to Joseph's brothers illustrate our riches in Christ?

6. Review the four ways in which Joseph's redemption of his brothers mirrors the way in which God redeems us. Are there other similarities you see in the story? How do they comfort you?

7. The author views vss. 25 – 28 as the end of exile for the family of Jacob. How is this perspective critical in later Jewish history? Why is it crucial for Christians today?

8. Was Jacob's reaction to the stunning news brought home by his sons one of unbelief or disbelief? What is the difference? Is it fair to say that the sheer wonder of gospel, once grasped, makes it sound too good to be true?

9. Do you believe that at this point the brothers finally told their father the whole truth? Why is it reasonable to believe they did? Why do you think Moses makes no mention of it?

10. What ultimately convinced Jacob to leave Canaan and travel to Egypt?

STUDY 15

Redemption, Part Three

CHAPTER 19: WHY WORSHIP FIRST?

CHAPTER 20: HE KNOWS YOUR NAME

Read Genesis 46: 1 – 27

1. This is now the sixth time God engaged Jacob. Does God still do this today? Have there been moments in your life where you were certain God was engaging you?

2. Why did Jacob choose Beersheba as the place to build an altar and offer his sacrifices? Are there such sacred places in your journey through life? Why are they so important?

3. The patriarchs often built altars at the defining moments of their lives. If you were to tell the story of your life by its altars, where would they be and what would they say?

4. Are the three promises God gave to Jacob (vss.3, 4) only relevant to him, or is there a way they are relevant to Christians today?

5. When you first read the list of the names of those who traveled down to Egypt (vss 8 – 25), what does it mean to you?

6. The author claims there are at least three reasons why all these names count to us. Do you agree or disagree with the three benefits he sees in our being shown this list? Are there other benefits you see?

7. How does Genesis 46: 1 – 27 enrich your view of the scope of the victory that flowed out of the redemption of Joseph's brothers? How does the vision of this family slowly making their way to Egypt bolster your determination to be an agent of redemption in the broken places in your world?

STUDY 16

Redemption, Part Four

CHAPTER 21: SON AND FATHER

CHAPTER 22: REDEMPTION'S BOUNTY

CHAPTER 23: REALLY?

Read Genesis 46: 28 — 47: 31; 50: 15 — 21

1. Why does reading the moment of Joseph's and Jacob's reunion move us to tears? What does it touch deep within us?

2. The author contends that the guiding star that shaped Joseph's entire life was his sonship to his father Jacob. Is this true? Was this true for Jesus? Is this also true for us and our heavenly father?

3. Is it true that Jesus redefined family?

4. Why is pleasing a father such a weight of glory for a child, as C. S. Lewis claims?

5. The author lists four bounties that flowed from the redemption of Jacob's family: property, prosperity, posterity and place. Which one resonates most deeply with you?

6. How does the scope of this bounty encourage you to work towards reconciliation in the broken relationships in your world?

7. How is the bounty of property (real estate) fulfilled in the lives of Christians? (Rev 21: 1 – 3)

8. Did Joseph exploit the Egyptians? How can slavery to Christ lead us into true and lasting prosperity?

9. When Jacob elevated Joseph, Manasseh and Ephraim, he ensured the glory of his posterity. How does Jesus do this for those who follow him? (Consider Acts 2: 39)

10. How does Jacob's death and funeral present a promise for us to cherish as we follow Jesus? (See 2 Corinthians 5: 1 – 10)

11. Why is grace so shocking? What ultimately cured the fear-filled hearts of the brothers after Jacob's death? How does this help us with our fears?

12. What truth in this entire study has most deeply impacted your heart?

The Devil's Dictionary

The Devil's
Dictionary

Ambrose Bierce

With an introduction by Roy Morris, Jr.

New York   Oxford
Oxford University Press
1999

Oxford University Press

Oxford   New York
Athens   Auckland   Bangkok   Bogotá   Buenos Aires   Calcutta
Cape Town   Chennai   Dar es Salaam   Delhi   Florence   Hong Kong   Istanbul
Karachi   Kuala Lumpur   Madrid   Melbourne   Mexico City   Mumbai
Nairobi   Paris   São Paulo   Singapore   Taipei   Tokyo   Toronto   Warsaw

and associated companies in
Berlin   Ibadan

Published by Oxford University Press, Inc.
198 Madison Avenue, New York, New York 10016

Oxford is a registered trademark of Oxford University Press

The Devil Alphabet from Bibliothèque Nationale de France, Paris.

Library of Congress Cataloging-in-Publication Data
Bierce, Ambrose, 1842-1914?
The devil's dictionary / by Ambrose Bierce: with an introduction by Roy Morris, Jr.
p. cm.
ISBN 0-19-512626-2 (cloth: alk. paper).—ISBN 0-19-512627-0 (paper: alk. paper).
1. English language—Dictionaries—Humor.
2. English Language—Semantics—Humor.
3. Vocabulary—Humor. I. Title
PS1097.D4   1998
423'.0207—dc21   98-22576

2004
25.00

CLOTH   10   9   8   7   6   5
PAPER   10   9   8

Printed in the United States of America
on acid-free paper

The Devil's Dictionary

Introduction

O f all the nicknames—mostly negative—that Ambrose Bierce acquired in the course of his career, one stands out as uniquely flattering: The West Coast Samuel Johnson. Most writers would have been pleased to find themselves mentioned, however briefly, in the same breath as the Great Cham, but Bierce was typically unimpressed. The problem, as he saw it, lay in Johnson's famous definition of patriotism as "the last refuge of a scoundrel." To Bierce's way of thinking, this was exactly wrong: "I beg to submit that it is the first." Nor would Bierce necessarily have agreed with Johnson's considered opinion that "no man but a blockhead ever wrote, except for money." While certainly not averse to being paid for his work, Bierce (like Johnson) wrote for many complex personal reasons, not least of which was a lifelong thirst for revenge upon a world that he felt—with some reason—had wounded him physically, spiritually, and emotionally. And while Johnson professed himself to be "more pained by ignorance than delighted by instruction," Bierce positively gloried in the ignorance of others, and he was only too happy to inflict upon "that immortal ass, the average man" a painful—if often hilarious—rod of correction.

The Devil's Dictionary was one of his most effective teaching tools. With the able assistance of "my scholarly friend, Mr. Satan," Bierce set out to challenge the most cherished institutions of American society: love, marriage, law, religion, politics, patriotism, and art. Wit was his weapon of choice, and The Devil's Dictionary remains one of the wittiest, if also one of the most deeply subversive, books in the English language. Readers would do well to keep in mind Kent's insightful warning to King Lear: "This is not altogether fool, my lord." For behind the word games and the mockery, the 998 definitions in *The Devil's Dictionary* comprise a deadly serious—and at times surprisingly personal—work of art. One modern critic has observed, with only slight exaggeration, that "each of these definitions, to some degree, may be said to define Bierce" himself. Certainly, the choice of words defined, as much as the definitions themselves, constitutes a sort of hidden autobiography, an indirect self-portrait of the artist as a not-so-young man at odds with his country, his family, his past, and himself. Such a reading, of course, requires a certain knowledge of the author's background. One does not become the devil's writing partner overnight.

In Bierce's case, the seeds of disquiet were planted early and deep. He was born on June 24, 1842, in the now-vanished frontier community of Horse Cave Creek, Ohio, the tenth of thirteen children (and the last to survive infancy) of intensely religious parents who had migrated west from Cornwall, Connecticut. When he was four the family moved again, to the tiny village of Warsaw in upstate Indiana, where Bierce spent the remainder of his distinctly unhappy childhood. From the start, his pious, sin-defying parents were as much an embarrassment to him as he was, no doubt, a puzzlement to them. His somewhat Dickensian father, Marcus Aurelius, was an odd mixture of religious zealot and closet aesthete, possessing along with a ramshackle farm and a forest of debts the largest collection of books in Kosciusko County. In fact, Bierce's own rather dandified name came from one of those books, a penny-dreadful play entitled *Ambrose Gwinett; or, A Sea-Side Story*, whose basic plot contrivance of the hero's surviving death by hanging would turn up again, albeit ironically, in Bierce's most famous story, "An Occurrence at Owl Creek Bridge." For reasons of his own, the elder Bierce gave all of his children names beginning with the letter *A*; Ambrose, true to form, always hated his.

For the most part, Bierce seems to have tolerated his father; his mother was another matter altogether. Laura Sherwood Bierce was a direct descendant of William Bradford, who had come over on the *Mayflower*. Besides having nine older children to care for—and three younger ones to bury—Mrs. Bierce faced the baffling and never-abating antipathy of blond-haired, blue-eyed Ambrose, who was as devilish-acting as he was angelic-looking. Both she and her husband seem to have made allowances for their youngest surviving child, excusing him from